Get a Grip on Your Grief!

Control your grief before it controls you.

Godfrey E. McAllister, Ph.D.

DEDICATION

Get a Grip on Your Grief!
is dedicated to

Leaders Communicating God's Love, Inc. (LCGL)

a 501(c)(3) non-profit, international, inter-denominational Christian ministry, charged with the mandate to **equip** and **build believers** in **Jesus Christ for spiritual battle** through **Spiritual Warfare Assertiveness Training (SWAT),**

in faithful obedience to the Great Commission (Matthew 28:19–20).

Get a Grip on Your Grief!

Much *of what is in this book*

you already know... but it helps to be reminded.

From ______________________________

To ______________________________

Grief is no respecter of gender, age, nationality, education, religion, or socio-economic status. Neither does grief make any appointments. The question is not if it will come, but *when it will come*—and how often. *Get a Grip on Your Grief!* will help you prepare, and prepare you to help others.

Godfrey E. McAllister

— Doctor Perspective —

Rights & Acknowledgments

Get a Grip on Your Grief!

Control your grief... before it controls you.

by Godfrey E. McAllister, aka, Doctor Perspective

Published by GodWill Publishers - March 2026
First run printed by Amazon in the United States of America.

ISBN: 978-0-9765781-5-4

Library of Congress Control Number: 2025922735

AI & Graphics Disclosure: This work was conceptualized, authored, and created by Godfrey E. McAllister, with research and limited editorial support provided by select artificial intelligence tools. The author retains full responsibility for editorial judgment and all final content decisions. All graphics were generated by ChatGPT/OpenAI under the author's instruction and guidance. All intellectual property rights to this work are reserved by the author.

The copyright owner and/or author may be contacted at
GodWill.Publishers@gmail.com
Visit https://Grief.GodfreyMcAllister.com

All praise, glory, and honor to God for His inspiration and overarching providential guidance throughout the production of this work.

Contents

Foreword ix
Preface xi
My Journal 1

Volume One 2

Even If It Feels So, You're Never Alone 2
A Gentle Beginning 2
When the World Stops 4
The Weight You Carry 6
What Your Body Knows 8
How the Mind Tries to Help 10
When Faith Feels Far Away 12
When People Say the Wrong Thing 14
When the World Moves On 16
When Helping Heals You 18
Finding Light You Did Not See Before 20
When Purpose Returns 23
Moments of Faith 25
Your Grief Recovery Journey in Perspective 29
Where You Are Right Now 29
What's Actually Happening Inside You 29
The Truth About Your Timeline 30
The Small Actions That Rewire Your Brain 30
The Four Seasons You'll Walk Through 31
What You Need From Others (And Yourself) 31
The Three Things That Will Carry You 31
Where You're Headed 32
One Final Truth 32

Volume Two 35

Chapter 1 36

What Grief Really Is 36
1.1 Beyond the Five Stages (A Modern Understanding) 36
1.2 What the Bible Says About Grief 37
1.3 Hope That Does Not Deny Pain (1 Thessalonians 4:13-18) 38
1.4 The Science of Sorrow - How the Brain Processes Loss 38

1.5 Faith and Feeling 39

Chapter 2 .... **47**

How Grief Affects Body, Mind, and Spirit 47

2.1 The Physiology of Shock & the Mind's Defenses 47

2.2 The First "Forty-Eight Hours" and their 3 D's 50

2.3 Physiological Aftershocks and the Search for Meaning 54

2.3.1 Coping Styles and Early Adaptation 56

Chapter 3 .... **60**

Pre-Trauma Grief Mitigation (PTGM): 60

3.1 The Theology of Preparedness 60

3.2 Building Resilience Before Loss 63

3.3 Spiritual, Emotional, & Cognitive Exercises for Readiness 66

3.4 The Theology of Preventive Comfort 69

Chapter 4 .... **76**

Resilience: The Strength You Already Have 76

4.1 Why Most People Recover Better Than They Expect 76

4.2 The Resilience Spectrum 80

4.3 Facing Toxic Positivity 83

4.4 The Interplay of Anger and Grief 87

Chapter 5 .... **94**

The Physiology of Grief - The Body Cries 94

5.1 Grief in Different Stories and Settings 94

5.2 The Biology of Bereavement 95

5.3 The Stress Cascade and Immune Collapse 96

5.4 The Silent Signals - When the Body Speaks for the Heart 97

5.5 Doctor Perspective's Pneumopsychosomatic Model 99

5.6 Healing the Whole Person 101

Chapter 6 .... **105**

Emotional Earthquakes 105

6.1 The Emotional Aftershocks 105

6.2 The Anger Within Grief 108

6.3 Guilt That Isn't Yours to Bear 111

6.4 Learning to Feel Again 113

Chapter 7 .... **118**

The Seasons of Sorrow 118

7.1 Winter - The Season of Numbness 118

7.2 Spring - The Season of Questions 123
7.3 Summer - The Season of Renewal 125
7.4 Autumn - The Season of Surrender 127
7.5 The Unbroken Circle 130

Chapter 8........ 132

When Faith Feels Far Away 132
8.1 The Silence of God........ 132
8.2 When Prayers Bounce Off the Ceiling 134
8.3 When the Bible Feels Closed 136
8.4 When Worship Feels Impossible 141
8.5 When You Cannot Feel God at All 145

Chapter 9........ 149

Finding Your Way Back 149
9.1 When Faith Feels Weak but Love for God Remains 149
9.2 When You Feel Guilty for Struggling Spiritually........ 153
9.3 Rebuilding a Spiritual Life at a Sustainable Pace........ 156
9.4 The Long View: Grief and Your Spiritual Identity 159

Chapter 10........ 165

Grief's Hidden Companions........ 165
10.1 The Five Stages of Grief: Origin, Limits, and Misuse 165
Where the Five Stages Came From........ 165
How the Model Is Commonly Misused........ 166
What Modern Grief Research Shows Instead 167
Why the Stages Persist (Despite the Evidence)........ 167
A More Accurate Way to Understand Grief Emotions 168
If You Have Been Measuring Yourself by the Stages........ 168
10.2 When Grief Becomes Anxiety........ 169
10.3 The Shadow of Depression........ 171
10.4 The Deep Ache of Loneliness........ 174
10.5 The Role of Community in Recovery 176
10.6 When Grief Needs Professional Help........ 182

Chapter 11 185

The Healing Journey: Growth Through Pain 185
11.1 Growing After Loss........ 185
11.2 Remembering Without Reliving........ 188
11.3 The Freedom of Forgiveness 191

11.4 Gratitude That Strengthens 194

Chapter 12 .... **199**

The Role of Faith and Science in Healing 199

12.1 How Therapy Works with Grief 199

12.2 How Belief Affects Biology 200

12.3 Hope and Neuroplasticity 202

12.4 The Convergence of Prayer, Medicine, and Mindfulness 203

12.5 Medication and Faith: Enemies or Partners? 206

Chapter 13 .... **209**

Being Present, Listening, and Available 209

13.1 What to Say (and What Not to Say) 209

13.2 The Power of Listening 210

13.3 The Compassionate Companion 211

13.4 Becoming a Bridge, Not a Bandage 213

13.5 Caring Without Burning Out - Self-Care for Helpers 214

Chapter 14 .... **218**

Living Beyond Loss 218

14.1 The Call to Meaning 218

14.2 Building New Traditions 220

14.3 How Hope Becomes Habit 221

14.4 7 Small Steps to an Emotional Reset 224

Appendix **228**

The Legitimacy of Communal Anger 228

What Makes This Grief Different 229

Righteous Anger Versus Destructive Rage 230

The Role of the Faith Community 231

A Word to Those Who Grieve with Rage 232

A Note for Pastors, Counselors, and Community Leaders: 233

My Journal 234

Support Contacts 236

About the Author 237

Glossary 239

Endorsements 249

The Sequel 251

Foreword

by Rev. Dr. Anthony Oliver
President, Caribbean Graduate School of Theology (CGST)
President, Caribbean Evangelical Theological Association (CETA)

It is both a privilege and a profound personal joy to write the Foreword to "Get a Grip on Your Grief! — Control Your Grief Before it Controls You" by Dr. Godfrey E. McAllister. I have known Dr. McAllister for over forty years, and during that time I have come to deeply respect his character, his faith, and his unwavering commitment to serving both God and humanity. This book reflects the man.

Dr. McAllister stands as a rare blend of spiritual maturity, professional excellence, and compassionate insight. As a believer for more than six decades, he has consistently demonstrated a life anchored in Scripture and shaped by enduring faith. His career as an internationally distinguished insurance sales producer is matched only by his enduring commitment to the personal welfare of his thousands of clients. His selfless activism as a fierce Consumer Advocate reinforced this commitment. His four years at the Jamaica Theological Seminary over fifty years ago helped to lay the foundation for a lifetime committed to interdenominational involvement with diverse groups of Believers in Jesus Christ, ranging from ultra conservative Christian Brethren to Pentecostals. His experience reflects a man who has navigated both corporate and personal landscapes with wisdom, integrity, and resilience.

These volumes emerge from that rich intersection of life experience, theological grounding, and thoughtful engagement with the fields of psychology and neuroscience. In Get a Grip on Your Grief!, Dr. McAllister addresses one of the most universal, yet deeply personal human experiences—grief. In our contemporary world, marked by loss on multiple fronts—whether through death, fractured relationships, economic hardship, or collective crises—grief has become an almost constant companion for many. Yet, despite its prevalence, it is often misunderstood, mishandled, or silently endured.

What distinguishes this work is its balanced and integrated approach. Dr. McAllister neither dismisses the emotional and psychological realities of grief nor reduces it to purely clinical categories. Instead, he brings together sound theological reflection and practical psychological and neuroscientific insight, offering readers a pathway toward understanding, managing, and ultimately overcoming debilitating grief. His writing is accessible yet profound, pastoral yet practical, and firmly rooted in the conviction that healing is both possible and necessary.

The title itself is both arresting and instructive: Get a Grip on Your Grief!. It signals urgency, responsibility, and hope. Dr. McAllister does not trivialize grief, nor does he suggest that it can be easily dismissed. Rather, he recognizes its power and seeks to equip readers with the tools to ensure that grief does not become controlling or destructive. In this sense, the book serves not only as a guide for those who are grieving but also as a resource for pastors, counselors, and caregivers who walk alongside others in their moments of pain.

Importantly, this work speaks into a critical need within the Church. Too often, communities of faith have struggled to adequately address the depth and complexity of human suffering.

Dr. McAllister's contribution helps to bridge that gap. He reminds us that the gospel speaks meaningfully into our grief—that the God we serve is not distant from our pain but present within it, offering comfort, strength, and restoration.

I commend this book to a wide audience. Whether you are personally navigating grief, supporting someone who is, or seeking to deepen your understanding of the human condition through the lenses of theology and psychology, you will find in these pages both guidance and hope.

Dr. McAllister has given us a timely and valuable gift. It is my prayer that this work will serve as an instrument of healing, renewal, and transformation for many.

Dr. Anthony Oliver, Ph.D.
President, Caribbean Graduate School of Theology (CGST)
President, Caribbean Evangelical Theological Association (CETA)

Preface

Grief has a way of arriving uninvited, rearranging everything it touches. Its tentacles have a global reach, and no one escapes. You may be grieving now. If it has never touched you, prepare. Very likely, it will someday. And even if you have grieved before, there is no guarantee that you will not grieve again. Grief could be seen as a side-effect of love.

This is why something as universal and as debilitating as grief demands our urgent attention. We cannot stop it. We cannot prevent it. But the better we understand it, the better we will cope with it and emerge stronger and more resilient on the other side. But there is more.

Paul reminds us in *2 Corinthians 1:3–4 (ESV)*: "Praise be to the God and Father of our Lord Jesus Christ, the Father of compassion and the God of all comfort, who comforts us in all our troubles, so that we can comfort those in any trouble with the comfort we ourselves receive from God."

Our compassionate God of all comfort has promised to comfort us. Why? So that we, in turn, may comfort others with the same comfort we ourselves have received. This means that when we are not on the receiving end of grief's ravages, we must be on the giving end of comforting reassurance.

This book was born out of years of observation, research, and personal encounters with loss. Born in Guyana and having spent my first twenty-one years there, I have seen Christians in grief, Muslims in grief, Hindus in grief, and even those who call themselves atheists in grief. In every instance, the face of grief is identical. Grief is not a religious phenomenon. It is a human experience.

My perspective is framed by my Biblical World-view, scientifically validated data, and my personal relationship with Jesus Christ. At the granular level, the principles and encouragement in this book work just as well for Muslims, Hindus, Christians, and even atheists, if you can set aside disbelief long enough to *get a grip on your grief.*

If you are Muslim or Hindu, this book will not attempt to convert you to Christianity, but it will help you get a grip on your grief. In doing so, it will also help you to help others. For the truth is that, regardless of the name or names assigned to God, He is the Creator of heaven and earth and all who dwell therein. He remains who He is, and was, and is to come, and He loves all His creatures regardless of the labels we attach to ourselves.

And a personal word to non-Christian readers: For every Christian principle or Scripture that I reference, feel free to replace it with one from your own sacred text that speaks equally or even more powerfully to your heart. My only concern is that you *get a grip on your grief.*

Get a Grip on Your Grief! consists of two volumes.

Volume One is written for the person currently caught in the grip of grief. Everything is stated in the simplest possible terms to make reading and application effortless. Every statement in Volume One is firmly rooted in the more detailed explanations and research findings in **Volume Two**. The difference lies not in content but in depth: Volume Two is an academic work, laced with authoritative opinions, medical and scientific validations, technical explanations, and source citations at the end of nearly every Chapter.

Volume Two is designed for those who are not currently grieving, as well as for professional grief therapists, counselors, pastors, and caregivers who must not only give advice but also *understand* the advice they give. Yet, because at one time or another we all find ourselves in the role of comforting the grieving, we understand the nature of that role and the resources and methods available to us.

The style employed is repetitive for the purpose of assimilation through repetition and reinforcement. All major themes surface multiple times across successive chapters. Whenever you read something and realize you have read this before, it was intentional. Learning is in progress.

Unfortunately, **Get a Grip on Your Grief!** comes too late for Job's three friends - Eliphaz, Bildad, and Zophar. It is just in time for anyone who mirrors their mindset. On the other hand, **Get a Grip on Your Grief!** fully aligns with the fourth and youngest of Job's visitors, Elihu. Read the account for yourself in the Book of Job.

Despite the solid medical, psychological, theological, and neuroscientific foundations of **Get a Grip on Your Grief!,** no part, nor the entirety of this book, is intended to replace or serve as a substitute for the advice of your licensed professional therapist or clinician. In fact, I strongly recommend that you share this book with your therapist and invite them to evaluate its general recommendations in light of your specific circumstances. And then you exercise your right to decide.

And now, a personal note for readers who identify as "born-again believers in Jesus Christ" or "Christians" as defined in Acts 11:19-30. You have God's Holy Spirit living in you. Because this book addresses a broad audience, I have not placed heavy emphasis on the decisive role that God's Holy Spirit plays in helping us get a grip on our grief. Yet He is officially referred to as *The Comforter*, and He is the active presence in *2 Corinthians 1:3–4*. I invite you to read on, and between the lines.

And for those who do not identify as born-again believers in Jesus Christ, that's okay. I respect your right of choice. However, if, as you read this book, you feel drawn to explore what it means to become a believer in Jesus Christ, visit us at **Leaders Communicating God's Love Inc.** online at https://lcgl.jesusisyouranswer.com/jesus-waits-you.

A Note on Biblical Terms: Mind, Soul, and Spirit:

Scripture presents the human person as an integrated tri-part being consisting of body, soul, and spirit (1 Thessalonians 5:23). Romans 12:2 introduces the mind, which functions as an aspect of the soul, specializing in thought, reflection, memory, and other psychological processes. In this book, body and spirit are used consistently. The term soul refers to the holistic experience of grief and personhood, while mind focuses on the soul's cognitive and psychological functions. This distinction reflects differences of function and emphasis, not a departure from Biblical anthropology. The spirit remains the dimension through which a person relates to God or other spiritual influences.

My Journal

Get a Grip on Your Grief!

Journal

Control your grief before it controls you.

Volume One

Even If It Feels So, You're Never Alone

A Gentle Beginning

I will never fully understand what you are going through, because your journey through grief is personal to you. The shape of your pain, the silence in your house, the moments that take your breath away. Those belong to you alone. But because God assures me that whatever you are facing, someone else has already faced it, I can try to imagine myself in your place. I can sit beside you for a while and remind you that you are not strange, not broken, and not forgotten.

When loss comes, it shatters the familiar rhythm of life. The days blur. Food tastes different, sleep hides from you, and even breathing feels like a task. You might wake up hoping it was all a bad dream, only to realize that the world has changed and no one asked your permission. That realization can feel unbearable. If that is where you are now, please know that there is no right way to feel. Tears, anger, confusion, even the numbness that frightens you, are all natural parts of the heart's protest against loss.

You do not have to rush to be strong. Strength in grief is not about pretending; it is about surviving one moment, one breath, one heartbeat at a time. The Bible never tells us not to cry. It tells us that God keeps track of our tears. He knows how much this hurts. You can talk to Him in whispers or even in silence. He hears both.

In these first days, your body may feel like it no longer belongs to you. It trembles, aches, and tires easily. This is how the body mourns. Drink water. Breathe slowly. Try to eat a few bites of something nourishing. Rest when you can, even if sleep won't come. These small acts are not selfish. They are survival.

Right now, the thought of "moving on" probably feels cruel. Don't move on. Just keep breathing. Time will move for you until you can move with it again.

I don't expect these words to erase your pain. They can't. But if they can hold a small light for you tonight, let that be enough. Grief has stolen so much already; don't let it take your hope, too.

Faith Window 1

"The Lord is close to the brokenhearted and saves those who are crushed in spirit." Psalm 34:18

Even when words fail, His nearness does not.

♥ Reflection 2

When the World Stops

When loss first strikes, it feels as if the whole world holds its breath. The air in the room changes. Ordinary sounds like footsteps, clocks, and voices seem far away, like they belong to someone else's life. Nothing fits, and nothing makes sense. You look around and wonder how everything outside can go on as if nothing happened.

I have seen that look before; the stillness in the eyes of someone whose world has just been rearranged by loss. I wish I could say the feeling passes quickly, but it doesn't. Time becomes strange. Hours stretch like rubber bands. Days collapse into each other. You forget what you ate, or if you did. It is as if your heart has been unplugged from the rhythm of life.

When this happens, your body and mind are protecting you. God designed us to slow down when our hearts are hit too hard. The numbness is not a failure of faith; it is mercy in disguise. It keeps you from drowning in the full weight of grief all at once. If you feel as though you're moving through fog, that's your soul catching its breath.

Sometimes you may even feel as though you're outside your own skin, as though you're watching yourself from across the room. That distance is another kind of mercy. The mind steps back so that the spirit can survive the first blow. You are not going crazy; you are standing inside a mystery too large for instant understanding.

You may find yourself staring at the same object for minutes without knowing why. You might walk into a room and forget why you came in.

The mind tries to keep life normal, but the heart knows better. This tug-of-war leaves you exhausted. Please don't scold yourself for it. You are not "losing it." You are surviving something that changes the way the human brain works.

In these early days, keep things simple. Drink water. Sit down often. Accept help even when it feels awkward. Let someone else answer the phone, cook a meal, or handle a small task. People want to help. They just don't know how. Giving them permission helps them and you.

If you wake at night with racing thoughts, whisper the name of God until your breathing slows. You don't have to recite polished prayers; a single word is enough. It could be *Jesus*, *Lord*, or simply *Help*. That is enough to invite peace into the chaos. The night may still be long, but you will no longer face it alone.

You may also notice that your thoughts drift toward guilt: *Could I have done more? Should I have seen it coming?* These questions are natural, but they rarely lead to peace. They are the mind's attempt to rewrite the story so that pain might make sense. Be gentle with yourself. The story cannot be rewritten, but healing can still be written on its pages.

And when you have no words for prayer, let stillness itself become prayer. God hears even what you cannot say. Scripture says that He remembers our frame and knows we are dust. That means He never expects you to hold yourself together when your world has come apart.

So, if all you can do today is sit and breathe, that is enough. The world may feel stopped, but God's compassion has not paused. Even in the silence after the storm, He is quietly rebuilding the strength that sorrow tried to steal.

Faith Window 2

"Be still, and know that I am God." *Psalm 46:10.* Even when everything stops, His care continues; His hands still hold what yours cannot.

♥ Reflection 3

The Weight You Carry

Grief is heavy in ways no one warns you about. It isn't only sadness. It's exhaustion that seeps into your bones, fog that settles over your thoughts, and a weariness that makes even small tasks feel impossible. You may wake up tired, move slowly through the day, and wonder why something as simple as making coffee feels like climbing a hill. This weight has nothing to do with weakness. It is the body's way of mourning.

When you love deeply, you also carry that love in your muscles, your heartbeat, and your breath. When the person you love is gone, that energy has nowhere to go. It lingers, pressing inward. Your chest tightens, your shoulders ache, your stomach feels hollow. This is what love in pain feels like. It becomes physical. Don't be alarmed by it. You are not falling apart; you are carrying love that has lost its daily destination.

Sometimes you will cry until you feel emptied out, and then more tears will come without warning. Let them. Tears are the body's language for what the tongue cannot say. Scientists tell us that tears carry stress hormones away from the body. Scripture tells us that God collects those tears in His bottle. Both truths are meant to comfort you. Your body is doing holy work when it weeps.

There will be days when you don't cry at all, and you might feel guilty for that. Don't. Grief changes shape moment by moment. Silence does not mean you've stopped caring; it means the soul is resting between storms. When that quiet comes, take it as a gift, not as betrayal. Breathe deeply. Let the body settle a little.

Weeping endures for the "night", but joy comes in the "morning"!

Try to give yourself more time than you think you need. If you need to sit, sit. If you need to lie down, do it. Rest is not laziness. It's repair. You cannot rebuild a house while it's still shaking from the earthquake. You have permission to do less right now. The weight will not always feel this heavy. Slowly, the heart begins to build new strength beneath the ache, like a muscle rebuilding after strain.

And as strange as it sounds, one day the tears that exhaust you now will become proof that love was real. You will remember that love is never wasted, even when it hurts. For now, though, your only task is to breathe, to rest, and to let God hold the weight you can't.

If the Weight Is Too Much

- Grief is heavy, but it should not destroy you. If you notice that:
- You often think about not wanting to live or about harming yourself.
- You cannot get out of bed, bathe, or eat for many days in a row.
- Fear, chest pain, or panic keep sending you to the emergency room.
- You are drinking or taking pills just to make it through the day.

Then please talk with someone who can help. It could be a doctor, a pastor, a counselor, or a trusted friend. You are not weak for reaching out. You are doing the bravest thing a hurting heart can do: refusing to suffer alone.

Faith Window 3

"Come to me, all you who are weary and burdened, and I will give you rest." *Matthew 11:28* You don't have to carry this weight alone.

Reflection 4

What Your Body Knows

Grief does not live only in your heart; it lives in your body too. Sometimes the ache sits behind your ribs, or in the back of your neck, or deep in your stomach where words can't reach. You may notice headaches that weren't there before, or a trembling that comes from nowhere. Even your breathing may change, as though your body itself is sighing. None of this means something is wrong with you. It means your body remembers the shock of loss and is trying, in its own language, to keep you safe.

When someone we love is gone, the body reacts as if danger has entered the room. Muscles tense. The heart beats faster. Sleep becomes shallow or disappears. These are survival responses; signals from a system that doesn't yet know the emergency has passed. In time, the body will learn that the threat has changed shape, but that takes patience and kindness. Right now, you are both the patient and the healer.

Let's look at the table on page 8 to get an idea of what is really happening inside you. Grief touches three connected parts of you: your **body**, your **mind**, and your **spirit**. They form a circle, not a ladder. Each one speaks and listens to the others.

This simple pattern is what I call the *Grief Response Matrix.* You don't have to memorize it, just notice it. When one part of you suffers, the others try to help. Sometimes the help feels clumsy. Your mind may push you to keep busy when your body needs rest. Your body may crave stillness while your spirit begs for prayer. Healing begins when you listen to them all.

Part of You	What It Does in Grief	How to Care for It
Body	Tightens, loses sleep, appetite shifts, *fatigue*	Breathe slowly, hydrate, stretch, rest
Mind	Replays moments, searches for meaning, questions	Write, talk, pray, let thoughts spill out
Spirit	Feels distant, strained, or angry toward God	Stay open; Scripture, song, or stillness can reconnect

When your shoulders tighten, that is the body's way of saying, *I am still carrying too much.* When your thoughts circle the same questions, that is your mind saying, *I need to make sense of this.* When you feel far from God, that is your spirit whispering, *I need to be found again.* Every part of you is trying to reach peace. None of these reactions makes you weak. They make you human.

You can start gently retraining your body to believe that safety still exists. Take three slow breaths. Feel the air enter your lungs and leave again. Drink a glass of water, not quickly but as an act of care. Go outside, even for a moment, and feel the ground under your feet. These are small ways of telling your body, *we are still alive.* And once your body calms, your mind and spirit will follow.

You are wonderfully made, and that includes how you heal. Grief may have unsettled everything, but nothing about your body's response is broken. God designed it to help you survive sorrow until peace returns to you.

Faith Window 4

"I praise you, for I am fearfully and wonderfully made." (*Psalm 139:14)* Your body still knows how to heal; it is one of God's quiet miracles.

How the Mind Tries to Help

Grief is not only an emotional storm; it is also a mental one. Your mind, desperate to make sense of what happened, begins to replay every detail. It searches for explanations, bargains with time, and tries to rewrite the story in ways that could have prevented the pain. This mental overactivity is not cruelty. It is protection. Your mind believes that if it can just understand the "why," the "what if," or the "how," it can restore order. But grief doesn't follow the rules of reason.

You may find yourself waking up in the night, replaying the same scene over and over. What you said, what you didn't say, what you might have done differently. The mind, once a faithful servant, becomes an overzealous guard. It scans for meaning, hoping that logic can mend a broken heart. Yet love is not logical, and neither is loss. The mind cannot repair what only the heart can grieve.

Still, your mind is trying to help. Think of it as a child holding a flashlight in a storm. The beam may flicker, but it's searching for a path. In the chaos of loss, the mind's goal is survival. It organizes tasks, manages people, and keeps your body moving when your spirit feels paralyzed. That's why in the earliest days, you may appear "strong." But this strength is often the mind's defense, which is a way to hold the pieces together until the soul can begin to process the truth.

Over time, your mind will shift from frantic searching to gentle remembering. The part that once shouted *"Why?"* will begin to whisper *"What now?"* That's the moment when healing starts to take root. You'll begin to see that understanding doesn't come from solving the loss, but from learning to live with it. The mind gradually accepts that the story didn't end where you wanted It simply turned a page you didn't expect.

Nature gives us a picture of this quiet adaptation. When a river is blocked by a fallen tree, the water doesn't stop. It gathers strength, finds another channel, and continues its flow. The new path may twist in different ways, but it remains the same river. Your mind, too, will find new channels and ways to think, remember, and hope again. At first, these channels are carved by tears, but one day they'll carry life instead of pain.

If your thoughts still circle restlessly, don't fight them. Let them circle. They will slow down when they're ready. Sometimes writing them down helps. Turning the storm into words gives the mind a place to rest. And when the same questions come again, remind yourself: *I don't have to solve everything to begin healing.* The mind's work is to understand, but the heart's work is to feel, and together, they will bring you back to peace.

Faith Window 5

"You will keep in perfect peace those whose minds are steadfast, because they trust in you." *Isaiah 26:3* Even when your thoughts race, God is patient with your searching mind.

When Faith Feels Far Away

There comes a point in grief when the faith you once stood on feels like sand. You know the words you used to sing, the prayers you used to pray, but they don't sound the same anymore. You whisper them, and they fall flat. You open your Bible, and the words blur. You try to believe, but your heart feels disconnected from what your mind still holds to be true. This season can feel like failure, but it isn't. It's what happens when pain speaks louder than understanding.

Even the most faithful people can lose their sense of connection in grief. Job did. David did. Jesus did, crying out, "My God, my God, why have You forsaken me?" The experience of distance from God does not mean God has left. It means you are standing in the fog between pain and comfort. Faith is still there. It just isn't loud right now. In these moments, you are not losing your faith; you are learning what faith really is: trust that remains when nothing feels certain.

Grief scrambles your senses. You may feel angry with God, or worse, nothing at all. Both are forms of relationship. Anger is a cry for fairness; numbness is the soul's temporary anesthesia. Neither disqualifies you from God's presence. He is not fragile. He will not retreat because your prayers sound raw or your silence feels cold. In fact, Scripture describes Him as "close to the brokenhearted." Sometimes His nearness is too gentle to feel, like air holding you up while you sleep.

Think of a seed buried deep in the earth. In darkness, it looks dead. No light, no sound, no movement. Yet within that hidden space, life is unfolding. The seed's shell must crack before anything new can grow. Faith works the same way. When your old understanding of God seems to shatter, it may be because a truer, deeper relationship is taking shape beneath the surface. Faith is not lost; it's being transformed.

If you can't pray, breathe. Each breath is a prayer without words. If you can't sing, listen. Someone else's song may carry you for now. If you can't read Scripture, rest in a single truth: *God is still here.* You don't have to reach for Him. He's already reaching for you. This is how faith survives the silence: not by noise or effort, but by presence.

In time, faith returns. Not as a sudden light but as a steady glow. You begin to see that God was not gone after all; He was simply sitting beside you in the dark, waiting for you to notice. When faith feels far away, it is not faith that has moved. It is your heart, walking through a valley it never chose. And even there, you are not alone.

Faith Window 6

"Even though I walk through the valley of the shadow of death, I will fear no evil, for you are with me." *Psalm 23:4* Faith isn't gone when you can't feel it; it's quietly holding you through the night.

When People Say the Wrong Thing

In times of loss, people often speak because silence makes them uncomfortable. They reach for words like a person groping in the dark, hoping to offer comfort but often bumping into your pain instead. You hear phrases like, *"They're in a better place,"* or *"At least you had time to say goodbye,"* or *"God needed another angel."* Those words might be meant kindly, but they can feel like sandpaper against an open wound. You nod politely because you know they mean well, but inside, something twists.

The truth is, most people have never been taught how to stand near someone else's grief. They mistake explaining for helping. But grief does not need explanations. It needs presence. The person who sits quietly with you in shared silence offers far more comfort than the one who tries to fill the space with answers. Yet, as the one who is grieving, you shouldn't feel obligated to protect everyone else from your pain. It is not your job to make others comfortable around your sorrow.

Still, those clumsy attempts at comfort can sting. You may replay the words later and feel a new wave of anger or sadness. That reaction is normal. It's your heart defending itself. You don't have to suppress that feeling, but you can choose how to carry it. Try to remember that most people speak from a place of helplessness, not cruelty. They're trying to bridge a gap they can't cross. Recognizing this doesn't erase the hurt, but it can keep bitterness from settling in.

Nature gives us an image here. When a large bird protects its young during a storm, its wings are wide open, catching both rain and wind. Some raindrops sting harder than others, but the bird doesn't close its wings. It knows that protection means enduring the weather, not avoiding it. In grief, you too are learning to stay open while things that hurt keep falling around you. Every awkward word you endure without hardening your heart is an act of quiet strength.

If someone's words truly wound you, it's okay to step back. You can say, "I know you mean well, but that's hard for me to hear right now." You're not being rude. You're being honest. And if you can't find the energy for even that, simply walk away and breathe. Protecting your peace is part of the healing process. Later, when you have more strength, you may even find compassion for those who spoke without understanding. They didn't know what to say because grief had never taught them its language.

And someday, you'll be the one who stands beside someone else in mourning. You'll remember what not to say. You'll understand that sometimes the best comfort is no words at all…just presence, listening, and gentle empathy. Your pain, even in this, is shaping you into someone wiser and kinder than before.

Faith Window 7

"The Lord is near to the brokenhearted and saves the crushed in spirit." *(Psalm 34:18).* When others don't know how to comfort you, remember that the One who truly understands already holds you close.

Reflection 8

When the World Moves On

There comes a moment when you realize that while your world has stopped, everyone else's has not. The sun still rises. The news still runs. People still talk about weekend plans and post photos of themselves smiling online. It feels like a quiet betrayal, as if the universe should have paused out of respect for your pain. But life has kept moving, and you're left trying to figure out how to live in a world that feels out of rhythm with your heart.

In the first days and weeks, you were surrounded. Calls came in, meals arrived, and prayers were said. But as time passes, the attention fades. People return to their routines, even those who love you deeply. They are not unkind. They are simply untrained in grief. They assume that because the service is over, the sorrow must have settled. What they don't see is that you're still waking up every day to the same silence, still relearning how to breathe without the one you've lost.

The loneliness that follows is not just about being alone; it's about feeling unseen. The world no longer mirrors your sadness. You walk through a grocery store and wonder how everyone else can move so easily. You hear laughter and feel both warmth and envy. This tension, wanting life to continue yet resenting that it has, is one of grief's strangest aches. It means your love was deep, and your loss is still teaching you how to live.

Nature understands this rhythm. After a storm, the sky clears, but the earth is still soaked. Flowers that look upright are still holding hidden water in their stems. Healing works like that, too. On the outside, you may seem steady, but inside, you're still holding rain. And that's all right. Healing never demands that you catch up with the world; it simply asks that you keep standing, even when you still feel drenched.

You may feel pressure to "move on." But moving on isn't the goal. Moving forward is. Moving on suggests leaving love behind; moving forward means carrying love with you into whatever comes next. Each small act, washing dishes, answering a message, watching a sunrise, is proof that you are learning to live again. You are not leaving your loved one behind; you are bringing them with you in new ways.

One day, you'll notice that the world no longer feels like an intruder. Its rhythm and yours will slowly begin to sync again. And you'll realize something beautiful. The world didn't forget you. It simply waited for you to find your footing again.

Faith Window 8

"Those who sow in tears shall reap with shouts of joy." (*Psalm 126:5)*
The world moves forward, and so will you. Not away from love, but deeper into it.

When Helping Heals You

Something surprising happens in the slow journey through grief: there comes a moment when, even though your own heart is still mending, you feel a quiet pull to reach out. It might begin with a small act, checking on someone else who's hurting, bringing a meal, sending a message, or simply listening without offering advice. That gentle tug is not a distraction from your pain; it is part of your healing. Helping others after loss is not about forgetting your sorrow. It's about discovering that compassion can carry you where strength alone cannot.

When you've walked through darkness, you develop eyes that see differently. You notice pain where others miss it. You recognize the heaviness in someone's voice because you've felt it yourself. This kind of awareness is a sacred gift, born from brokenness. And when you use that gift to comfort someone else, something remarkable happens. You begin to feel your own heart knit together in new ways. It's as if God takes the thread of your grief and uses it to mend another person's wound, and in doing so, He repairs part of yours.

Psychologists have found that serving others reduces anxiety and strengthens emotional resilience. But long before research confirmed it, Scripture already taught it: *"Carry each other's burdens, and in this way you will fulfill the law of Christ."* When you step outside yourself to lighten another's load, your brain begins to release chemicals of calm and connection. What once felt like isolation now feels like belonging again. The very act of giving becomes the medicine you didn't know you needed.

Of course, helping others doesn't mean denying your own pain. You cannot pour from an empty cup. It's about sharing from your overflow, not your reserve. Some days, that may mean a prayer whispered from your pillow for someone else who is grieving. Other days, it might mean volunteering, mentoring, or simply being the presence you once wished for. Every act of compassion, no matter how small, is a declaration that love still has a voice in your story.

In nature, rivers offer a quiet lesson in this truth. When heavy rains fill them beyond their banks, they overflow into the surrounding soil, watering dry ground and fostering new life. The river doesn't stop flowing; it simply widens its reach. Your grief can do the same. When you allow your compassion to overflow into someone else's dry places, your own soul becomes fertile again. You may never have chosen this sorrow, but you can choose what grows from it.

As you give, you'll find that healing doesn't mean erasing the past. It means transforming it into something that blesses others. You become part of the comfort God promises to the world. The same arms that once hung limp in sorrow now reach outward in grace. And though your heart will always remember what was lost, it will also learn to rejoice in what love can still create.

Faith Window 9

"Blessed be the God of all comfort, who comforts us in all our troubles, so that we can comfort those in any trouble." (*2 Corinthians 1:3–4*) When you share comfort, healing moves through you and always multiplies beyond you.

♥ Reflection 10

Finding Light You Did Not See Before

When the heavy fog of grief begins to lift, it often happens in small, almost invisible ways. You may notice that one morning, the air smells sweeter. Or that a song you once couldn't bear to hear now makes you smile. These are gentle arrivals of light, fragile but real. At first, they might feel strange, even wrong, as if joy has no right to visit your sorrow. But joy doesn't cancel grief; it redeems it.

You may wrestle with guilt the first time you laugh again. It can feel like betrayal, but it isn't. It's love finding a new way to breathe. The same heart that broke from love is the one that's learning how to live again because of love. Healing doesn't mean forgetting. It means remembering without collapsing. Each moment of light is proof that loss cannot erase life.

The light often comes disguised as ordinary things: the taste of coffee, the warmth of a pet resting near you, a neighbor's kindness, the way rain sounds against a window. These are not accidents. They are reminders that even in brokenness, beauty still exists. And when you let yourself notice them, something inside of you shifts. You begin to trust that hope can return, even if it arrives quietly.

This is where intentional practice helps, not as a strict routine, but as a rhythm of grace. You are not commanding yourself to heal; you are inviting healing to meet you. The following small steps are designed to reawaken your body, mind, and spirit gently. You can practice any of them, in any order, as often as you wish within seven days. There is no schedule. Only a reminder that you are still capable of life.

The 7 Small Steps to Emotional Reset

(Practice any, as often as you wish, within seven days (no order required.)

- **A slower breath.** Place a hand on your chest. Inhale through your nose for four counts, hold for two, exhale for six. Do this five times. Nothing dramatic, just air moving in and out. Your body hears the message: we are safe enough to breathe again.
- **A glass of water.** Loss dries everything: eyes, throat, even thoughts. Drink slowly. Feel the swallow. Dehydration disguises itself as dread; water softens its edges. This is care in its simplest form.
- **A name for the feeling.** Say it out loud or write it down: angry, frightened, numb, lonely. Naming does not enlarge pain; it gives it shape. Once named, feelings become something you can hold instead of something that holds you.
- **A step outside. Stand at the door or on the porch**. Notice one living thing. It could be a leaf, a bird, or a slice of sky. Let the world remind you that life continues, not as a betrayal of your love, but as its context.
- **A reach toward someone.** Send a short message: "Today is hard." You don't need to explain. Connection breaks isolation's spell. If no one is around, write a note to yourself for tomorrow: "I made it through today."
- **A moment with meaning.** Hold an object that carries your story. It could be a photo, a watch, a recipe card, or a tool. Whisper, "Thank You." Gratitude doesn't erase ache, but it keeps love visible when memory stings.
- **A gentle rest. Lie down without guilt.** Set a three-minute timer if sleep won't come. Close your eyes anyway. Rest repairs what sorrow loosens. Your worth is not measured by productivity right now.

These steps are not about finishing grief. They're about remembering life. Repeat them whenever your heart feels heavy; repetition helps bring restoration.

As you practice, you may notice that peace doesn't stay all day. It drifts in and out like sunlight through trees. That's how healing works: it visits before it settles. But every visit strengthens you. The light that once startled you will soon feel natural again. And when it does, you'll know that your heart has not only survived. It has begun to shine.

Faith Window 10

"Weeping may endure for a night, but joy comes in the morning." *(Psalm 30:5)* Joy doesn't replace sorrow; it grows beside it until you realize both were part of love's design.

♥ Reflection 11

When Purpose Returns

One of grief's quiet miracles is that, somewhere down the road, purpose begins to stir again. At first, it feels impossible. You can barely make it through a day without tears. How could life ever have meaning again? But purpose doesn't come all at once, and it doesn't always come with fanfare. It begins as a whisper, a small spark of curiosity, a faint desire to do something that matters again. It might occur to you: *Maybe I could help someone else. Maybe I could finish what we started. Maybe I could live in a way that honors their memory.*

Purpose after loss doesn't erase your pain. It gives it direction. It's the shift from asking *"Why did this happen?"* to *"What can I do with what I've learned?"* That's when sorrow begins to transform into wisdom. You start to see that grief, as unwanted as it was, has taught you how fragile life is, how precious people are, and how short time can be. Those lessons become sacred tools for living differently, more intentionally, more tenderly, more awake.

Sometimes this rediscovered purpose takes the shape of service: helping others who walk a similar road. Other times, it's found in creativity, advocacy, or simply living your life with deeper gratitude. You may not build a foundation or write a book; your purpose might be to love your family better, to forgive more freely, or to see beauty in places you once ignored. No purpose is small when it grows from compassion.

Nature illustrates this perfectly. When a storm damages a tree, it doesn't stop growing. Instead, it bends toward the light in new directions. The scar remains, but so does the growth. Some branches grow stronger because of where they broke. You, too, are learning to bend toward the light and to stretch into a version of yourself that couldn't exist before loss. The person you were before loved deeply; the person you are becoming loves even deeper.

Finding purpose again doesn't mean the grief is over. It means that love has matured into something that gives back. You begin to see your loved one's influence in your choices, your values, and your compassion. You live in a way that carries their legacy forward. In that sense, death does not end the story. It passes the pen to you. You become the living continuation of what you both shared.

If you feel that stirring of purpose, don't rush it. Let it unfold gently. Ask God to guide it, to breathe direction into your desire. You may be surprised by where it leads. What began as brokenness can become a blessing, not only for you, but for others who will one day draw strength from your journey.

Faith Window 11

"And we know that in all things God works for the good of those who love Him." *(Romans 8:28)* Purpose doesn't replace grief; it redeems it, turning pain into compassion, and sorrow into strength.

♥ Reflection 12

Moments of Faith

Faith in the midst of grief rarely looks like confidence. More often, it looks like trembling hope. Yes, the kind that prays through tears and holds on by a thread. You may not feel strong. You may not even feel faithful. But faith is not the absence of doubt; it's the decision to keep trusting when nothing makes sense. It's whispering, *"God, I still believe You're here,"* even when silence fills the room.

In grief, faith is often found in moments, not in mountains. It lives in small acts of surrender: the sigh that releases fear, the prayer that begins with *"I don't understand,"* the choice to get out of bed and face another day. These moments may seem insignificant, but heaven notices. Jesus said faith the size of a mustard seed can move mountains (Matthew 17:20). That means even the faintest flicker of trust still carries power. You don't have to feel faith to have it. You only have to refuse to let go of it.

Over time, these fragile moments of faith begin to gather strength. You start to remember times when God carried you before, when comfort came just when you needed it most. You recall the people who showed up unexpectedly, the words that spoke peace when everything felt shattered. Each memory becomes a small altar of gratitude, a reminder that you were never abandoned. The God who walked with you in the valley has not changed His address.

Faith is not a shortcut through grief. It is the steady companion that keeps you from being swallowed by it. It doesn't erase pain; it transforms it. It allows sorrow to be seen through the eyes of eternity, where love is never wasted, and loss is never final. As faith deepens, peace makes quiet visits to your heart, sometimes for just seconds at a time. Then, gradually, those seconds into minutes, and one day you realize that peace has moved in and decided to stay.

Think of a candle in a dark room. One tiny flame can't eliminate all the shadows, but it changes the atmosphere. The darkness is still there, but it no longer owns the room. Your faith is that candle. Each prayer, each verse remembered, each sigh of trust adds a little more light. You don't need to banish every shadow. You need to keep the flame alive.

When you can't pray, whisper your pain. When you can't sing, hum the silence. When you can't see the road ahead, trust the One who walks beside you. Faith isn't about understanding everything. It's about knowing that you're not alone in anything. And in those quiet, sacred moments of faith, your spirit begins to breathe again.

Faith Window 12

"The Lord is near to the brokenhearted and saves the crushed in spirit." *(Psalm 34:18)* Faith doesn't always shout. Sometimes it simply whispers, *"God is still here."*

♥ Reflection 13

Full Circle Healing

How Body, Mind, and Spirit Work Together

You first met this idea early in the book, when we talked about what your body knows. Then, your body felt like the battlefield. It felt tight, restless, heavy, and tired. Your mind was the storm, and your spirit seemed far away. Now, near the end of this journey, it's time to see the whole picture again, not as a list of what hurts, but as a living circle of healing. The same parts of you that once trembled in pain are now learning how to work together in peace.

Grief may have broken your rhythm, but it never destroyed your design. You were created as one being with body, mind, and spirit. Each plays a role in helping you find your way home again. Healing is not a race toward "better." It's the slow cooperation of all three parts of you finding balance after the storm. When one falters, another quietly helps. That's why small progress counts. Each breath, each prayer, each decision to keep going is a sign of the circle repairing itself.

The **body** speaks first. It tells you when you've carried too much. The ache in your shoulders, the fatigue, the shallow breath are all your body's way of saying, *"I'm still remembering."* But now, instead of bracing against it, you can listen. You've learned to rest when needed, to breathe more deeply, to honor the tension as a sign that you're still alive and still capable of healing.

The **mind** joins next. It once spun in confusion, replaying the loss, searching for answers. Now it begins to slow. It starts asking gentler questions: *What still matters? What can I do with what remains?* The mind learns that understanding doesn't mean solving the loss. It means finding meaning within it. Slowly, it becomes a companion again rather than a critic.

And then the **spirit**, once silent, begins to hum again. You may notice it in a tear that feels cleansing rather than heavy, or in the stillness that suddenly feels peaceful rather than empty. That's the voice of the spirit returning, reminding you that you were never truly alone. The same God who comforted you in the valley is still here, guiding your circle back toward light.

Here's a simple way to see what's happening:

Part of You	In the Beginning	Now, in Healing
Body	Tense, exhausted, restless, numb.	Calming, resting, remem*bering safety.*
Mind	Overthinking, searching, doubting.	Accepting, focusing, discovering meaning.
Spirit	Silent, distant, questioning.	Reawakening, trusting, quietly strong.

This is the same you, only steadier, softer, more whole. The pieces didn't vanish; they realigned. Healing isn't about going back to who you were before the loss. It's about becoming the person who can carry both love and loss at once. You've walked through pain, found grace in the dark, and learned that even broken things can become beautiful when held by God's hands.

When you breathe now, your body remembers peace. When you think now, your mind seeks hope. When you pray now, your spirit feels heard.

This is what it means to come full circle.

Faith Window 13

"He restores my soul." Psalm 23:3 The same God who held you in pieces now holds you whole.

Your Grief Recovery Journey in Perspective

From Tragedy to Triumph in Time

Where You Are Right Now

Your world has shattered. The pain feels permanent. You wonder if you'll ever feel whole again. You're exhausted, numb, or overwhelmed. And sometimes all three in the same hour. This is normal. This is grief doing what grief does. And here's what you need to know:

Your brain and body are already working to heal you, even when you can't feel it happening.

What's Actually Happening Inside You

Right now, three systems are responding to your loss:

Your BODY is in survival mode. Your heart races, sleep breaks, appetite vanishes. This isn't weakness. It's your nervous system treating loss like a physical threat. It's protecting you the only way it knows how.

Your MIND is searching desperately for answers. Why? What if? If only? These loops aren't failures of faith. They're your brain trying to restore order to a world that suddenly makes no sense.

Your SPIRIT feels distant, silent, or angry. Prayer feels empty. Scripture feels closed. God feels far. This doesn't mean you've lost your faith. It means you're walking through the valley where faith is tested, refined, and deepened.

All three are connected. When one suffers, the others try to help. When one heals, the others follow. You are not broken. You are a masterpiece under repair.

The Truth About Your Timeline

Grief doesn't move in stages. You won't go through denial, then anger, then bargaining, then depression, then acceptance in neat order. Real grief **oscillates**. You swing between facing the pain and rebuilding life, sometimes within the same day. Both movements are necessary. Both are healthy.

Most people stabilize faster than they expect. Not because the pain vanishes, but because resilience is built into your design. You are more durable than you know.

The Small Actions That Rewire Your Brain

Here's the neuroscience that changes everything: **hope is not a feeling you wait for. It's a neural network you build through repetition.**

Every time you take one small action, neurons fire together in your brain. It could be one breath, one prayer, one verse read, one glass of water, or one moment of gratitude. Do it again tomorrow, and those neurons begin to wire together. Keep going, and within 8 weeks, what feels like discipline today becomes automatic tomorrow.

Week 1-2: You're planting seeds. The pathways are fragile, but they're forming. Your brain releases tiny dopamine signals, chemical whispers that say, "do that again."

Week 3-4: Repetition strengthens the pathways. What once required all your willpower now takes slightly less. Hope flickers, even if you don't trust it yet.

Week 5-8+: The network matures. Pathways connect to each other. Prayer triggers peace without effort. Scripture brings comfort automatically. Resilience becomes your new baseline.

This isn't wishful thinking. It's Hebb's Law from 1949: *neurons that fire together wire together.* Your brain is designed to rewire itself. All you have to do is cooperate with small, repeated acts of turning toward life.

The Four Seasons You'll Walk Through

Grief moves in cycles, like seasons:

WINTER is numbness and shock. You're still. You're protected. This is your body conserving strength.

SPRING is questions and searching. Why did this happen? What does it mean? You're waking up, even when it hurts.

SUMMER is renewal returning. Joy flickers. Service feels possible. Hope steadies. You're living again, not just surviving.

AUTUMN is surrender and gratitude. You release what you can't control. You bless what was. You trust what's ahead.

You'll revisit seasons. Winter may return in July. That's not failure. That's the rhythm of healing. The difference is that each time you cycle through, you carry more strength.

What You Need From Others (And Yourself)

From others: No explanations. Not sermons. Just **presence**. Someone who sits with you in silence. Someone who listens without fixing. Someone who brings a meal, holds space, and doesn't rush you.

From yourself: Permission to be exactly where you are. Permission to cry on good days. Permission to laugh without guilt. Permission to rest without shame. **You don't have to perform recovery for anyone.**

From God: He is closer than you feel. When prayers bounce off the ceiling, He's catching them. When faith feels weak, He's holding what you can't. *"The Lord is near to the brokenhearted and saves the crushed in spirit"* (Psalm 34:18). Near, not distant. Saving, not spectating.

The Three Things That Will Carry You

1. Small daily rhythms. Not grand plans. Just breathe slowly for three minutes. Drink water. Read one verse. Call one friend. Let these micro-actions build the neural infrastructure for tomorrow's hope.

2. Safe community. You cannot heal in isolation. One anchor person. One weekly check-in. One group that doesn't rush you. Healing multiplies in connection.

3. Meaning-making over time. Eventually, the question shifts from "Why did this happen?" to "What can I do with what I've learned?" That shift is grace at work. Your pain has taught you things others desperately need to hear. Your compassion will become someone else's lifeline.

Where You're Headed

You won't return to who you were before the loss. You'll become someone deeper. Someone who knows the valley and learned that God walks there too. Someone whose tears carved channels where compassion now flows. Someone whose faith survived the furnace and came out refined.

Grief doesn't destroy love. It proves it. The ache you carry is the weight of love that has nowhere to land. One day, that love will find new expression: in service, in memory, in how you treat the next grieving soul you meet.

You will laugh again without betraying what you lost. **You will hope again** without erasing who you loved. **You will live again** because love never commanded you to stop.

One Final Truth

Right now, you're standing at the bottom of a dark valley. You can't see the path forward. But **every small step you take today is building a bridge you can't see yet.** Every breath prayer lays one neural pathway. Every verse read strengthens one connection. Every tear cried releases one burden.

Your brain is rewiring. Your body is recalibrating. Your spirit is being refined. And God, whether you feel Him or not, is reconstructing your shattered heart into something that can hold both sorrow and joy, both memory and hope, both loss and life.

You are not falling apart.

You are being rebuilt.

And the One who began this work **will finish it.**

"He heals the brokenhearted and binds up their wounds."

Psalm 147:3

Weeping endures for the "night", but joy comes in the "morning"!

"Weeping may tarry for the night, but joy comes with the morning."
Psalm 30:5

"I am making all things new."
Revelation 21:5

You will survive this.
You will heal from this.
You will grow through this.

One small step at a time.

In the kindest and gentlest ways possible, I have tried to say, Get a Grip on Your Grief, before it gets a grip on you. Grieving has benefits, but only after you have experienced a trauma. Think of grieving as your subconscious attempt to mitigate the severity and pain of the trauma you encountered. That makes grieving good, but only because the trauma was bad. Without a trauma to trigger it, no one would wake up one sunny morning with just the right temperature, with food in the fridge, money in the bank, physically fit, and all family members living in harmony and prosperity, and say, "Let me grieve". That is because there is nothing inherently good in grieving itself. On the contrary, it wearies us, depletes our energy, and, in acute cases, may even compromise our will to live if left unmanaged.

It is for this reason that we must make an effort as lovingly as we can, to get a grip on our grief before it gets a grip on us and controls our thoughts and actions. In this book, you will learn that when designing our physical and spiritual structures, God made provision for automated grief mitigation. Just as the body self-heals physiologically, so, spiritually, mentally, and emotionally, our mind and spirit, when affected by grief, are programmed to self-heal, but not without our doing our part.

When there is a minor wound on our hand or foot, the body heals itself as blood clots form a protective scab, inflammation helps fight infection and start repair, new skin grows underneath, and the scab falls away once the tissue is fully restored. We must resist the temptation to prematurely disturb the scab before the healing process is complete. To do otherwise will prolong the wound's healing time.

Similarly, the wounds associated with grief will self-heal over time, but we need to cooperate with the process and ensure that we expose ourselves only to those who are able and willing to do so. But how can we cooperate with what we do not fully understand? Get a Grip on Your Grief! seeks to answer most of the questions about grief you may have, or may never have thought about. Volume Two complements Volume One in every way, but seeks to address most of the issues that are sometimes difficult to resolve or even understand.

Feel free to read Volume One over and over. If you wish to understand anything about the fascinating masterpiece God created you to be, then begin Volume Two. Of course, if you are a pastor, counselor, practical caregiver or licensed therapist… then Volume Two is definitely for you.

END of Volume One

Volume Two

Chapter 1

What Grief Really Is

1.1 Beyond the Five Stages (A Modern Understanding)

Grief is not a sequence to be completed but a lived reality that unfolds across mind, body, and spirit. Popular models have long held that sorrow progresses through identifiable stages, yet real human grief rarely follows a neat progression. People loop, skip, and collide through emotions that overlap, recur, and resist resolution. When grief is framed as a linear process rather than a dynamic experience, mourners often feel confused or inadequate, not because they are grieving wrongly, but because the model itself is insufficient.

When believers try to force themselves through those five compartments, they begin to think they are failing spiritually.[1] The Bible tells a different story. David went from panic to praise within the same Psalm (Psalms 13 & 32). Jeremiah declared that God's mercies are new every morning, right after saying, "My soul is bowed down within me." Even Jesus, who knew resurrection was near, still groaned in His spirit and wept at Lazarus's tomb (John 11:33-35). Scripture shows that faith does not cancel emotion; faith sanctifies emotion by bringing it into the presence of God.[2]

The Greek verb *embrimaomai* (ἐμβριμάομαι), translated "groaned," conveys indignation or deep inner turmoil, and not mere sadness, but visceral distress, even anger at death itself. This is the same word used for a horse snorting in battle. John layers three emotional responses: Jesus was "deeply moved" (*embrimaomai*), "troubled" (*tarassō* - agitated, stirred), and then "wept" (dakryō - the quiet tears of grief, not the loud wailing of *klaiō*). Christ's tears were neither a lack of faith nor emotional incontinence. They were the incarnate God entering fully into human loss, feeling death's wrongness in His sinless spirit. He wept knowing the resurrection was minutes away because grief is the proper human response to the rupture death creates, and Jesus sanctified that response by experiencing it Himself.

The modern church often teaches victory but not process. It preaches the cross and the empty tomb but tends to overlook the Saturday of silence in between.[3] Yet that in-between day is where most mourners live. It is the space between "It is finished" and "He is risen." Grief is holy ground because it exposes what we truly believe about God's character when explanations are gone.

1.2 What the Bible Says About Grief

From Genesis to Revelation, God records human sorrow with dignity.[4] Abraham mourned Sarah and buried her with honor. Joseph wept over Jacob. Moses lamented Israel's rebellion. David's tears for Absalom echo through history. And the shortest verse in Scripture, which is "Jesus wept", reminds us in John 11:35 that the Incarnate Son entered the full range of human feeling.

Biblical grief is not merely emotional discharge; it is covenant conversation.[5] When the Psalmist says in Psalm 34:18, "The Lord is near to the brokenhearted and saves the crushed in spirit," he reveals a God who draws closer, not farther, when hearts collapse. Tears become prayer when offered toward Him.

Lament is grief with direction. It begins in pain but moves toward petition and eventually to praise, even if praise sounds cracked. Job questioned God, yet God said Job had spoken rightly. Jeremiah wrote Lamentations amid ruins, and God preserved it as Scripture. Heaven keeps every honest cry because it proves relationship has not been severed. Even silence before God is dialogue when the heart remains turned toward Him.

Modern psychology now describes lament as an essential step in trauma recovery: naming what hurts in a safe relationship rewires the brain's fear circuits. Scripture taught that centuries earlier.[6] The human nervous system calms when truth is spoken in trust.[7] Faith and neuroscience meet in the same design.

1.3 Hope That Does Not Deny Pain (1 Thessalonians 4:13-18)

Paul's words in 1 Thessalonians 4:13, "that you may not grieve as others do who have no hope," are often misread as a command not to cry. He did not forbid grief; he forbade hopelessness. Hope is the companion of pain, not its replacement.

Hope that denies sorrow becomes delusion; hope that walks through sorrow becomes endurance. When Jesus wept at Bethany, He knew resurrection was minutes away (John 11:35). Still, He let His humanity tremble. He did not hurry His tears. This shows believers that divine certainty does not erase human ache.

True Christian hope is covenant memory. It is the recollection that the God who raised before will raise again.[8] It stands on history, not sentiment. Grief without hope collapses inward; grief with hope leans forward. Faith does not say, "It doesn't hurt." Faith says, "It hurts, but God remains."

Every mourner eventually reaches a fork in the road between pretending and trusting. Pretending numbs the pain temporarily but deepens isolation. Trusting invites God into the chaos. Pain shared with Him becomes transformed pain; pain denied becomes despair.

Hope is not a mood; it is muscle memory built through worship. Each act of praise under pressure trains the soul to believe again. The tomb is empty, yet the tears of Good Friday were real. The Christian learns to hold both truths at once. Resurrection is promised, and suffering is acknowledged.

1.4 The Science of Sorrow - How the Brain Processes Loss

Modern science gives language to what Scripture already implied: grief is embodied theology.[9] When the heart breaks, chemicals and neurons echo the cry of the soul.[10] Researchers now speak of the vagus nerve, the body's main calming pathway, which slows the heart during prayer and soft worship.[11] Brain scans show the amygdala quieting when Scripture is read aloud in rhythm.[12] Even sleep patterns begin to normalize through expressive writing practices.[13]

Physicians call one manifest *stress cardiomyopathy*, popularly "broken-heart syndrome." The left ventricle weakens after extreme emotional shock,[14] yet recovery improves when patients engage in spiritual practices that evoke peace.[15] Science is tracing the fingerprints of grace.

David once said in Psalm 32:3, "When I kept silent, my bones wasted away." He described what later came to be called psychosomatic depletion. Unspoken grief consumes energy; expressed grief releases healing hormones.[16] The pneumopsychosomatic truth is this: when the spirit finds voice, the psyche organizes, and the body obeys. God designed coherence across domains.

The tears we call weakness are chemical evidence that love has matter. Cortisol falls, immunity rises,[17] and hope alters heart rhythms measurable on an EKG.[18] The gospel of healing runs deeper than emotion. It is biology responding to belief.

1.5 Faith and Feeling

1.5.1 The Psalm of Unanswered Pain (Psalm 88)

Psalm 88 ends in darkness. No resolution, no chorus of victory. God allowed that unfinished lament into His canon to prove that He can handle unfinished people. Faith is not tidy. It sometimes ends a day with "Why, Lord?" instead of "Hallelujah." That Psalm gives believers permission to keep praying when no answer comes. It teaches that honesty itself is worship.

"But I, O Lord, cry to You; in the morning my prayer comes before You."

Even when morning brings no relief, prayer itself becomes oxygen. Faith is not the absence of pain; it is persistence within pain.

When the Noise Fades…

Grief often intensifies after the funeral when silence replaces sympathy. Emergency grief runs on adrenaline; honest grief begins when adrenaline runs out.[19] Do not mistake exhaustion for regression. You are now facing the real landscape of loss. It is the place where emotion becomes form.

Joseph's Compassionate Tears

After Jacob's death, Joseph led the formal mourning of Egypt (Genesis 50:1-14). Later, when his brothers feared that his kindness would expire with their father's memory, they sent a fabricated plea for mercy. "Joseph wept when they spoke to him." (Genesis 50:17 ESV) His tears were not weakness but empathy. He grieved that his brothers still lived chained to guilt, though forgiveness had already been given. Mature grief feels sorrow for those still bound to the past, yet chooses mercy over resentment. Joseph comforted them and "spoke kindly to them." His reaction shows that grief can evolve from anguish into compassion; pain transfigured into gentleness.

The Body's Protest

If you are still crying months or years later, it means the attachment was profound. Your nervous system is arguing with the new reality. It says, "You changed the world I lived in." The human brain forms maps of relationships; when the map is torn, it fires alarms through the muscles, stomach, and breath. When death erases the person, the map remains.[20] This is not a weakness. It is designed. God hard-wired remembrance into flesh so that love would never become abstract.

Physical grief is often misdiagnosed as illness: the tight chest, the sudden exhaustion, the forgetfulness. Yet each symptom is the body's sermon, preaching that love mattered.[21] When the mourner learns to treat the body kindly by providing hydration, movement, sleep, and simple nourishment, he cooperates with grace instead of resisting it. Elijah collapsed under the broom tree not because he lacked faith but because he lacked calories (1 Kings 19:5-7). The angel did not quote a verse; he served a meal. Spiritual restoration is not dependent on physical stamina, but is facilitated by it.

When Anger Speaks…

Anger during mourning frightens many believers. They confuse it with rebellion. But anger often testifies that something sacred has been violated.

It is grief's thunderclap announcing that meaning was torn away.[22] Suppressed anger festers; expressed anger can become intercession. David asked, "How long, O Lord?" Jeremiah cried, "Why is my pain unceasing?" Habakkuk shouted, "Will You not hear?" Jesus Himself cried from the cross, "My God, My God, why have You forsaken Me?" Faith that never questions is not strength. It is numbness.

The way to redeem anger is to give it vocabulary before God. To shout inside His presence is safer than to smile outside of it. Unspoken rage poisons relationships; confessed rage purifies worship. The believer who dares to speak honestly discovers that divine patience is wider than human fear.

The Identity Earthquake

Loss not only removes people; it removes roles. The widow must learn who she is apart from the shared pronoun *we*.[23] The parent who loses a child must renegotiate every sentence of self-definition. These are not psychological luxuries; they are survival necessities.

Israel faced a similar crisis after exile. They asked, "How shall we sing the Lord's song in a foreign land?" Identity trembles when the environment changes. God answered not with a new title but with His presence: "Fear not, for I have redeemed you; I have called you by name, you are Mine" (Isaiah 43:1). The antidote to identity loss is divine ownership. You are still known. You are still chosen. The pronouns change; the covenant does not.

When Guilt Rewrites Memory

Almost every mourner rehearses the *if only* chorus: *If only I had called... If only I had stayed...* Guilt masquerades as responsibility because it gives the illusion of control. If the past were your fault, then the future could be fixed by penance. But God alone holds the past. Psalm 31:15 declares, "My times are in Your hand." The phrase includes yesterday as well as tomorrow.

Self-forgiveness is not sentiment. It is theology. Refusing to forgive yourself is declaring that your standard of justice is higher than Calvary's. Once forgiveness is received vertically, it must also be applied inwardly. Worship breaks the tyranny of retroactive blame.

A Story That Could Be Yours

In a counseling session, a retired schoolteacher, whom I will call *Monica*, confessed that she still sets two plates at supper three years after her husband's death. "I'm not pretending he's coming back," she said. "I'm reminding myself that love leaves evidence." That ritual does not trap her; it tethers her to gratitude. Psychologists call this a *continuing bond*; a healthy integration of memory rather than a denial of death.[24]

Monica's practice echoes biblical truth. Jesus spoke of Abraham, Isaac, and Jacob as living unto God (Matthew 22:32). Covenant relationship transcends burial. Love continues in the presence of God and in the behavior of those who remain. The Christian hope is not amnesia but resurrection memory. Every good thing is redeemed; nothing is truly lost.

Two Lies and Two Truths

Lie #1: "You're alone."

Truth: You are part of a fellowship of the wounded who became healers. Naomi said, "Call me Bitter," yet through Ruth, her lineage birthed a king. Elijah prayed for death under a broom tree, yet God sent him to anoint successors. Paul confessed "great sorrow and unceasing anguish," yet his letters still build churches. The Bible is not a gallery of the invincible; it is a hospital record of survivors.

Lie #2: "You will feel like this forever." **Truth:** Pain has seasons. The sharp edge dulls; the scar remains as testimony. The body relearns safety, the mind relearns focus, and the spirit relearns joy. Valleys have exits. "Weeping may tarry for the night, but joy comes with the morning" (Psalm 30:5).

Moving Forward...Not Moving On

To "move on" sounds like betrayal; to "move forward" means continuation. Forward motion carries memory, not denial. Joseph named his son Ephraim, which meant "God has made me fruitful in the land of my affliction." He did not rename Egypt; he redeemed it.

Believers move forward when they transform remembrance into ministry. The parent who lost a child starts a scholarship fund. The widow comforts others at funerals. The once-broken become architects of consolation. This is not replacement. It is resurrection work inside time.

Paul modeled the rhythm. He acknowledged pain: "Demas has deserted me", but kept writing letters that would outlive him. He did not bury feeling; he baptized it into purpose.

The Healing Power of Story

Telling the story aloud reorders chaos. Each retelling integrates emotion and meaning until the two walk together. When you speak of the one you lost in the present tense - "She loves roses," "He plays the piano beautifully", you are not denying reality. You are affirming that influence transcends mortality.

Outsiders may correct you: "Don't you mean *loved*?" You need not comply. Love and influence are verbs that never retire. Their seed remains in your character, your humor, your ethics. You are living proof of their investment. The mourner becomes a walking archive of grace.

Spiritual and Physical Care as One

True ministry does not silence tears; it nourishes the body that produces them. Elijah's angel said, "Rise and eat, for the journey is too much for you." 1 Kings 19:7. The spirit cannot endure when the body collapses. Jesus Himself fed hungry crowds as He taught them, even though He knew their focus was on physical food (John 6:26). The pattern holds: hydration, rest, worship. Caring for the physical is obedience, not vanity. Holistic compassion is holiness in motion.

Four Simple Survival Prayers

Breathe: "God, I am still here."

Admit: "God, I am not okay."

Ask: "God, sit with me in this hour."

Act: "God, help me do one good thing today, even if I am still limping."

These prayers shorten the distance between despair and dialogue. They are anchors for days when language fails. Even whispering them trains the heart to turn upward rather than inward.

The Faith of the Limping

You do not need to feel strong to be faithful. Wanting to want God still counts. A trembling hand reaching toward heaven still counts. In the courtroom of grace, a groan is admissible evidence. Limping does not disqualify you; it identifies you as one who wrestled and lived.

In Genesis 32:24-32, we learn that Jacob limped after Peniel, yet Scripture calls him Israel, meaning "one who struggles with God and prevails." The limp became the proof of encounter. Likewise, every believer who survives loss carries a mark that heaven interprets as a sign of victory. Strength is not walking without pain; it is walking, anyway.

Faith Window 1

Prayer for the Valley

"Lord Jesus, teach me to weep without hopelessness, to remember without idolizing, to wait without doubting. When I cannot stand, hold me up. When I cannot sing, hear my silence as song. Let my limp be evidence that grace still works.

Chapter 1 Endnotes

1 Exline, J. J., Park, C. L., Smyth, J. M., & Carey, M. P. (2011). Anger toward God: Social-cognitive predictors, prevalence, and links with adjustment to bereavement and cancer. Journal of Personality and Social Psychology, 100(1), 129-148.

2 Kapic, K. M. (2018). Embodied hope: A theological meditation on pain and suffering. IVP Academic.

3 Swinton, J. (2007). Raging with compassion: Pastoral responses to the problem of evil. Eerdmans.

4 Brueggemann, W. (2002). The Psalms and the life of faith. Fortress Press.

5 Card, M. (2005). A sacred sorrow: Reaching out to God in the lost language of lament. NavPress.

6 van der Kolk, B. A. (2014). The body keeps the score: Brain, mind, and body in the healing of trauma. Viking.

7 Pennebaker, J. W., & Smyth, J. M. (2016). *Opening up by writing it down: How expressive writing improves health and eases emotional pain* (3rd ed.). Guilford Press.

8 Wright, N. T. (2008). Surprised by hope: Rethinking heaven, the resurrection, and the mission of the church. HarperOne.

9 O'Connor, M.-F. (2019). The grieving brain: The surprising science of how we learn from love and loss. HarperOne.

10 O'Connor, M. F. (2019). Grief: A brief history of research on how body, mind, and brain adapt. Psychosomatic Medicine, 81(8), 731-738.

11 Porges, S. W. (2011). The polyvagal theory: Neurophysiological foundations of emotions, attachment, communication, and self-regulation. W. W. Norton & Company.

12 Newberg, A. B., & Waldman, M. R. (2009). How God changes your brain: Breakthrough findings from a leading neuroscientist. Ballantine Books. [Classic study on neural effects of religious practices].

13 Pennebaker, J. W., & Smyth, J. M. (2016). Opening up by writing it down: How expressive writing improves health and eases emotional pain (3rd ed.). Guilford Press.

14 Templin, C., et al. (2015). Clinical features and outcomes of Takotsubo (stress) cardiomyopathy. New England Journal of Medicine, 373(10), 929-938.

15 Ai, A. L., Park, C. L., Huang, B., Rodgers, W., & Tice, T. N. (2007). Psychosocial mediation of religious coping styles: A study of short-term psychological distress following cardiac surgery. Personality and Social Psychology Bulletin, 33(6), 867-882.

16 Slavich, G. M., & Irwin, M. R. (2014). From stress to inflammation and major depressive disorder: A social signal transduction theory of depression. Psychological Bulletin, 140(3), 774-815.

---

17 Vingerhoets, A. J. J. M. (2013). Why only humans weep: Unraveling the mysteries of tears. Oxford University Press.

18 McCraty, R., & Shaffer, F. (2015). Heart rate variability: New perspectives on physiological mechanisms, assessment of self-regulatory capacity, and health risk. Global Advances in Health and Medicine, 4(1), 46-61.

19 O'Connor, M. F., & Arizmendi, B. J. (2021). Neuropsychological correlates of complicated grief in older spousally bereaved adults. The Journals of Gerontology: Series B, 76(1), 95-100. https://doi.org/10.1093/geronb/gbaa005

20 Sbarra, D. A., & Hazan, C. (2008). Coregulation, dysregulation, self-regulation: An integrative analysis and empirical agenda for understanding adult attachment, separation, distress, and recovery. Personality and Social Psychology Review, 12(2), 141-167.

21 Stroebe, M., Schut, H., & Stroebe, W. (2007). Health outcomes of bereavement. The Lancet, 370(9603), 1960-1973.

22 Boelen, P. A., Lenferink, L. I. M., Nickerson, A., & Smid, G. E. (2018). Evaluation of the factor structure, prevalence, and validity of disturbed grief in DSM-5 and ICD-11. Journal of Affective Disorders, 240, 79-87.

23 Neimeyer, R. A. (Ed.). (2001). Meaning reconstruction and the experience of loss. American Psychological Association.

24 Klass, D., Silverman, P. R., & Nickman, S. L. (Eds.). (1996). Continuing bonds: New understandings of grief. Taylor & Francis

Chapter 2

How Grief Affects Body, Mind, and Spirit

2.1 The Physiology of Shock & the Mind's Defenses

Why the Body Reacts Before the Mind Understands

When devastating news strikes, the body outruns the intellect. Long before words or theology appear, the nervous system fires the **Acute Stress Reaction (ASR)**. This built-in emergency reflex floods the bloodstream with adrenaline and cortisol, redirecting oxygen to the heart and muscles. Pupils widen; digestion halts; the heart pounds like a war drum.[25] It is God's pre-programmed survival code saying, *"Live first. Interpret later."*

The Grief Response Matrix

Dimension	Immediate Shock Response	→	Ongoing Adaptation
BODY	↑ Racing heart (elevated bpm) ↑ Shallow breathing ↑ Muscle tension ↓ Digestive shutdown	→	• Cortisol elevation • Immune suppression • Fatigue/exhaustion
MIND (Psyche)	⊖ Prefrontal cortex impairment △ Memory impairment ↓ Narrowed attention △ Difficulty deciding • Sense of unreality	→	• Intrusive thoughts • Rumination loops • Search for meaning • Cognitive fog • Reorganizing reality
SPIRIT	• Numb to God's presence • Prayer feels empty • Faith questions arise • Spiritual numbness	→	• Lament becomes prayer • Meaning slowly returns • Faith shifts shape • Hope gradually restored

The Grief Response Matrix shows how loss activates all three dimensions simultaneously. • Early responses protect; ongoing adaptations rebuild. Timeline is non-linear.

* Pneumopsychosomatic Model: Pneuma (πνεῦμα) = Spirit · Psyche (ψυχή) = Mind/Soul · Soma (σῶμα) = Body • The three dimensions activate simultaneously and interact continuously. Responses are non-linear.

Scripture validates this biology. When Jacob believed Joseph was dead, "he refused to be comforted" (Genesis 37:35 ESV). Ezekiel admitted, "I sat where they sat, overwhelmed" (Ezekiel 3:15). Job's friends sat in silence seven days (Job 2:13)

The Hebrew phrase translated "sat with him" (yashav ʾēṣel) means more than physical proximity. It denotes deliberate companionship, sitting alongside as equals. The seven days match the prescribed period of intense mourning (shiva) in ancient Near Eastern practice, during which mourners sat on the ground, rent their garments, and abstained from normal comforts.

Job's friends "did not speak a word to him, for they saw that his suffering was very great". Their silence was not awkwardness but sacred witness. Only when they broke this silence with theodicy and accusations (Chapters 4-31) did they become "miserable comforters" (Job 16:2). Their presence was incarnational ministry; their explanations became injury. This text establishes a biblical precedent: sometimes the most theological thing you can do is close your mouth and open your presence.

Long before medical textbooks, the Bible captured the same freeze response neurologists now chart on brain scans.[26]

Inside the Storm - What the Brain Actually Does

In a flash, the **amygdala** sounds its alarm. The hypothalamus releases chemical messengers; the **sympathetic nervous system** mobilizes energy.[27] Within seconds, the reasoning center, the **prefrontal cortex**, goes offline. That blackout explains why mourners often say, “It felt unreal.[28]” Time fractures, memory splinters, and people forget entire hours. This amnesia is not failure; it is divine anesthesia. The Creator shields consciousness from more than it can safely bear.

Neurologists describe it as a protective circuit; pastors call it mercy. Denial is often labeled the first “stage” of grief, but physiologically, it is a stabilizer.[29] God restrains awareness until the heart is strong enough to absorb the truth. What looks like numbness may actually be heaven’s form of shock absorption.

How the Mind Protects the Spirit

The **limbic system,** which is the seat of emotion, and the **hypothalamus**, which is the regulator of hormones, form a delicate bridge between the physical and the spiritual.[30] When that bridge shakes, grace steadies it. Psalm 34:18 promises, “The Lord is near to the brokenhearted and saves the crushed in spirit.” Modern science would call that stabilization; faith calls it presence.

A retired teacher, *Monica*, once described the moment she was told of her husband’s sudden passing. She remembered gripping a countertop, unable to speak. “Everything inside me froze,” she said. Yet her whispered, “Lord, help me breathe,” triggered the body’s natural braking system, which is the **parasympathetic response.** It slowed her breathing and released trembling. The physical and the spiritual met at a single word: *Lord.*[31]

What Actually Helps in the First Hours

Containment Before Counsel. In the shock phase, logic cannot lead. A calm presence lowers cortisol faster than clever words. Comfort begins with safety, not speech.[32]

Rhythm Before Reflection. Elijah's recovery started with food and sleep before divine conversation (1 Kings 19:4-8). Basic care restores biology so that belief can function.

Permission to Be Human. Many grievers apologize for "not being strong." Reassure them: trembling does not mean unbelief. Even Jesus trembled in Gethsemane.

Medical studies confirm that crying, sighing, and trembling are the body's ways of discharging energy safely.[33] Suppressing those actions delays healing. Psalm 56:8 says God "keeps our tears in His bottle." That verse dignifies biology itself, tears as therapy ordained by design.

The Hebrew noun "*nōʾd*" refers to a leather flask or skin bottle used to store water or wine. God is pictured as carefully collecting and preserving each tear, like precious liquid. But the verse adds a second image: "Are they not in your book?" The word "*sēper*" means scroll or written record. Tears are not only collected but catalogued, numbered, remembered. This dual metaphor, liquid treasure and written record, reveals God as both emotionally engaged and cognitively attentive. He values tears enough to save them, and He keeps detailed accounts.

Ancient Near Eastern lament practices sometimes involved collecting tears in small bottles placed in tombs, making this metaphor viscerally real to David's audience. The Psalmist is saying: your grief is not wasted, not forgotten, not invisible. Every tear is witnessed, valued, and eternally remembered by the One who sees.

Faith Within the Biology of Pain

"Be still and know that I am God" (Psalm 46:10) is not a command to freeze but an invitation to surrender control while chaos rages (Psalm 46:2).

The Psalm contrasts collapsing nations with confident believers. Stillness is not stunned paralysis; it is conscious trust.

When Jesus said, "My soul is overwhelmed with sorrow to the point of death" (Matthew 26:38 NIV), His sweat became like drops of blood, which is a rare physiological condition called hematidrosis, and is produced by extreme stress.[34] Heaven itself entered humanity's chemistry. To be human and hormonal is not to be faithless; it is to be fearfully and wonderfully made (Psalm 139:14).

When Calm Returns and Grace Begins

Eventually, the **parasympathetic system** releases the body from siege. Blood pressure falls; muscles unclench; tears flow freely.[35] Each tear is a signal: the alarm is ending. The soul begins to re-inhabit its own body. In this stage, remembrance, not reaction, takes over.

Many believers misjudge this calm, assuming numbness means distance from God. In reality, it is restoration. God designed the human frame for ebb and flow. Grief and grace will trade shifts at the same watchtower. The body's chemistry, when allowed to complete its God-given cycle, becomes a miniature testimony of resurrection: life re-emerging from emotional death.

Early bereavement reactions show widespread physiological disruption (cortisol, sleep, immunity, hemodynamics), yet most people gradually stabilize without chronic pathology.[36] Every person who survives the first day of loss has already lived through a private miracle. Survival itself is grace in motion. The rhythm of shock, release, and stillness whispers the same truth biology and theology agree upon: we are crafted for recovery.

2.2 The First "Forty-Eight Hours" and their 3 D's

Disbelief, Denial, and Disorientation

When Reality and Reflex Collide

The first two days after a loss are unlike any other span of time. People speak in fragments, move mechanically, and describe the hours as a fog. In clinical language, this is the **acute bereavement window**.[37] The mind's reasoning center struggles to process data that the senses have already delivered.[38] Grief in this stage behaves like an electrical surge. The system overloads before it stabilizes.

Loved ones often recall standing at a hospital bed or hearing the phone ring and thinking, *"This can't be true."* That sentence is not denial; it is the brain's first safety valve.[39] Psychologists call it **cognitive dissonance**, the gap between information and comprehension.[40] In Scripture, we see it when the women came to Jesus' tomb and were "startled and frightened" though He stood before them (Luke 24:37). Shock made belief momentarily impossible.

Disbelief - The Mind's Emergency Brake

Disbelief and moderate denial reduce acute spikes in autonomic arousal (BP, panic) and allow the psyche to absorb loss in increments;[41] external structure and simple tasks help the nervous system exit survival mode.

Disbelief keeps the psyche from collapsing. It allows the mourner to breathe, sign papers, answer questions, and survive the day's logistics. Neurologically, it is the prefrontal cortex that throttles emotional input until cortisol levels begin to drop. Pastorally, it is mercy in disguise. Jacob stared at Joseph's blood-stained coat and said, "Surely I will go down to Sheol mourning for my son" (Genesis 37:35). His declaration was not accurate, yet it was honest; the brain could not yet reconcile evidence and hope.

During disbelief, external structure matters more than conversation. Simple tasks such as hydration, rest, and light movement help the nervous system exit survival mode. The presence of another person who neither preaches nor analyzes can restore orientation faster than medication. In this stage, ministry is measured in proximity, not profundity.

Denial - A Protective Story

When disbelief softens, but acceptance still feels lethal, denial takes over.[42] It is not lying; it is pacing. The mourner rehearses sentences such as, *"He's still at work,"* or *"She'll walk through the door any moment."* Psychiatrists note that moderate denial correlates with lower blood-pressure spikes and fewer panic episodes in early grief. The body is teaching the soul to face pain in increments.

Scripture shows this pacing of compassion. Thomas doubted until he touched the wounds; Jesus did not shame him but met him where evidence and faith could merge (John 20:27). Likewise, God gives each heart its own timetable for re-entry into reality. For some, denial lasts hours; for others, weeks. What matters is not its duration but that it gently yields to truth.

A widow once told me, "For two days I set his plate at the table." She was not losing faith; she was training her nervous system to eat without guilt. Denial, handled tenderly, becomes rehearsal for acceptance.

Disorientation - The World Without Coordinates

High emotional stress can affect the vestibular system and balance, creating dizziness and "falling into a hole" sensations; grounding techniques (slow breathing, sensory focus) help re-engage orientation.

When disbelief and denial wane, orientation collapses. This is the moment many describe as *"falling into a hole."* Time, appetite, and memory blur. The **vestibular system**, which governs balance, actually shows altered patterns under high emotional stress. That is why mourners often sway, stumble, or feel "light-headed."[43] The body quite literally cannot find its footing.

Spiritually, this vertigo mirrors the Psalmist's cry, "All Your waves and breakers have swept over me" (Psalm 42:7). The language is nautical; the sense is drowning. Yet verse 8 follows with equilibrium: "By day the Lord commands His steadfast love." In other words, divine constancy steadies human instability.

What Stabilizes the Soul in Disorientation

Predictable Routines. Eating at regular times, maintaining light exercise, and avoiding major decisions give the body cues of safety.

Grounding Techniques. Counselors teach slow breathing, naming nearby objects, or touching textured surfaces to re-engage sensory orientation. Biblically, this aligns with the incarnational truth that faith is not disembodied.

Guided Lament. Lamentations 3 moves from chaos to confidence through structured sorrow. Writing or speaking prayers of complaint channels confusion toward communion.

Companionship. Romans 12:15 commands, "Weep with those who weep." Shared orientation creates emotional homeostasis.

When Faith Feels Absent

Many believers equate the numbness of early grief with a lack of faith. In truth, the Spirit often works beneath perception. Romans 8:26 assures that "the Spirit Himself intercedes for us with groanings too deep for words." In trauma language, this is **implicit regulation**, the unseen alignment of body and soul through divine empathy. The one who feels faithless may actually be most carried.

Disorientation gradually yields to coherence when spiritual meaning begins to return. Hope flickers not as a sermon but as a scent. Isaiah 61:3 calls it "the oil of gladness instead of mourning." Oil implies slow absorption. Early grief demands patience with grace itself.

Pastoral and Clinical Consensus

Clinicians and chaplains increasingly agree that these first forty-eight hours set the trajectory of long-term recovery. Those who are permitted by others and themselves to express disbelief, denial, and disorientation without shame develop fewer chronic stress disorders months later.[44] Those forced to "be strong" too soon risk unresolved grief syndromes. God's wisdom and neuroscience converge: truth must arrive at the pace of love.

Transition to Stabilization

When the second sunrise arrives, the chemistry of emergency begins to ebb. The mourner's body temperature steadies, heart rate slows, and the first coherent memory of the loss forms. This is the bridge between crisis and comprehension. Psalm 30:5 captures it perfectly: "Weeping may endure for a night, but joy comes with the morning." Joy here is not laughter; it is oxygen. The first full breath after disbelief is itself a resurrection rehearsal.

2.3 Physiological Aftershocks and the Search for Meaning

When the Storm Seems Over, but the Waves Keep Coming

Most mourners assume that once the funeral ends, the body will calm down. Instead, many discover new symptoms such as palpitations, exhaustion, dizziness, or a sense that the world tilts to the side. Medicine calls these **physiological aftershocks**. They are the body's delayed echo of trauma: stress hormones that were useful during crisis continue to circulate after the threat has passed.[45]

In the days or weeks following a loss, the **autonomic nervous system** can misfire, confusing routine events for danger.[46] A knock at the door may spike adrenaline; a quiet house may trigger unease. This is not weakness; it is biology catching up to reality. Psalm 6:6 describes David "weary with moaning," a line that captures the collision between emotion and exhaustion. Modern science confirms what Scripture already recognized: grief drains both the spirit and the cells.

The Body's Slow Reset

Cortisol, the chemical of endurance, does not vanish on command. It must be metabolized through sleep, hydration, and gentle movement. This is why even faithful believers can feel "hungover" from sorrow. Fatigue is not faithlessness; it is chemistry in recovery. Clinical imaging shows reduced activity in the brain's **default-mode network** days after acute loss. This network governs reflection and meaning-making; its quieting explains the blankness many describe as *"feeling nothing."*[47]

Spiritually, that silence is a pause between verses. When Elijah lay under the broom tree wishing for death, God did not debate with him; He sent food, water, and rest (1 Kings 19:5–8). The divine prescription matched the physiological need. Rest restores worship as surely as prayer restores hope.

Heartache, Literally

Grief's metaphors often prove literal. Cardiologists now recognize **stress-induced cardiomyopathy**, sometimes called *broken-heart syndrome*. Intense emotion causes the heart's left ventricle to balloon temporarily, producing chest pain indistinguishable from a heart attack.[48] Most cases heal within weeks, but the reminder is profound: sorrow leaves fingerprints on flesh.

For pastors and clinicians alike, this knowledge reframes ministry. The mourner clutching the chest is not merely poetic. A prayer, a presence, or even slow breathing in company may lower blood pressure more effectively than solitude. Compassion has measurable cardiology.

Neural Echoes of Love and Loss

Grief does not only deactivate; it rewires. Neuroimaging reveals that circuits once activated by affection continue to fire in the absence of it, producing both longing and comfort. This is why memory can hurt and heal simultaneously. When Jesus told His disciples, "Sorrow has filled your heart… but your sorrow will turn into joy" (John 16:6,20), He acknowledged this neurological truth: love carves deep grooves that cannot be erased, so God fills them with new meaning rather than erasing them.

In practice, this means that recurring dreams, phantom sensations, or sudden tears months later are normal. They are the brain's maintenance of connection until faith redefines presence. Paul's assurance that "to be absent from the body is to be present with the Lord" (2 Corinthians 5:8) offers the believer a neuro-spiritual anchor: continuity without contact.

The Search for Meaning

Aftershock eventually yields to reflection. Humans cannot live long in chaos; we instinctively ask *why*. This question, often feared, is essential to healing. Meaning-making converts pain into narrative, narrative into testimony. Psychologists term this **post-traumatic growth**, but believers know it as sanctification through suffering.[49] Romans 8:28 is not a slogan but a slow revelation: God weaves even biochemistry into the fabric of redemption.

2.3.1 Coping Styles and Early Adaptation

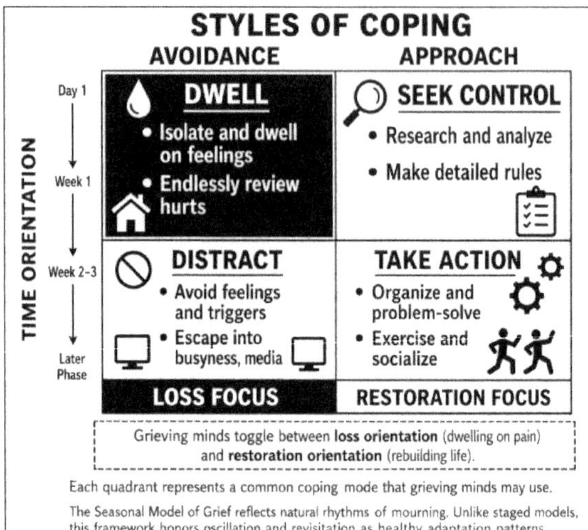

Each quadrant represents a common coping mode that grieving minds may use.

The Seasonal Model of Grief reflects natural rhythms of mourning. Unlike staged models, this framework honors oscillation and revisitation as healthy adaptation patterns.

Grief expresses itself through recognizable coping styles that reflect how a person engages pain over time. Some **dwell** in loss through emotional isolation. Others **seek control** by analyzing and organizing. Some **distract** themselves to avoid overwhelming feelings, while others **take action** by rebuilding routines and relationships (see Grief Response Matrix). Research also recognizes additional patterns such as meaning-making, oscillation, and resilience. But these four modes capture the most common early responses and help normalize the shifting ways mourners adapt as body, mind, and spirit regain equilibrium.

These coping styles do not replace the body's ongoing recovery; they operate within it. As grief continues, physiology, memory, and meaning remain intertwined, shaping how the nervous system, emotions, and faith gradually recalibrate.

Practical meaning emerges in simple ways. It could be a journal entry, a letter never mailed, an act of service done in memory of the one lost. Each gesture signals that love still exerts creative force. In that sense, the body participates in theology: hands that once trembled now build, plant, or comfort. The nervous system learns that movement itself is hope.

Integrating Body and Spirit

True recovery requires honoring both biology and belief. Ignoring the body's alarms spiritualizes what should be treated; ignoring the spirit medicalizes what must be consecrated. The Psalmist who wrote, "You have kept count of my tossings; put my tears in Your bottle" (Psalm 56:8) joined data with devotion. He trusted that heaven records what medicine measures.

Every tear, every spike in pulse, every sigh belongs to a God who heals through wholeness.

For counselors, pastors, and physicians alike, the task is alignment: teach the mourner to listen to the body without worshiping it, to name emotions without idolizing them, and to let faith interpret physiology. When body and spirit cease arguing, peace follows naturally.

Faith Window 2

God's Healing Rhythm

Grief is the wound time cannot stitch, but grace can. God never promised that faith would erase pain; He promised that His presence would transform it. The same Spirit who hovered over chaos in Genesis still hovers over broken hearts, shaping meaning from confusion. When the waves of sorrow feel endless, His rhythm of healing begins quietly: breath after sob, sunrise after sleepless night.

Every heartbeat that continues after loss testifies to divine intention. Life is still entrusted to you. The body's gradual recovery mirrors the soul's slow resurrection. God designed them to heal in concert, not in conflict. Where science measures cortisol and adrenaline, heaven measures trust and endurance. Each tear that falls is a verse in the song of restoration; each sigh becomes a prayer too deep for words.

In this rhythm, denial turns to discovery, and pain begins to pulse with purpose. "He heals the brokenhearted and binds up their wounds" (Psalm 147:3). To walk through grief with God is to keep time with the One who writes beauty into ashes and makes even chemistry serve His mercy. Listen closely: within your trembling chest beats the cadence of hope.

Looking Ahead

As the body stabilizes and the fog of early grief lifts, memory awakens. Faces, sounds, and shared moments begin to return. At first painfully, then redemptively. Chapter 3 explores this sacred terrain: how memory reconstructs reality, how faith reframes remembrance, and how God uses the mind's recall to rebuild identity. When memory and mercy meet, the mourner discovers that remembrance itself becomes a ministry.

Chapter 2 Endnotes

25 McEwen, B. S., & Gianaros, P. J. (2011). Stress- and allostasis-induced brain plasticity. Annual Review of Medicine, 62, 431-445.
Litz, B. T., & Carmassi, C. (2023). Defining and assessing the RDoC constructs of acute threat ("fear") and potential threat ("anxiety") in trauma-exposed people. Depression and Anxiety, 2023, 1-12. https://doi.org/10.1155/2023/1566419

26 :. Porges, S. W. (2021). Polyvagal theory: A biobehavioral journey to sociality. *Comprehensive Psychoneuroendocrinology, 7*, 100069. https://doi.org/10.1016/j.cpnec.2021.100069

27 .. LeDoux, J. E. (2015). Anxious: Using the brain to understand and treat fear and anxiety. Viking.

28 Arnsten, A. F. T. (2015). Stress weakens prefrontal networks: Molecular insults to higher cognition. Nature Neuroscience, 18(10), 1376-1385.

29 Bonanno, G. A., & Burton, C. L. (2013). Regulatory flexibility: An individual differences perspective on coping and emotion regulation. Perspectives on Psychological Science, 8(6), 591-612.

30 Sapolsky, R. M. (2015). Stress and the brain: Individual variability and the inverted-U. Nature Neuroscience, 18(10), 1344-1346.

31 Porges, S. W. (2011). The polyvagal theory: Neurophysiological foundations of emotions, attachment, communication, and self-regulation. W. W. Norton.

32 Coan, J. A., Schaefer, H. S., & Davidson, R. J. (2006). Lending a hand: Social regulation of the neural response to threat. Psychological Science, 17(12), 1032-1039.

33 Vingerhoets, A. J. J. M. (2013). Why only humans weep: Unraveling the mysteries of tears. Oxford University Press.

34 Holoubek, J. E., & Holoubek, A. B. (1996). Blood, sweat and fear: A classification of hematidrosis. Journal of Medicine, 27(3-4), 115-133.

35 Thayer, J. F., & Lane, R. D. (2000). A model of neurovisceral integration in emotion regulation and dysregulation. Journal of Affective Disorders, 61(3), 201-216.

36 Buckley, T., Sunari, D., Marshall, A., Bartrop, R., McKinley, S., & Tofler, G. (2012). Physiological correlates of bereavement and the impact of bereavement interventions. Dialogues in Clinical Neuroscience, 14(2), 129-139.

37 Shear, M. K. (2015). Clinical practice. Complicated grief. New England Journal of Medicine, 372(2), 153-160.

38 Arnsten, A. F. T. (2015). Stress weakens prefrontal networks: Molecular insults to higher cognition. Nature Neuroscience, 18(10), 1376-1385.

39 Bonanno, G. A., & Burton, C. L. (2013). Regulatory flexibility: An individual differences perspective on coping and emotion regulation. Perspectives on Psychological Science, 8(6), 591-612.

40 Stroebe, M., & Schut, H. (2010). The dual process model of coping with bereavement: A decade on. OMEGA — Journal of Death and Dying, 61(4), 273-289.

41 Bonanno, G. A., Papa, A., Lalande, K., Westphal, M., & Coifman, K. (2004). The importance of being flexible: The ability to both enhance and suppress emotional expression predicts long-term adjustment. Psychological Science, 15(7), 482-487.

42 Shear, M. K., Reynolds, C. F., Simon, N. M., Zisook, S., Wang, Y., Mauro, C., & Skritskaya, N. (2016). Optimizing treatment of complicated grief: A randomized clinical trial. JAMA Psychiatry, 73(7), 685-694. https://doi.org/10.1001/jamapsychiatry.2016.0892

43 Balaban, C. D., & Thayer, J. F. (2001). Neurological bases for balance-anxiety links. Journal of Anxiety Disorders, 15(1-2), 53-79. [Documents vestibular-emotional connections]

44 Bonanno, G. A., & Kaltman, S. (2001). The varieties of grief experience. Clinical Psychology Review, 21(5), 705-734.

45 O'Connor, M.-F., Wellisch, D. K., Stanton, A. L., Eisenberger, N. I., Irwin, M. R., & Lieberman, M. D. (2008). Craving love? Enduring grief activates brain's reward center. NeuroImage, 42(2), 969-972.

46 Pfefferbaum, B., & North, C. S. (2020). Mental health and the Covid-19 pandemic. New England Journal of Medicine, 383(6), 510-512.

47 Gündel, H., O'Connor, M.-F., Littrell, L., Fort, C., & Lane, R. D. (2003). Functional neuroanatomy of grief: An fMRI study. American Journal of Psychiatry, 160(11), 1946-1953.

48 Templin, C., et al. (2015). Clinical features and outcomes of Takotsubo (stress) cardiomyopathy. New England Journal of Medicine, 373(10), 929-938.

49 Tedeschi, R. G., & Calhoun, L. G. (2004). Posttraumatic growth: Conceptual foundations and empirical evidence. Psychological Inquiry, 15(1), 1-18.

Chapter 3

Pre-Trauma Grief Mitigation (PTGM):

Preparing the Heart Before It Breaks

3.1 The Theology of Preparedness

Why Preparation Matters to Faith

Preparation for loss is not pessimism; it is wisdom. Jesus never promised a life free from pain. He promised His presence *through* it. "In this world you will have trouble," He said, "but take heart, I have overcome the world" (John 16:33). The theology of preparedness begins with accepting that adversity is not an interruption of God's plan but a Chapter within it.

Modern psychology calls this *anticipatory adaptation*. It is the mind's ability to rehearse adversity and build emotional elasticity before impact.[50] Scripture anticipated this principle centuries ago: Joseph stored grain in years of plenty, Noah built an ark in sunshine, and Jesus prepared His disciples for His own crucifixion long before Gethsemane. In each instance, divine foresight transformed disaster into testimony.

Faith that prepares is not fearful faith; it is fortified faith. To "prepare the heart before it breaks" is to train trust before trauma, ensuring that when crisis comes, faith responds faster than fear.

Suffering as a Certainty, Not an Accident

Peter wrote, “Do not be surprised at the fiery ordeal that has come on you to test you, as though something strange were happening to you” (1 Peter 4:12).

Peter uses “*pyōsis*”, a rare word meaning "burning" or "conflagration," which appears elsewhere in the New Testament only in Revelation 18:9, 18 to describe the burning of Babylon. This is not minor discomfort, but a consuming fire. The phrase “*mē xenizesthe*” literally means "stop thinking of it as foreign/strange/alien". The present imperative with negative suggests they were already treating suffering as “xenon” (strange), and Peter commands them to stop. The verb “*dokimazō*” (to test) carries metallurgical overtones: refining precious metals by fire to remove impurities.

Peter, writing to believers facing Neronian persecution, reframes suffering from invasion as a formative experience. He anticipates his readers' shock ("how strange!") and preemptively corrects it: this is not foreign territory. It's the pathway every disciple walks. In 1 Peter 5:7, he continues: "Cast (*epirripsantes*, aorist participle, "having hurled") all your anxiety upon Him." The verb is violent and urgent, not "gently place" but "throw with force." The Christian life is neither a masochistic embrace of pain nor a shocked denial. It's a realistic expectation met with urgent dependence.

The unprepared believer treats suffering as a foreign invasion; the prepared believer sees it as familiar terrain patrolled by grace.

In theological terms, preparedness honors the doctrine of *providence*. God’s sovereignty does not exempt us from pain; it assures us that pain will never be pointless. This conviction turns every potential loss into a classroom where faith is not merely professed but proved.

Theology gives believers language before tears steal words. Those who study suffering in the light of Scripture find that when calamity arrives, lament becomes fluent rather than foreign. Preparation thus shifts grief from chaos to covenant and into a planned participation in the redemptive work of God.

Jesus as Model of Anticipatory Strength

The Gospels portray Christ as the ultimate practitioner of PTGM. In Luke 9:22, He told His disciples plainly that He would “suffer many things… and be killed.” Yet He faced this knowledge without despair. His preparedness was rooted not in fatalism but in fellowship: "Not my will, but Yours be done" (Luke 22:42). In John 12:27, Jesus not only demonstrates his preparation for His ultimate suffering, but He indicates that He is fully prepared for it. Yet, a short time later in the Garden of Gethsemane, as the full weight of your sins and mine, and that of the whole world began to descend on Him, three times He pleaded with His Father, "let this cup pass from me!" If, after preparation, the agony was "unbearable", could you imagine how much more unbearable it would have been if Jesus had not prepared for it?

Neurologically, this anticipatory acceptance stabilizes the body's stress systems.[51] Spiritually, it repositions the soul from protest to participation. Jesus' advanced awareness did not remove pain, but it prevented panic. The Cross was agony, but it was never a surprise.

Believers who internalize this model learn to interpret forewarning not as dread but as divine mercy. It is God's way of rehearsing hope before the curtain rises on suffering.

The Heart as the Battlefield of Readiness

Preparation begins in the heart, which is the seat of emotion, conviction, and decision. Proverbs 4:23 instructs, "Above all else, guard your heart, for everything you do flows from it." Guarding does not mean hardening; it means training tenderness to survive trauma.

Emotional readiness involves acknowledging life's fragility without succumbing to anxiety. Faith transforms foreboding into formation. When David wrote, "Even though I walk through the valley of the shadow of death, I will fear no evil," he spoke as one who had already walked the valley in prayer before his feet touched it in reality. The shadow lost its power because belief had already built its lantern.

Counselors call this **cognitive pre-appraisal**; theologians call it meditation; Scripture calls it wisdom.[52] Whatever the name, it is the alignment of thought and spirit before impact.

Training the Soul Before the Test

Every believer can cultivate disciplines that make the spirit crisis-resilient: daily thanksgiving, memorization of Scripture, and community connection. Each act deposits strength for future withdrawal. The soldier who drills in peace fights with instinct in war.

Paul's admonition in Ephesians 6, "put on the full armor of God", is essentially PTGM in Biblical language. Armor is useless if donned mid-battle. Spiritual disciplines are preventive equipment: worship trains breath; Scripture sharpens discernment; fellowship rehearses comfort. When grief arrives, the soul already knows its choreography.

Even secular resilience training mirrors this truth. Studies show that those who consciously rehearse coping strategies before tragedy recover more quickly physiologically.[53] Heaven and neuroscience agree: preparedness is preventive mercy.

The Blessing Hidden in Preparation

To prepare is to trust that God's promises will hold even when life does not. Isaiah 26:3 assures, "You keep him in perfect peace whose mind is stayed on You." The Hebrew phrase for 'stayed' implies a deliberate leaning, not collapse, but resting weight intentionally—the theology of preparedness, therefore, centers on where the heart leans before it breaks.

Those who prepare through prayer, Scripture, and service discover that the breaking itself becomes birthing. Out of readiness grows revelation; out of surrender comes strength. God does not waste preparation. Every quiet rehearsal of trust today is a prophecy of stability tomorrow.

Faith in Action

Preparedness is not the end of prevention; it is the foundation. Once the heart understands the theology of readiness, the mind must learn resilience in practice. Section 3.2 explores how believers can **build emotional and cognitive resilience before loss**, transforming faith from fragile sentiment into a durable strategy.

3.2 Building Resilience Before Loss

Resilience as a Spiritual and Biological Reality

Resilience is not stoicism; it is sanctified elasticity. To be resilient is to bend under pressure without breaking, to adapt without abandoning faith. Isaiah captures this beautifully: "When you pass through the waters,

I will be with you; and through the rivers, they shall not overwhelm you" (Isaiah 43:2). The promise is not avoidance but accompaniment.

Modern research defines resilience as the ability to recover equilibrium following disruption.[54] Scripture goes further — it declares that equilibrium is not self-generated but Spirit-sustained. Paul confessed, "We are hard pressed on every side, but not crushed... struck down, but not destroyed" (2 Corinthians 4:8–9). That contrast is the biblical signature of resilience: fragile clay vessels carrying indestructible treasure.

The Foundations of Faith-Based Resilience

Three principles anchor biblical resilience: *trust, training, and togetherness.*

Trust - the conviction that God is both sovereign and good. Without trust, suffering breeds despair; with it, suffering breeds depth. Proverbs 3:5 commands, "Trust in the Lord with all your heart and lean not on your own understanding." Trust reframes trauma by giving it context within eternity.

Training - the intentional development of endurance through spiritual discipline. "Solid food is for the mature, who by constant use have trained themselves to distinguish good from evil" (Hebrews 5:14). Spiritual habits like prayer, fasting, and reflection strengthen emotional muscles before a crisis. Neuroscience affirms this; repeated contemplative practices thicken neural pathways of calm and reduce panic reflexes.[55]

Togetherness - resilience rarely grows in isolation. Ecclesiastes 4:12 reminds us, "A cord of three strands is not quickly broken." Community provides both external stability and mirrored hope. In shared faith, personal endurance becomes corporate grace.

When Strength Looks Like Weakness

Many grievers interpret tears or trembling as spiritual failure. Yet resilience is not the absence of emotion; it is the stewardship of it. Jesus Himself wept at Lazarus's tomb, though He knew resurrection was minutes away. His tears teach that divine confidence does not erase human compassion.

Emotional resilience means permission to feel deeply without losing direction. The Psalmist oscillated between despair and praise. "Why, my soul, are you downcast?" (Psalm 42:5 NIV) Yet he still ended in worship. The capacity to move between weeping and worship is the rhythm of a resilient believer. Science calls it *emotional flexibility*; Scripture calls it *steadfastness.*

Physical Habits That Reinforce Spiritual Strength

Resilience is embodied faith. The nervous system, not just the spirit, must learn peace.[56] Breathing exercises, slow walks, balanced nutrition, and regular sleep are not secular distractions but sacred disciplines. When Elijah fled from Jezebel, the angel of the Lord did not start with a sermon but with food and rest (1 Kings 19:5–8). Restoration of the body precedes the revelation of the spirit.

The modern term for this cooperation is **psychophysiological coherence,** which refers to the harmony between body rhythms and emotional states.[57] Gratitude journaling, singing hymns, or engaging in communal worship all synchronize heart rate and respiration, reducing stress hormones.[58] The believer who treats the body as a temple rather than a tool honors God through resilience itself.

Mental Frames That Withstand Loss

Cognitive reframing, or renewing the mind, changes emotional responses to stress; directing attention toward gratitude and past deliverance builds resilience circuits.[59]

Resilient minds interpret suffering through a divine narrative. Instead of asking, "Why me?" the trained soul asks, "What now, Lord?" This shift from analysis to alignment transforms the mental battlefield. Psychologists term this *cognitive reframing*; Scripture describes it as "renewing the mind" (Romans 12:2).[60]

Renewed minds recall God's faithfulness selectively. They rehearse deliverance stories, not disasters. David strengthened himself in the Lord (1 Samuel 30:6) by remembering past victories. Memory becomes a weapon when guided by faith. As neurons re-fire along paths of gratitude, despair loses its grip.

Community as a Buffer and Mirror

Strong perceived social support and religious participation lower inflammatory markers, reduce the risk of complicated grief, and support better psychological outcomes after bereavement.

Community is God's design for durable healing. In isolation, grief magnifies; in connection, it redistributes. Galatians 6:2 commands, "Bear one another's burdens, and so fulfill the law of Christ." Bearing is not rescuing; it is reinforcing.

Research confirms that perceived social support reduces both inflammatory response and depressive relapse after bereavement.[61] Fellowship literally alters chemistry. Spiritually, it restores a sense of belonging and dispels despair. In the body of Christ, resilience becomes contagious.

The Spiritual Mechanics of Rebound

Resilience does not mean bouncing *back* to what was; it means bouncing *forward* into who God is shaping you to become. Job did not regain the same life; he received a redeemed one. The theology of rebound is not replacement but renewal. "Behold, I make all things new" (Revelation 21:5).

Every act of endurance writes prophecy: that suffering will not have the final word. The believer who learns to stand again becomes living evidence that resurrection power operates daily, not just on Easter morning.

Anchored in Christ

Having explored the habits and community that fortify believers before loss, we now turn inward again. Section 3.3 examines how faith actively **reframes memory**, transforming painful recall into sacred remembrance, which is the heart of redeemed remembering.

3.3 Spiritual, Emotional, & Cognitive Exercises for Readiness

When crisis strikes, the human spirit, mind, and body instinctively seek balance. Yet true readiness isn't built in the storm. It is forged in seasons of peace. A life that anticipates loss without being ruled by fear learns to train the soul, discipline the emotions, and renew the mind daily. These disciplines form a threefold cord that is not easily broken (Ecclesiastes 4:12 ESV).

Spiritual Exercises - Preparing the Inner Life

The spirit is the control tower of the believer's entire being. To prepare it for the unpredictable winds of grief, spiritual readiness must become habitual, not reactive. Key practices include:

Scripture Saturation

Letting the Word dwell richly in us (Colossians 3:16 ESV) reshapes how we interpret loss. Reading, memorizing, and praying Scripture aloud tunes the heart to God's perspective before tragedy distorts our perception.

Daily Worship and Surrender

Worship is not only a celebration but also a calibration. Each act of surrender resets the believer's focus, teaching that God remains sovereign even when life is not safe. Jesus modeled this in Gethsemane when He prayed, "Not My will, but Yours be done" (Luke 22:42 ESV).

Intercessory Readiness

Learning to pray for others during their valley seasons builds empathy and faith muscle. Those who have interceded for others grieve differently; their hearts have already been trained in compassion and trust.

Quiet Trust.

Isaiah 30:15 reminds us that "in quietness and trust is your strength." Spiritual readiness is not frantic activity but cultivated calm, anchored in God's unchanging nature.

Emotional Exercises - Strengthening the Heart's Resilience

Emotional readiness involves learning how to feel deeply without being destroyed by those feelings. Believers are not called to emotional denial but to disciplined stewardship of emotion.

Naming Emotions Honestly.

Denial weakens resilience. The Psalms demonstrate how naming sorrow, anger, or confusion before God releases healing. David's candor - "Why, my soul, are you downcast?" (Psalm 42:5 NIV) - invites honest self-examination before divine restoration.

Practicing Gratitude in Minor Losses

Training begins in small daily disappointments. Gratitude for what remains conditions the heart for the day something precious is taken. Paul's admonition to "give thanks in all circumstances" (1 Thessalonians 5:18 ESV) is not a cliché but an emotional discipline.

Building Safe Circles

Emotional strength multiplies in a community. Grief shared is grief lightened. Creating trusted spaces, prayer partners, support groups, and mentors helps prevent emotional isolation, which can magnify pain.

Controlled Vulnerability

Readiness means knowing when to open up and to whom. Jesus Himself had twelve disciples, but confided in Peter, James, and John at His darkest hour (Matthew 26:37-38 ESV). Controlled openness avoids both suppression and oversharing.

Cognitive Exercises - Renewing the Mind

The mind interprets every event through the filters of past experience, belief, and expectation. If those filters are clouded by fear or fatalism, even faith can be misapplied.

Meditative Reflection.

Regularly revisiting God's past faithfulness creates mental reference points of hope. Psalm 77 shows Asaph doing precisely this: recalling God's deeds to regain perspective when overwhelmed.

Truth Reframing.

When pain tempts us to say, "I can't survive this," biblical truth reframes it: "I can do all things through Him who strengthens me" (Philippians 4:13 ESV). Reframing trains thought patterns to submit to Scripture rather than circumstance.

Cognitive Sabbath.

Periodically disconnecting from mental clutter, digital noise, endless news, or even ministry overload restores equilibrium. "Be still, and know that I am God" (Psalm 46:10 ESV) invites cognitive quiet, not paralysis but purposeful rest.

Hope Visualization.

The imagination can serve faith or fear. Mentally picturing redemption after loss conditions the brain toward expectation rather than despair. Hebrews 11 portrays faith as envisioning unseen realities until they shape behavior.

Integrated Readiness - The Pneumopsychosomatic Balance

When the spiritual, emotional, and cognitive systems work in harmony, believers enter what I call *pneumopsychosomatic balance*. This is wholeness across spirit, mind, and body. Medical science notes that anxiety heightens cortisol levels and inflammation; Scripture adds that "a tranquil heart gives life to the flesh" (Proverbs 14:30 ESV). True readiness, therefore, becomes both a spiritual discipline and a physiological safeguard.

Faith-filled thinking calms the nervous system; gratitude stabilizes emotion; prayer lowers blood pressure; and forgiveness reduces chronic stress responses. Each is a divine prescription embedded in creation's design.[62]

Faith Window 3 Part 1

Preparing Before the Storm

"The prudent see danger and take refuge, but the simple keep going and pay the penalty." Proverbs 27:12 (NIV)

Readiness is not fear; it is faith, foresight. To practice preparedness is to trust God enough to plan wisely, and to trust Him even more when plans must yield to providence.

3.4 The Theology of Preventive Comfort

Grief does not surprise God, and it should not dismantle the believer who walks with Him. Scripture presents comfort not only as a remedy after loss but as a formation before loss. Jesus told His disciples, "In the world you will have tribulation; but take heart; I have overcome the world." The grammar is preventive: *take heart now* because My victory already stands. Preventive comfort, then, is the ongoing ministry of the Triune God; Father promising His presence, the Son securing our peace, and the Spirit applying consolation daily.

Covenant before crisis

From Eden's exile to the exile of Judah, God's word arrives before calamity with promises of nearness: "Fear not, for I am with you" (Isaiah 41:10). The comfort precedes the pain because covenant precedes the valley. Pastoral studies show that *anticipated support* reduces trauma intensity; believers who already expect God's steadying presence display faster emotional stabilization.[63]

Incarnation as comfort

Divine consolation is not an abstract mood but embodied nearness. "The Word became flesh and dwelt among us." In Jesus, God's compassion takes on pulse and breath. The Cross adds depth: our Savior faced suffering with lucid obedience and joy set before Him. For the disciple, contemplating Christ's passion trains the heart to interpret future loss through redemption rather than randomness. Clinical, meaning-making research mirrors this: suffering borne within a coherent story predicts better outcomes than does suffering perceived as meaningless.[64]

Paraclete within

Preventive comfort is also inward. The Spirit, *paraklētos*, the One called alongside, guards us with a peace that surpasses understanding. Paul's verb in Philippians 4:7 is military: peace *garrisons* the heart and mind. Prayer and petition with thanksgiving are not emergency hacks; they are a daily practice that strengthens parasympathetic tone, lowering physiological arousal.[65]

Comfort as discipleship, not denial

The valley is real; so is the Shepherd. Preventive comfort rejects two errors: naïve triumphalism ("pain can't touch me") and fatalistic despair ("pain defines me"). Instead, it embraces *trained tenderness* and lament that breathes faith. The Psalms model this integration of honest sorrow braided with remembered mercy. The affect-labeling literature affirms the wisdom that naming grief while orienting toward stabilizing truth reduces limbic reactivity.[66]

Community as carrier wave

Comfort multiplies in the Body of Christ. Before the crisis, believers weave *habits of 'withness'*: worship, table fellowship, prayer agreements, and testimony. These practices create a social buffer that mitigates isolation when bereavement comes. Cohort studies consistently show lower loneliness indices and more rapid grief recovery among those embedded in faith communities.[67] The church becomes a living memory of God's faithfulness when our own memory trembles.

Sacraments and symbols.

The Lord's Table and baptism are not sentimental ceremonies; they are anchors, or you might even say, visible words. They fix the heart to objective grace. Approached regularly in faith, they tutor the imagination: I am united to Christ; His death and resurrection hold me. This sacramental imagination fortifies believers against collapse by reframing identity around Christ rather than around what is later lost.[68] The one obvious difference is that baptism is required only once, whereas the "Lord's Table" or Holy Communion ought to be celebrated as often as possible. In the case of baptism, the consciousness of its significance ought to be a daily lived experience.

Eschatological oxygen.

Finally, preventive comfort lifts the gaze. Christian hope is not wishful thinking but a promise anchored in an empty tomb. Paul weighs present pain against future glory and finds the scales outrageous: "not worth comparing." Hope reorients appraisal; it does not trivialize pain, but it prevents pain from monopolizing meaning. Longitudinal work on religious coping shows that future-oriented hope is associated with lower inflammatory markers and better sleep. These are somatic echoes of theological truth.[69]

Practicing comfort now

Daily Presence: ten unhurried minutes of quiet prayer, breathing the Jesus Prayer; peace rehearsed becomes peace remembered.[70]

Testimony Rehearsal: once a week, recall aloud a past deliverance and how God met you; this builds a mental library for tomorrow's valley.[71]

Table of Mercy: receive Communion regularly; meditate on union with Christ as your core identity.[72]

Comfort Distribution: comfort someone each week. Call, visit, pray; giving comfort strengthens your own capacity to receive it.[73]

The Comfort Continuum: Comfort is not merely what God *does* after sorrow; it is who He *is* with you before it arrives. Train with Him now. Then, when the waters rise, you will discover the peace He already placed in your path.

Faith Window 3 Part 2

Before the Valley Comes

"When you pass through the waters, I will be with you; and through the rivers, they shall not overwhelm you."

Isaiah 43:2 (ESV)

This passage reflects an ancient psychological truth validated by modern science: anticipating steady companionship reduces the intensity of trauma.[74] In spiritual terms, God's presence precedes the crisis; in human terms, inner assurance precedes resilience. Across faith traditions, those who internalize a sense of divine nearness or transcendent meaning consistently exhibit greater emotional recovery and post-traumatic growt

Chapter 3 Endnotes

50 Southwick, S. M., Vythilingam, M., & Charney, D. S. (2005). The psychobiology of depression and resilience to stress: Implications for prevention and treatment. Annual Review of Clinical Psychology, 1, 255-291.

51 Peters, A., McEwen, B. S., & Friston, K. (2017). Uncertainty and stress: Why it causes diseases and how it is mastered by the brain. Progress in Neurobiology, 156, 164-188.

52 Folkman, S., & Lazarus, R. S. (1988). Coping as a mediator of emotion. Journal of Personality and Social Psychology, 54(3), 466-475.

53 Meichenbaum, D. (2017). Stress inoculation training: A preventative and treatment approach. In D. Meichenbaum (Ed.), The evolution of cognitive behavior therapy (pp. 117-140). Routledge.

Park, C. L., Russell, B. S., Fendrich, M., Finkelstein-Fox, L., Hutchison, M., & Becker, J. (2020). Americans' COVID-19 stress, coping, and adherence to CDC guidelines. Journal of General Internal Medicine, 35(8), 2296-2303. https://doi.org/10.1007/s11606-020-05898-9

Eisma, M. C., Tamminga, A., Smid, G. E., & Boelen, P. A. (2023). Acute grief and rumination in response to the death of a loved one: A network analysis. Journal of Psychopathology and Clinical Science, 132(3), 351-362. https://doi.org/10.1037/abn0000803

54 Kalisch, R., Baker, D. G., Basten, U., et al. (2017). The resilience framework as a strategy to combat stress-related disorders. Nature Human Behaviour, 1(11), 784-790.

55 Fox, K. C. R., Dixon, M. L., Nijeboer, S., et al. (2016). Functional neuroanatomy of meditation: A review and meta-analysis. Neuroscience & Biobehavioral Reviews, 65, 208-228.

56 Porges, S. W. (2021). Polyvagal theory: A biobehavioral journey to sociality. Comprehensive Psychoneuroendocrinology, 7, 100069. https://doi.org/10.1016/j.cpnec.2021.100069

57 McCraty, R., Atkinson, M., Tomasino, D., & Bradley, R. T. (2009). The coherent heart: Heart-brain interactions, psychophysiological coherence, and the emergence of system-wide order. Integral Review, 5(2), 10-115.

58 McCraty, R., & Shaffer, F. (2015). Heart rate variability: New perspectives on physiological mechanisms, assessment of self-regulatory capacity, and health risk. Global Advances in Health and Medicine, 4(1), 46-61. https://doi.org/10.7453/gahmj.2014.073

59 Gross, J. J., & John, O. P. (2003). Individual differences in two emotion regulation processes. Journal of Personality and Social Psychology, 85(2), 348-362.

60 Beck, J. R., & Demarest, B. (2005). The human person in theology and psychology. Kregel Academic.

61 Hostinar, C. E., Sullivan, R. M., & Gunnar, M. R. (2014). Psychobiological mechanisms underlying the social buffering of the hypothalamic-pituitary-adrenocortical axis: A review of animal models and human studies across development. Psychological Bulletin, 140(1), 256-282.

62 Koenig, H. G. (2012). Religion, spirituality, and health: The research and clinical implications. Templeton Press.

63 Park, C. L. (2005). Religion as a meaning-making framework in coping with life stress. Journal of Social Issues, 61(4), 707-729.

64 Park, C. L. (2010). Making sense of the meaning literature: An integrative review of meaning making and its effects on adjustment to stressful life events. Psychological Bulletin, 136(2), 257-301.

65 Newberg, A. B., & Waldman, M. R. (2009). How God changes your brain: Breakthrough findings from a leading neuroscientist. Ballantine Books.

66 Lieberman, M. D., Eisenberger, N. I., Crockett, M. J., Tom, S. M., Pfeifer, J. H., & Way, B. M. (2007). Putting feelings into words: Affect labeling disrupts amygdala activity in response to affective stimuli. Psychological Science, 18(5), 421-428.

67 Brown, S. L., Nesse, R. M., House, J. S., & Utz, R. L. (2004). Religion and emotional compensation: Results from a prospective study of widowhood. Personality and Social Psychology Bulletin, 30(9), 1165-1174.

68 Smith, J. K. A. (2009). Desiring the kingdom: Worship, worldview, and cultural formation. Baker Academic.

69 Ai, A. L., Pargament, K. I., Kronfol, Z., Tice, T. N., & Appel, H. (2010). Pathways to postoperative hostility in cardiac patients: Mediation of coping, spiritual struggle and interleukin-6. Journal of Health Psychology, 15(2), 186-195.

70 Ware, K. (1997). The power of the name: The Jesus Prayer in Orthodox spirituality. In C. Jones, G. Wainwright, & E. Yarnold (Eds.), The study of spirituality (pp. 584-594). Oxford University Press.

71 Pals, J. L. (2006). Narrative identity processing of difficult life experiences: Pathways of personality development and positive self-transformation in adulthood. Journal of Personality, 74(4), 1079-1110.

72 Torrance, J. B. (1996). Worship, community and the triune God of grace. IVP Academic.

73 Brown, S. L., Nesse, R. M., Vinokur, A. D., & Smith, D. M. (2003). Providing social support may be more beneficial than receiving it: Results from a prospective study of mortality. Psychological Science, 14(4), 320-327.

74 Pargament, K. I., Koenig, H. G., & Perez, L. M. (2000). The many methods of religious coping: Development and initial validation of the RCOPE. Journal of Clinical Psychology, 56(4), 519-543.

Chapter 4

Resilience: The Strength You Already Have

4.1 Why Most People Recover Better Than They Expect

Most bereaved people follow a resilient trajectory: acute distress that stabilizes relatively quickly, with stable functioning as the modal outcome; resilience and recovery are distinct from chronic grief.[75]

Grief shrinks the horizon. In the first weeks after a loss, the future can look like a blank wall with no doorway, and no light. Yet across cultures, ages, and kinds of loss, a consistent finding emerges: **most people regain their footing sooner, and more fully, than they fear.** That does not trivialize sorrow; it rightly sizes resilience. The pain is real, but so is the mind–body capacity to steady itself, helped by love, routine, and meaning. For readers of faith, this matches an ancient claim: *"Weeping may endure for a night, but joy comes in the morning"* (Psalm 30:5). For readers of any background, the science stands on its own: human beings are built to bend without breaking.

The Hebrew verb *"yalin"* (endure/lodge/tarry) suggests a temporary guest staying overnight. Weeping is not a permanent resident but a passing visitor. The parallelism intensifies the contrast: "weeping" *(bekī* - audible crying) and "night" (ereb - evening, darkness) are set against "joy" (*rinnāh* - a ringing cry, shout of joy) and "morning" *(bōqer* - dawn, the breaking of light). Yet verse 5a contains a crucial theological premise often skipped: "For His anger is but for a moment, His favor is for a lifetime." The grief

David describes here is specifically covenantal discipline, not random suffering. God's corrective anger (ʼap̱) is momentary; His favor (*rāṣôn* - acceptance, delight) is lifelong. Earlier in the Psalm, David declares, "The Lord is near to the brokenhearted" (Psalm 34:18), where the Hebrew *"qārôḇ"* means not mere spatial proximity but covenant nearness, active engagement. God doesn't observe broken hearts from a distance; He draws close to intervene. The promise isn't that morning erases night's reality, but that weeping, though real and prolonged, has an appointed end, and the God who is "near" ensures that dawn will come.

Dispelling the "universal breakdown" myth.

The fallacy many believe is that everyone passes through the same fixed "stages," and if you don't, you're suppressing. That is not supported by modern evidence.[76] Large longitudinal studies show **multiple healthy trajectories**, from brief, intense waves of grief to quieter adaptation, with **chronic, disabling grief being the minority pattern.**[77] You are not "doing it wrong" if your tears come less often than your neighbor's, or if you have a day that suddenly feels almost normal. Variation is not avoidance; it is how resilience often looks.

What helps most people adapt?

Several ingredients repeatedly show up in those natural recovery patterns:

Social buffering: a safe, supportive presence dampens the brain's threat response. Even small, nonverbal contact, sitting nearby, holding a hand, reduces physiological arousal and the felt sense of being overwhelmed.

Flexible coping - Healthy grievers "oscillate". They face the loss for a while, then deliberately turn toward ordinary tasks such as laundry, sorting bills, or a short walk, before turning back again. This back-and-forth, not nonstop confrontation, is linked to better adjustment.

Emotion regulation (not repression) - Naming a feeling, breathing through it, and reframing its meaning are skills the brain can learn; they quiet the amygdala and recruit prefrontal circuits that help us choose responses rather than react automatically.

Meaning-making - People who can locate their loss within a larger story of love, service, legacy, faith, or a renewed purpose, recover faster and carry fewer symptoms long-term.

What the brain is doing

Neuroimaging has shown that grief activates pain and yearning networks; over time, circuits for memory, planning, and meaning begin to counterbalance raw distress.[78] This **neuroplastic** shift is not denial; it is healing at a cellular level. New connections are supporting new stability. For readers who draw on Scripture, this is one way to understand promises like, *"When you pass through the waters, I will be with you"* (Isaiah 43:2): presence does not erase pain; it keeps pain from having the last word.

Resilience is not stoicism.

Tears are not the enemy; **getting stuck** is. Suppressing grief can raise anxiety and stress-related symptoms. Resilience, by contrast, allows emotion its moment, then gently guides the day back toward life-giving habits. Even brief returns to routine signal safety to the nervous system. For some, prayer, Scripture reading, or quiet contemplation serve this role; for others, a walk with a friend or tending a garden does the same work of "grounding." The common thread is **a rhythm that includes both sorrow and restoration**.

Calibrating expectations

None of this means everyone "bounces back" quickly, or that timelines should be policed. Some losses cut deeper, some contexts are harsher, and some people, because of prior trauma, limited support, or biological vulnerability, need clinical help.[79] Compassion requires **room for outliers**. At the same time, knowing that most mourners improve within months protects against a second wound: the fear that today's intensity is forever. Whether you pray, journal, talk with a counselor, or lean into family, you are cooperating with processes the brain and soul are prepared to carry.[80]

A humane, evidence-guided posture

For friends, pastors, chaplains, clinicians, and caring neighbors, the mandate is simple: **be near, be patient, be practical.** Offer presence before advice. Invite the griever for a short walk before a long talk. Help with one concrete task, such as meals, a ride, or a form, before exploring "big meanings." In time, meaning will come; forcing it too soon can backfire. Respect different grief rhythms, watch for signs of complicated grief, evidenced by persistent, impairing yearning and functional decline, and refer for care when needed. Most of all, by tone, by showing up, keep conveying that there is **nothing defective** about needing time, and nothing doomed about taking small steps.

For those who look to Jesus, the shortest verse in Scripture, *"Jesus wept"* (John 11:35), offers both validation and direction: tears acknowledged, action resumed. For those who do not, the same wisdom holds in secular terms: emotion honored, function restored.

When the horizon shrinks, borrow the eyes of those who have walked ahead. There is a doorway in the wall. You may not see it yet, but your heart, and the people beside you, will help you find it.

Faith Window 4 Part 1

Psalm 34:18 (ESV)

"The Lord is near to the brokenhearted and saves the crushed in spirit."

Resilience is not the absence of breaking. It is what happens when breaking does not have the final word. The Psalmist's words, written from a cave of despair, speak to both the believer and the skeptic who has ever felt life collapse inward. *"The Lord is near"* does not describe a sentimental closeness; it is the declaration of a God who steps into the wreckage.

His nearness is not proven by preventing the wound but by sustaining the wounded.

Even when faith feels thin, the very ache for meaning is evidence of life still moving within.[81] From a Christian perspective, that impulse is the Spirit's whisper, reminding us that pain can become a passage. From a universal human view, it is the same unseen strength that keeps the lungs breathing when the heart wants to stop. The verse bridges both worlds, the divine and the human, showing that comfort is not passive but active.

Resilience, then, is a partnership between God's presence and human participation. We do not wait idly for rescue; we walk while we are being carried. For the mourner who prays, this verse is a promise. For the mourner who simply endures, it is still true: you are not abandoned in your breaking, and your breaking is not the end of your becoming.

4.2 The Resilience Spectrum

Resilience is often spoken of as though it were a single trait, something people either possess or lack. In truth, it functions more like a **spectrum,** a continuum of human adaptability that varies from moment to moment and from one kind of loss to another. Some days, the bereaved can face the world; other days, they can barely face themselves. The difference does not mean they have failed. It means that resilience flexes with the weight of reality.

Modern psychology confirms that resilience is not a rare gift but a *common grace*. Studies by Dr. George Bonanno of Columbia University demonstrate that the majority of mourners, though deeply shaken, regain stability faster than they predict.[82] His research introduced the idea of "resilience trajectories," showing that recovery does not move in straight lines but through waves: decline, stabilization, partial recovery, and renewed strength. These findings echo biblical truth: *"A righteous man falls seven times and rises again"* (Proverbs 24:16, ESV). Falling is expected; rising is assured.

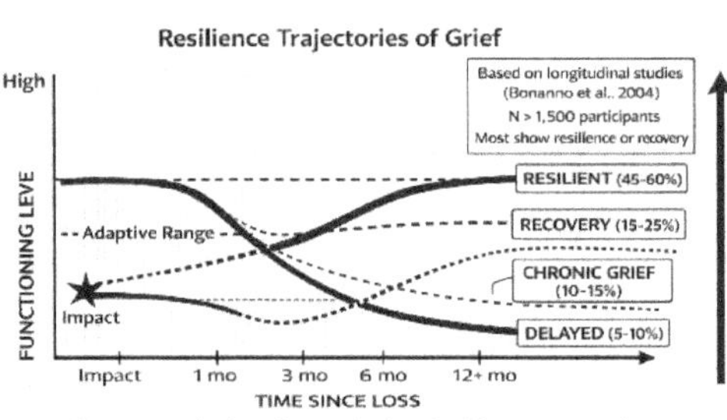

Resilience trajectories show diverse paths through grief. Contrary to popular belief, most bereaved individuals maintain or quickly regain functioning. Chronic impairment affects a minority.

Resilience as Dynamic Equilibrium

Resilience is less about toughness than *rebalancing*. Grief is the body's and mind's attempt to restore internal order after the emotional nervous system has been struck by lightning.[83] The stress hormones released during early loss gradually recede, and the parasympathetic system begins to rebuild calm.[84] In that sense, healing is a biological obedience to divine design. The Creator built recovery into the circuitry of human life; our task is to cooperate with what He already engineered. That cooperation involves rest, nutrition, prayer, and social connection. All of these stabilize the system that God made.

Spiritual equilibrium parallels physical equilibrium. Faith does not erase grief but keeps it from becoming chaos. Scripture never calls us to deny pain; it calls us to discover peace *within* it (John 14:27). Those who attempt to "stay strong" by suppressing emotion often find themselves breaking internally, while those who allow tears to flow find release. Resilience grows when the heart stops fighting the reality of loss and begins to live truthfully inside it. This is not resignation; it is acceptance bathed in hope.

The Spectrum in Practice

On one end of the spectrum are the **emotionally immobilized**. These are those so stunned that life's routines collapse. At the center are the **oscillators**, people who alternate between coping and collapse. At the far end are the **adaptive mourners**, who integrate loss into a sense of purpose. Most people move through all three zones, often within a single week. Knowing this helps remove guilt from the equation. It allows the grieving to stop measuring their progress against a calendar and start measuring it against compassion for themselves.

The biblical witness supports this spectrum view. Consider Elijah under the broom tree (1 Kings 19:4–8). Exhausted, despairing, and suicidal, he represents the immobilized end. God's response was neither rebuke nor lecture but rest and nourishment. Only later did the whisper of divine presence reignite Elijah's courage. That sequence of collapse, care, and clarityis the essence of resilient faith. Even the prophet's recovery was gradual; resilience unfolded, not exploded.

The Hidden Allies of Resilience

Resilience also draws from hidden reservoirs: **meaning, connection, and memory**. Meaning reframes suffering, connection shares its weight, and memory redeems it. When we recall earlier survivals and times we thought we would not make it, but did, our nervous system gains proof that survival is possible again. This is why testimony, in both church and therapy, is powerful medicine. The story we tell ourselves about pain determines whether pain imprisons or propels us.

In this sense, resilience becomes a form of worship. It is gratitude enacted under pressure. Every step forward, be it making a meal, answering a call, or opening a curtain, is a quiet "thank You" that life continues. Faith adds one more layer: the belief that God's strength works best in weakness (2 Corinthians 12:9). Resilience is not heroic self-sufficiency; it is divine partnership with human perseverance.

Practical Pathways to Strength

Researchers identify four daily actions that strengthen resilience: **restoration, reflection, relationship, and routine**.[85] Restoration involves sleep, hydration, and nutrition, all necessary for the body's maintenance of balance. Reflection keeps the mind honest before God, through journaling or prayer. Relationship reconnects the heart to others so that isolation cannot become identity. Routine re-anchors life in small certainties: a morning walk, a consistent bedtime, a Scripture read aloud. Each of these acts tells the brain that order still exists, and the spirit that life is still worth living.

These principles harmonize with Isaiah's promise: *"Those who wait for the Lord shall renew their strength; they shall mount up with wings like eagles"* (Isaiah 40:31). The word "renew" in Hebrew, *chalaph*, means "to exchange." We do not create strength; we exchange weakness for divine sufficiency. Resilience is that sacred exchange happening again and again inside the wounded heart. In a moment of deficiency, God's assurance to Paul was, "My grace is sufficient for you. For my power is made perfect in weakness." (2 Corinthians 12:9-10).

Healthy and Unhealthy Dependence on Others

Life was never meant to be lived alone, and the presence of others in our lives is a reality. In times of grief, weakness, and felt need, for many it is intuitive to look to others for support. However, caution is required. The distinction must be drawn between adaptive dependency, a healthy reliance on others, and maladaptive dependency. Adaptive dependency can protect against prolonged grief, while maladaptive dependency is linked with more complicated bereavement.[86] Healthy dependence means accepting help while still taking small steps on your own. Unhealthy dependence expects others to carry what only God and time can heal.

In a different context, Scripture parallels this concept of limited reliance on others in Galatians 6:2&5 - Bear one another's burdens, and so fulfill the law of Christ... For each will have to bear his own load."

When Pain Crosses the Border Into Thought

Grief does not end when the tears dry; it evolves. If resilience describes the body and soul learning to stand again, the next step is to face toxic positivity and explore how well-meaning people can unintentionally hinder that process. Authentic strength, we will see, is honest strength.

4.3 Facing Toxic Positivity

In today's culture of relentless optimism, grief often collides with a well-meaning but damaging form of denial called *toxic positivity*. It is the compulsion to silence sorrow, to replace lament with slogans, and to hide pain behind a smile. It is the pressure to "stay positive" and suppress negative emotion.[87] It promotes emotional suppression and shame. It can worsen psychological distress. The reality is that grief requires honest emotional processing. While encouragement is healthy, suppression is not. Toxic positivity denies the legitimacy of suffering and short-circuits the healing process.

When someone says, "At least he's in a better place," "Everything happens for a reason," or even "God is good," it may sound spiritual, but it often minimizes real pain. Studies in affective neuroscience show that when emotions are invalidated, the brain's anterior cingulate cortex (responsible for emotional regulation) becomes hyperactive, producing greater stress and slower recovery.[88] Emotion, like a physiological wound, must be cleaned before it can close. To ignore it is to risk infection of the mind.

The grief process needs space for the full spectrum of emotion without shame. This includes shock, anger, guilt, and even numbness. Psychologists call this *emotional granularity*, the ability to name and distinguish what one feels. People who can articulate their sorrow, rather than suppress it, display better immune function and cardiovascular stability. Naming emotion activates the prefrontal cortex, calming the amygdala, the brain's alarm center, and restoring balance.

Theologically, the Psalms model emotional honesty. Nearly half of them are laments. The writers do not rush to optimism; they begin with anguish, confusion, and complaint. Psalm 42:9 cries, *"I say to God, my Rock, 'Why have you forgotten me?'"* Yet lament often resolves into trust, not because the pain vanishes, but because God meets His people in the middle of it. Authentic faith does not erase feeling; it redeems it.

For those outside the Christian tradition, the principle still stands: healing requires acknowledgment, not avoidance. Buddhist mindfulness calls this *equanimity* and refers to meeting suffering without judgment. In secular therapy, it appears as *radical acceptance*, facing what is, without forcing premature resolution. Across disciplines, truth-telling about pain is the beginning of peace.

In pastoral care, the remedy for toxic positivity is not pessimism but permission to grieve, to cry, to feel human again. Counselors can model this by using language that validates rather than corrects: "This must hurt deeply," or "You have a right to miss them." Validation does not prolong grief; it gives it boundaries. People who feel seen and heard metabolize sorrow faster than those told to "move on."

Authentic hope, then, is not the absence of tears but their transformation. The Gospel does not command silence but invites surrender: *"Blessed are those who mourn, for they shall be comforted."* (Matthew 5:4, ESV) That comfort is not a denial of loss. It is divine companionship within it.

As one clinical study concluded, **suppressing emotion increases sympathetic arousal and delays the physiological return to baseline**.[89] But confession, whether emotional or spiritual, reduces cortisol, lowers blood pressure, and enhances immune resilience. When the mourner stops pretending, the body stops overreacting.

The paradox of grief is that strength emerges through surrender. True resilience is not built by ignoring pain but by integrating it—naming it, feeling it, offering it to God (or to truth, for the nonreligious), and allowing it to mature into compassion. Toxic positivity says, "Smile, it's over." Healthy faith says, "Cry! It matters."

And only after we have truly cried can the soul begin to breathe again.

Detoxify Toxic Positivity

Grief is heavy. Toxic positivity says, "Don't show it." It sounds like faith or strength, but it pressures hurting people to hide their pain. Sentences like "Everything happens for a reason," "God won't give you more than you can handle," or "Stay strong" may mean well, yet they can make sorrow feel wrong. When pain is denied, healing slows.

Healthy encouragement is honest. It does not rush people. It makes room for sadness and tears. Brain studies show why this matters. When we are "shushed" emotionally, the brain's alarm center (the **amygdala**) stays stirred up, while the thinking, calming part (the **prefrontal cortex**) has a harder time helping us settle down. In simple words: pretending you're fine keeps your body on high alert.

Naming feelings helps. Psychologists call this *emotional granularity*. It uses clear words like "I feel angry," "I feel numb," or "I feel guilty," rather than vague words like "bad" or "off." Naming feelings is not a weakness; it is a tool. It signals the thinking brain to step in and dial down the alarm brain. This lowers stress and helps the body recover.

The Bible does not demand smiles. Almost half the Psalms are laments. God gave us these prayers to show that *saying the hard thing to Him is still a sign of faith*. David asks, "Why?" Jeremiah weeps. Jesus Himself wept at a friend's grave. Scripture never calls tears a lack of belief. It calls them *truth*. For readers from other faiths, or from none, the same principle holds: honest grief is the starting line of healing. Many therapies call this *acceptance*: facing what is, without pretending.

Why do we slide into toxic positivity? Often, we are afraid of our own pain or of saying the wrong thing to others. Cheerful slogans feel safe. But they can become masks that hide, rather than heal. Real comfort chooses presence over pep talks. "I'm here." "This hurts." "You're not alone." These short lines open a door for breath and calm to return.

What churches and families can do.

Make space for lament. Read a Psalm of sorrow out loud. Allow silence. Light a candle. Ask, "What would honoring your loved one look like this week?" Avoid timelines like "You should be better by now." Healing is not a deadline; it is a journey. In small groups, teach people to sit with pain before speaking about hope. Hope that comes too soon can feel like pressure, not promise.

What individuals can do.

Permit pain. If tears come, let them come. Your nervous system is discharging stress.

Use simple words. "Today I feel angry." "This morning I felt okay; now I feel empty." Naming is calming

Create a gentle routine. Eat, move, rest, and pray (or reflect) at set times. Routine tells your body that life is still safe.

Invite a witness. Ask one trusted person to check in. Being seen reduces the brain's alarm signals.

Pray honest prayers. If you follow Jesus, pray like the Psalmists: say the truth and then ask for help. If you are not a Christian, try a short daily reflection: "What hurts? What helped, even a little?" Both pathways lower inner load

What not to say to the grieving.

"It was God's plan." (This often lands as blame on God.)

"They wouldn't want you to be sad." (It denies love's weight.)

"At least…" (Anything after "at least" usually shrinks someone's story.) Instead, try: "This matters." "Tell me about them." "I'm not in a hurry."

Faith and Science Agree: suppression backfires.

Studies show that suppressing emotions raises blood pressure and keeps stress hormones elevated. People feel "wired and tired"—exhausted but unable to rest. By contrast, *expressive writing* (10–15 minutes of truthful journaling over three days) has been shown to reduce stress and improve immune markers.[90] It gives sorrow a safe place to go.

Toxic positivity says, "Smile so I can feel okay." Healthy hope says, "Speak so you can heal." The difference is compassion. Compassion has time. It listens. It does not argue. It does not quote a verse to end a conversation. It stands beside you until you can stand again.

For Christians, comfort is a Person, not a pep talk. *"Blessed are those who mourn, for they shall be comforted."* (Matthew 5:4) The promise is not that pain disappears at once, but that God draws near in it. For readers outside the faith, the principle still holds: people recover faster when they are allowed to be human, and when their pain is met with patience rather than pressure.

A simple daily practice:

Sit for three minutes.

Breathe slowly: in for four counts, out for six.

Speak one true sentence about your loss.

Name one small mercy you noticed today.

Ask for help from God or from a friend. This is not a fix. It is a light. Small lights guide tired feet.

Tears are not the enemy of strength. They are the river that carries us there. And only after we have truly cried can the soul begin to breathe again.

4.4 The Interplay of Anger and Grief

Anger often surprises mourners. They expect tears but not rage. Yet anger is one of grief's oldest companions.[91] It erupts when love collides with loss, and when something once whole is torn apart, and no explanation seems good enough. For counselors and caregivers, anger is not rebellion; it is protest. It shouts what words cannot yet reason out: *"This should not have happened."* I will even venture to say that anger may be thought of as grief with teeth.[92]

Anger wears many faces. It may be loud and explosive, or quiet and cold. Some aim it at doctors, family members, or God. Others turn it inward and call it guilt. The target changes, but the source is the same: love wounded and searching for justice. Modern neuroscience confirms that anger and grief share overlapping brain circuits. When we lose someone, the brain areas that signal *attachment threat*, the amygdala and anterior cingulate cortex, fire in patterns nearly identical to those seen in physical pain.[93] Anger, then, is not sin by default. It is the mind's alarm that something precious has been violated.

The physiology of protest

When anger rises, stress hormones surge. Heart rate and blood pressure climb. Muscles tighten, preparing for a fight. In small doses, this energy can help a mourner push through the fog of early loss. It makes it possible to plan a funeral, meet paperwork deadlines, or defend boundaries against unhelpful intrusions. But when anger becomes chronic, cortisol and adrenaline linger, draining immunity and increasing cardiac risk.[94] The same reaction meant to protect now begins to harm.

The psychology of meaning

Anger asks questions no tidy theology can silence: *Why them? Why now? Why not me?* Suppressing those questions does not erase them; it drives them deeper, where they can ferment into bitterness. Healthy processing requires a safe listener, someone who will not correct too quickly. Research on "constructive anger expression" shows that when mourners can voice anger in the presence of empathy, emotional intensity drops and insight rises. The goal is not to justify rage but to translate it into truth.

Anger, Justice, Mercy, and Healing

Integrating justice-seeking anger with forgiveness and mercy aligns with clinical findings that meaning-making and balanced emotional expression support adaptation after violent or preventable losses.[95] We are all created in the image and likeness of God. True, some of that image has been tarnished and compromised, but the fundamentals still remain. When we perceive that justice has not been served, we should feel angry. Quite often, at points in the journey of grief, we may feel that it is God who is unjust. The challenge is for us to restrain our words to questioning and investigation, never to accusation. And yet, even when we foolishly and falsely accuse God, as we learn from the life of Job, God is merciful and even accommodating.

The cycle of anger against God and of falsely accusing Him is complete when He gently reminds us of His mercies and loving kindness towards us. And as we think of how much God has forgiven us, we begin to cool into an attitude of gratitude to God for all His goodness to us, none of which we merited. And as He floods our hearts with His mercy, we become inclined to also be merciful and forgiving of others.

The spiritual dimension.

Scripture permits feeling anger while warning against its rule. *"Be angry and do not sin; do not let the sun go down on your anger."* (Ephesians 4:26 ESV) The verse does not command calm; it commands stewardship. Even prophets raged. Jeremiah cried out against injustice; Jesus wept and overturned tables. These were not acts of rebellion but of alignment; anger harnessed for righteousness rather than revenge. Faith teaches that God's shoulders are broad enough for honest complaint. He would rather hear a raw lament than a polite pretense.

For readers of other faiths, similar wisdom can be found elsewhere. Buddhist teaching names anger as a "second arrow". It describes the wound we added to the first. Mindfulness helps the sufferer notice the surge, breathe, and let it pass before it burns others. In secular therapy, this corresponds to *affect labeling* and *self-compassion*: noticing the emotion, naming it, and choosing a non-destructive response.[96] The principle is universal. Acknowledge, pause, redirect. Constructive expression of anger (lament, honest speech, channeling into action) is healthier than suppression or explosive discharge and is compatible with faith.

Practical counsel for caregivers.

Do not argue with anger. Reflect it: *"I can hear how unfair this feels."*

Stay grounded. Slow your own breathing; calm is contagious.

Differentiate between protest and hostility. Protest seeks understanding; hostility seeks harm.

Invite expression in safe form; journaling, physical activity, prayer, or guided imagery.

Affirm that faith and fury can coexist. God is not threatened by emotion.

Practical counsel for mourners....

Write a letter you will never send. Say everything. Then decide what to keep.

If anger targets God, say so. Scripture is full of such prayers.

Move your body. Anger stored in muscles becomes fatigue. Walk, stretch, breathe.

Seek reconciliation where possible, and release where it is not possible. Forgiveness is not approval; it is unclenching the fist of the heart.

The turning point.

When anger is heard, it changes temperature. What was hot becomes honest. The mourner moves from shouting *at* God to talking *with* Him, from blaming life to blessing memory. Pastoral counselors note that this moment often marks renewed trust. Physically, breathing slows, shoulders drop, and cortisol subsides. Spiritually, the sufferer begins to trade the demand for answers for the presence of peace.

To lose anger too soon is to lose momentum for healing; to hold it too long is to poison hope. The balance is found in transformation. Let righteous protest become purposeful compassion. Many who once shouted at heaven later build foundations, counsel others, or comfort new mourners. Their anger, refined by grace, becomes fuel for mercy.

Anger, then, is not the enemy of grief but its twin. Both cry out for what was lost and for what still matters. When guided wisely, anger opens a door, not to vengeance, but to vision. Through that door, the grieving heart begins to find its strength again.

Faith Window 4 Part 2

"The Lord Is Near to the Brokenhearted" (Psalm 34:18)

"The Lord is near to the brokenhearted and saves the crushed in spirit." Psalm 34:18 (ESV)

Grief has a way of making people feel far from everyone, even from God. Silence fills the room; prayers feel like echoes. Yet this verse tells a different story. Nearness does not mean the pain ends; it means you are not alone in it. When your heart

breaks, God does not stand at a distance waiting for composure.
He moves closer.

David wrote Psalm 34 after fleeing danger, hiding in caves, and pretending to be someone else to survive. His fear was real, his failures recent, and his reputation in ruins. Still, he could say, "God is near." That is the paradox of faith: divine presence can share the same space as human pain. The broken heart does not push God away; it attracts Him.

For counselors and caregivers, this verse is not only theology. It is therapy. People heal faster when they believe they are not alone. Modern neuroscience agrees: the brain's stress center calms when we sense safe connection. The believer names that connection *God*; others may name it *love*, *community*, or *peace that passes understanding.* The result is the same. Hope begins to breathe again.

For the Christian, God's nearness has a face. Jesus wept at a tomb before He ever spoke a single word of resurrection. He did not skip sorrow; He sanctified it. To be "saved" in this verse is more than rescue from despair; it is restoration of dignity. The crushed spirit is not discarded but lifted and reshaped. Grief becomes the workshop where grace does its quietest miracles.

So, when hearts break and voices falter, this promise still stands: **God is nearer than the tears that fall.** Not to erase them, but to catch them. Not to rush you, but to redeem what pain tried to destroy. And in that nearness, sometimes wordless, sometimes whispered, the healing begins

Chapter 4 Endnotes

75 Bonanno, G. A., Wortman, C. B., & Nesse, R. M. (2004). Prospective patterns of resilience and maladjustment during widowhood. Psychology and Aging, 19(2), 260-271.

76 Stroebe, M., & Schut, H. (2021). Bereavement in times of COVID-19: A review and theoretical framework. Omega-Journal of Death and Dying, 82(3), 500-522.

77 Bonanno, G. A., & Kaltman, S. (2001). The varieties of grief experience. Clinical Psychology Review, 21(5), 705-734.

78 O'Connor, M. F., Wellisch, D. K., Stanton, A. L., et al. (2008). Craving love? Enduring grief activates brain's reward center. NeuroImage, 42(2), 969-972.

79 Boelen, P. A., & Smid, G. E. (2017). Disturbed grief: Prolonged grief disorder and persistent complex bereavement disorder. BMJ, 357, j2016.

80 Currier, J. M., Neimeyer, R. A., & Berman, J. S. (2008). The effectiveness of psychotherapeutic interventions for bereaved persons. Psychological Bulletin, 134(5), 648-661.

81 Park, C. L. (2010). Making sense of the meaning literature: An integrative review. Psychological Bulletin, 136(2), 257-301.

82 Bonanno, G. A. (2004). Loss, trauma, and human resilience: Have we underestimated the human capacity to thrive after extremely aversive events? American Psychologist, 59(1), 20-28.

83 Prigerson, H. G., Boelen, P. A., Xu, J., et al. (2021). Validation of the new DSM-5-TR criteria for prolonged grief disorder. World Psychiatry, 20(1), 96-106.

84 O'Connor, M. F., Wellisch, D. K., Stanton, A. L., Olmstead, R., & Irwin, M. R. (2012). Diurnal cortisol in complicated and non-complicated grief. Psychoneuroendocrinology, 37(5), 725-728.

85 Southwick, S. M., & Charney, D. S. (2018). Resilience: The science of mastering life's greatest challenges (2nd ed.). Cambridge University Press.

86 Denckla, C. A., Mancini, A. D., Consedine, N. S., Milanovic, S. M., Bornstein, R. F., Bewley, K. E., Galfalvy, H. C., Oquendo, M. A., & Bonanno, G. A. (2011). Adaptive and maladaptive dependency in bereavement: Distinguishing prolonged and resolved grief trajectories. Journal of Nervous and Mental Disease, 199(6), 444-450.

87 Quintero, S., & Long, J. (2019). Toxic positivity: The dark side of positive vibes. The Psychology Group. https://thepsychologygroup.com/toxic-positivity/

88 Lieberman, M. D., Eisenberger, N. I., Crockett, M. J., Tom, S. M., Pfeifer, J. H., & Way, B. M. (2007). Putting feelings into words: Affect labeling disrupts amygdala activity in response to affective stimuli. Psychological Science, 18(5), 421-428.

89 Gross, J. J., & Levenson, R. W. (1997). Hiding feelings: The acute effects of inhibiting negative and positive emotion. Journal of Abnormal Psychology, 106(1), 95-103.

90 Pennebaker, J. W., & Smyth, J. M. (2016). Opening up by writing it down: How expressive writing improves health and eases emotional pain (3rd ed.). Guilford Press.

91 Zech, E., & Arnold, C. (2021). Attachment and emotion regulation in bereavement. Journal of Loss and Trauma, 26(5), 447-467.

92 Zech, E., & Arnold, C. (2021). Attachment and emotion regulation in bereavement: A systematic review. Journal of Loss and Trauma, 26(5), 447-467.

93 Eisenberger, N. I. (2012). The pain of social disconnection: Examining the shared neural underpinnings of physical and social pain. Nature Reviews Neuroscience, 13(6), 421-434.

94 Chida, Y., & Steptoe, A. (2009). The association of anger and hostility with future coronary heart disease: A meta-analytic review of prospective evidence. Journal of the American College of Cardiology, 53(11), 936-946.

95 Neimeyer, R. A., & Sands, D. C. (2011). Meaning reconstruction in bereavement: From principles to practice. In R. A. Neimeyer, D. L. Harris, H. R. Winokuer, & G. F. Thornton (Eds.), Grief and bereavement in contemporary society (pp. 9-22). Routledge.

96 Neff, K. D., & Germer, C. K. (2013). A pilot study and randomized controlled trial of the mindful self-compassion program. Journal of Clinical Psychology, 69(1), 28-44.

Chapter 5

The Physiology of Grief - The Body Cries

The Body Cries What the Soul Can't Say

5.1 Grief in Different Stories and Settings

Not all grief is carried on equal ground. A widow in a crowded village, a single father in an unsafe neighborhood, and a professional in a quiet suburb may all weep over the death of a child, but the pressures around them are not the same. Access to food, medical care, safe housing, and an understanding community all change how the body and mind weather sorrow.

Culture also shapes what is "allowed." Some families grant generous space for tears and anger; others reward only silence and quick recovery. In some cultures, grief is sung in the streets; in others, it is hidden behind polite smiles. The biology of grief is shared, but the story it unfolds in is different. Good pastoral care and wise therapy pay attention to both.

When you read the research or the Scriptures in this book, remember: God sees not only your pain but also the conditions that surround it.[97] He understands the extra weight that poverty, racism, migration, or isolation can add to an already broken heart. His compassion takes your entire situation into account.

5.2 The Biology of Bereavement

Grief does not live in the mind alone. It moves through the bloodstream, echoes in the pulse, and leaves fingerprints on the nervous system.[98] When loss strikes, the body interprets it as danger, a biological emergency that disrupts nearly every major organ system. What many mistake for "just sadness" is actually a measurable physiological state.[99] The body mourns too.

In the first hours and days after loss, the human body releases a cascade of stress hormones — primarily **cortisol, adrenaline, and norepinephrine.**[100] These are survival chemicals designed for fight-or-flight. In bereavement, however, there is no enemy to confront and no escape route to run. The body's emergency response has nowhere to go. As a result, stress hormones linger, circulating at abnormal levels for days or weeks.[101]

Clinical studies from institutions such as Harvard Medical School and the Mayo Clinic confirm that **cortisol levels in recently bereaved individuals can double or triple** the baseline, causing elevated heart rate, blood pressure spikes, muscle tension, and sleep disruption.[102] These physiological effects mirror those of acute trauma. In essence, **grief behaves like a prolonged state of emergency**, except the threat is invisible and internal.

The **immune system** also takes a hit. Bereaved spouses and parents show significantly reduced lymphocyte activity, leaving them more vulnerable to infections. A famous 1977 British study found that widows were more likely to catch colds and experience slow wound healing in the months following their loss. This immune suppression has since been termed "Bereavement-Related Immune Suppression," a biological marker of bereavement.[103]

Interpretive Bridge - The Body Keeps the Score

Every tear shed is a chemical event. Crying activates the parasympathetic nervous system and releases stress-related hormones through tears, providing physiological relief.[104] Emerging research suggests that crying may also stimulate the release of oxytocin and endogenous opioids, the body's natural soothing agents, particularly when it occurs in supportive social contexts where the person feels safe and understood. The calming effects appear strongest when crying is witnessed with empathy rather than criticism or isolation.[105]

Yet chronic suppression of emotion can prevent this natural recovery cycle. When mourners "keep strong" by bottling feelings, the unspent cortisol remains un-neutralized, and physical health deteriorates.[106]

In this way, the statement "time heals all wounds" is only partially true. It is **expressed emotion**, not time alone, that helps healing to happen.

Even Scripture acknowledges the body's participation in grief. When Job sat in ashes, scraping his sores (Job 2:8), his physical agony mirrored his emotional devastation. David described his grief as bones wasting away (Psalm 32:3). These were not poetic exaggerations. They were ancient observations of the same psycho-biological truth that science now confirms: **the body suffers what the soul cannot articulate.**[107]

5.3 The Stress Cascade and Immune Collapse

The **stress cascade** begins the moment the bereaved perceives loss. Two major systems drive it. These are the **sympathetic nervous system (SNS)** and the **hypothalamic–pituitary–adrenal (HPA) axis**.[108]

The SNS floods the bloodstream with adrenaline and norepinephrine. Breathing quickens, pupils dilate, and blood diverts from the digestive system to the muscles. The HPA axis, meanwhile, sends chemical signals from the brain's hypothalamus to the adrenal glands, which then release cortisol — the primary stress hormone.[109] Cortisol suppresses inflammation and sharpens alertness in the short term, but chronic exposure can break down tissues, weaken immunity, and impair memory.[110]

Within days of profound grief, the HPA axis often becomes **dysregulated**. Sleep cycles break down, digestion falters, and immune markers drop.[111] Over time, this dysregulation can produce lasting conditions such as hypertension, irritable bowel syndrome, and cardiac arrhythmia.

A 2014 study in *Circulation: Journal of the American Heart Association* coined the term "**Broken Heart Syndrome**" (Takotsubo cardiomyopathy), a temporary heart failure triggered by emotional shock.[112] It primarily affects women and mimics a heart attack, though arteries remain clear. This demonstrates that intense emotional pain can **literally reshape the heart muscle.**

Interpretive Bridge - The Silent Saboteur

Because these changes happen invisibly, mourners often blame themselves for "not coping well." They do not realize their fatigue, chest tightness, or digestive upset are not weakness but **somatic echoes** of grief.

The prophet Elijah, after losing his sense of mission and emotional equilibrium, collapsed under a broom tree and prayed to die. God's first response was not a sermon but **rest and food** - "Get up and eat, for the journey is too much for you" (1 Kings 19:7 NIV). Divine care began with physiological restoration. Only after nourishment did God address Elijah's despair. This illustrates a profound principle: **spiritual renewal often begins with biological repair.**

Medical evidence confirms it. Chronic cortisol elevation suppresses white blood cell production, allowing pathogens to thrive. It also disrupts the gut microbiome, affecting nutrient absorption and serotonin synthesis — chemicals crucial for emotional balance.[113] Thus, grief can precipitate depression not merely by sadness but by **biochemical depletion**.

To heal from loss, the body must first regain a sense of safety. That means rest, hydration, nutrition, and gentle movement, not guilt for being human.

5.4 The Silent Signals - When the Body Speaks for the Heart

When people cannot or will not speak their sorrow, the body does the talking. Physicians call this **somatization**, that is, the process by which psychological pain manifests as physical symptoms. In the bereaved, these signals often include chest pain, headaches, gastrointestinal distress, skin breakouts, or sudden muscle tension. The heart may race, or breathing may tighten for no apparent reason. The body becomes the voice of the voiceless soul.

Many cultures intuitively recognize this link. Traditional Jewish mourning rituals, for example, include tearing garments that served as a tangible release of internal anguish. Similarly, ancient African practices of wailing, drumming, and rhythmic movement externalize the pain so it does not stay trapped in the body. Modern psychology echoes this wisdom, teaching that **safe physical expression**, such as weeping, walking, or creative activity, prevents emotional energy from becoming physiological toxicity.

Listening to the Body's Sermon

Grief's physical manifestations are not betrayals of faith; they are sermons preached by the body. They remind us that we were created as integrated beings comprising spirit, mind, and body, and that what harms one dimension reverberates through the others.

In Psalm 38:8 (NIV), David lamented, "I am feeble and utterly crushed; I groan in anguish of heart." David employs three distinct Hebrew terms for his condition: *"nāp̄ag"* (feeble - properly "to grow numb," used of limbs losing sensation), *"dāḵā'"* (crushed - violently shattered, used elsewhere of breaking pottery), and *"šā'ag̱"* (groan - the roaring of a lion, not a quiet sigh). This is total-person collapse: physical numbness, emotional shattering, and vocal agony. In Psalm 62:8, David moves from lament to invitation: "Pour out (*shāp̄aḵ)* your heart before Him." The verb means to spill, empty completely, like overturning a vessel; not measured confession but complete evacuation. The noun *"lēḇāḇ"* (heart) in Hebrew psychology encompasses mind, will, and emotion, that is, the entire inner person.

David is not saying "tell God some of your feelings"; he's saying "upturn your entire interior life before Him like dumping water from a jar." The implicit theology: God is strong enough to receive what would overwhelm human listeners, and intimate enough to invite the unfiltered contents of your interior world. No screening process is required before approaching Him. Come with the mess.

Modern neuroscience reinforces this biblical anthropology. The **anterior cingulate cortex**, which processes emotional pain, overlaps with the same neural pathways that process physical pain. When heartbreak is described as "gut-wrenching," it is not a metaphor. It is neurology. Brain imaging confirms that emotional rejection or bereavement activates the same pain centers as a burn or fracture.

Thus, when the bereaved say, "It hurts everywhere," they are telling the truth. The ache that seems to live in muscle and marrow is the echo of a heart struggling to translate sorrow into chemistry. Yet even in that ache, the Creator has built hidden, merciful help. Every tremor, every tear, every sigh is the body's way of calling for integration and repair.

Grief, then, is not only evidence that love once lived. It is evidence that life itself still moves within. The same nervous system that reels from pain also carries the signals of recovery. In God's design, the very physiology that makes us vulnerable to heartbreak also equips us to heal.

5.5 Doctor Perspective's Pneumopsychosomatic Model

The Trinity of Healing (Spirit, Mind, Body)

While preparing a teaching series for Leaders Communicating God's Love Inc., I coined the term "PneumoPsychoSomaticism"[114] and its derivatives. a framework I'm developing that examines the interplay between the spiritual, psychological, and physical dimensions of human experience.

Human experience is ***pneumopsychosomatic***—spirit, mind, and body act together. **Healing requires alignment across all three.**

The human person is not a collection of separate compartments but a single, three-dimensional organism: **spirit**, **mind**, and **body**. Scripture consistently presents the human person as a unified, tri-part being - body, soul, and spirit (1 Thessalonians 5:23). Within this biblical framework, the soul (Hebrew *nephesh*, Greek *psychē*) refers to the inner self - the seat of identity, will, emotion, and lived experience. The mind *(nous)*, by contrast, is not a separate "fourth part," but a functional aspect of the soul: the soul's capacity for thought, reflection, memory, and renewal (Romans 12:2). Modern medicine often focuses on the body; psychology addresses the mind; theology speaks to the spirit.

Yet grief makes it impossible to treat any one of the three without the others. To heal the bereaved heart, these three must speak to one another once again. This integrated framework, the *Pneumopsychosomatic Model*, honors the full design of humanity.

Spirit: The Transcendent Core

The *pneuma*, or spirit, is the seat of meaning, conscience, and connection to God. When death intrudes, it is the spirit that cries, "Why?" Grief wounds faith because it challenges ultimate order. If this dimension is neglected, healing becomes mechanical rather than transformative. Jesus Himself, facing Lazarus's tomb, wept before He spoke the word of resurrection (John 11:35-43). His tears were a spiritual identification with human loss.

Soul (mind): The Interpreter and Integrator

The *psyche* translates experience into perception. It labels sensations, organizes memories, and constructs narrative. In grief, the mind often misfires, looping through "if only" and "why me." Cognitive neuroscience shows that repetitive rumination activates the brain's default-mode network, trapping mourners in cycles of guilt and confusion. Scripture anticipated this: *"As a man thinks in his heart, so is he"* (Proverbs 23:7 KJV). Cognitive renewal through Scripture meditation, journaling, or counseling can help rewire these loops toward hope.

Body: The Responder and Messenger

The *soma* houses both spirit and mind. Its cells store emotional memory. Physical acts of prayer, such as kneeling, raising hands, and breathing deeply, translate faith into physiology. Scientists call this **embodied cognition**; believers, worship. When the body participates in spiritual practices, measurable biological changes follow: lowered heart rate, balanced cortisol levels, improved immunity.

Interpretive Bridge - The Circle of Reciprocity

Each dimension ministers to the others. The spirit gives the mind meaning; the mind gives the body instruction; the body gives the spirit expression. Break the circle and healing stalls. Restore it, and the journey to wholeness resumes. Paul captured this divine symmetry: *"May your whole spirit, soul, and body be kept blameless at the coming of our Lord Jesus Christ"* (1 Thessalonians 5:23 NIV). True recovery is therefore not merely emotional regulation but **spiritual recalibration**.

5.6 Healing the Whole Person

Recovery from grief cannot rely on prayer alone, nor on therapy alone, nor on rest alone. Each contributes part of the remedy. The whole person must be engaged, because grief is a whole-person injury.

Restoring the Spirit

Healing begins when the bereaved re-establish trust in God's character. This is not unquestioning optimism but the re-anchoring of belief after a storm. The Psalms offer a manual for this process: cry, lament, remember, and praise. Every honest complaint in Scripture ends with *"yet will I trust You."* Worship is thus rehabilitation for the spirit: it re-aligns the compass of faith to true north.

Renewing the Mind

Cognitive healing follows spiritual realignment. Practices such as gratitude listing, Scripture memorization, and pastoral counseling help replace intrusive thoughts with constructive ones. Neuroscientific studies show that daily gratitude journaling activates the prefrontal cortex—the area responsible for emotional regulation.[115] Paul's exhortation in Philippians 4:8 (NIV) anticipates this: *"Whatever is true, whatever is noble, whatever is right... think about such things."* The mind trained on goodness becomes medicine to the emotions.

Rehabilitating the Body

The body's recovery is slower but sure. A nutritionally rich diet high in omega-3s and antioxidants reduces inflammation linked to chronic grief. Gentle exercise releases endorphins that counter cortisol. Restorative sleep rebalances neurotransmitters. These are not secular add-ons to faith; they are God's engineering instructions. Elijah's angelic caregiver did not preach. He baked a cake (1 Kings 19:6). Physical renewal was the prelude to renewed mission.

Grace as Biochemistry

Grace does not bypass biology; it moves through it. The same divine energy that forgives sin also stabilizes the heartbeat. When believers pray, "Lord, restore my soul," the Holy Spirit engages neural pathways, hormonal systems, and immune responses. Healing is not magic. It is **incarnational**: spirit entering matter. In that sacred interface, grief's power begins to fade.

Faith Window 5

"He Restores My Soul" (Psalm 23:3)

David's confession in Psalm 23 is more than poetry. It is physiology redeemed. *"He restores my soul"* describes renewal of the *nephesh*, the life-breath that animates body and mind. When God restores the soul, He re-tunes every system to harmony. The Shepherd leads not only beside still waters but **within** them, quieting adrenal surges, soothing anxious thoughts, oxygenating the weary heart.

The promise of restoration is not escapism; it is **divine homeostasis,** the return of balance after chaos. Every heartbeat that slows, every sigh that releases tension, every tear that finds peace is evidence that the Shepherd still tends His flock. Science observes recovery; faith names its Source.

Chapter 5 Endnotes

97 Brown, W. S., & Strawn, B. D. (2021). The physical nature of Christian life: Neuroscience, psychology, and the church. Cambridge University Press.

98 Fagundes, C. P., & Wu, E. L. (2020). Matters of the heart: Grief, morbidity, and mortality. Current Directions in Psychological Science, 29(3), 235-241.

99 Fagundes, C. P., & Wu, E. L. (2020). Matters of the heart: Grief, morbidity, and mortality. Current Directions in Psychological Science, 29(3), 235-241.

100 Seiler, A., & von Känel, R. (2020). The psychobiology of bereavement and health: A conceptual review from the perspective of social signal transduction theory of depression. Frontiers in Psychiatry, 11, 565239.

101 O'Connor, M. F., Wellisch, D. K., Stanton, A. L., Olmstead, R., & Irwin, M. R. (2012). Diurnal cortisol in complicated and non-complicated grief. Psychoneuroendocrinology, 37(5), 725-728.

102 Buckley, T., Sunari, D., Marshall, A., Bartrop, R., McKinley, S., & Tofler, G. (2012). Physiological correlates of bereavement and the impact of bereavement interventions. Dialogues in Clinical Neuroscience, 14(2), 129-139.

103 Bartrop, R. W., Lazarus, L., Luckhurst, E., Kiloh, L. G., & Penny, R. (1977). Depressed lymphocyte function after bereavement. The Lancet, 309(8016), 834-836.

104 Gračanin, A., Bylsma, L. M., & Vingerhoets, A. J. J. M. (2014). Is crying a self-soothing behavior? Frontiers in Psychology, 5, 502. https://doi.org/10.3389/fpsyg.2014.00502

105 Bylsma, L. M., Croon, M. A., Vingerhoets, A. J. J. M., & Rottenberg, J. (2020). When and for whom does crying improve mood? A daily diary study. Emotion, 20(7), 1280-1295. https://doi.org/10.1037/emo0000633

106 Pennebaker, J. W., & Smyth, J. M. (2016). Opening up by writing it down (3rd ed.). Guilford Press.

107 Koenig, H. G., King, D. E., & Carson, V. B. (2012). Handbook of religion and health (2nd ed.). Oxford University Press.

108 Russell, G., & Lightman, S. (2019). The human stress response. Nature Reviews Endocrinology, 15(9), 525-534.

109 Smith, S. M., & Vale, W. W. (2006). The role of the hypothalamic-pituitary-adrenal axis in neuroendocrine responses to stress. Dialogues in Clinical Neuroscience, 8(4), 383-395.

---

110 McEwen, B. S., & Akil, H. (2020). Revisiting the stress concept: Implications for affective disorders. Journal of Neuroscience, 40(1), 12-21.

111 O'Connor, M.-F., Wellisch, D. K., Stanton, A. L., Eisenberger, N. I., Irwin, M. R., & Lieberman, M. D. (2008). Craving love? Enduring grief activates brain's reward center. NeuroImage, 42(2), 969-972.

112 Templin, C., et al. (2015). Clinical features and outcomes of Takotsubo (stress) cardiomyopathy. New England Journal of Medicine, 373(10), 929-938.

113 Foster, J. A., & McVey Neufeld, K. A. (2013). Gut-brain axis: How the microbiome influences anxiety and depression. Trends in Neurosciences, 36(5), 305-312.

[114] I have coined the term 'pneumopsychosomaticism' to describe this tripartite relationship between spirit (pneuma), mind (psyche), and body (soma), which I explore more fully in a forthcoming work.

115 Fox, G. R., Kaplan, J., Damasio, H., & Damasio, A. (2015). Neural correlates of gratitude. Frontiers in Psychology, 6, 1491.

Chapter 6

Emotional Earthquakes

Shock, Anger, Guilt & Numbness

6.1 The Emotional Aftershocks

Grief does not erupt once and settle. It moves in pulses, one might say, emotional tremors that strike when the mind least expects them. After the initial impact of loss, the nervous system continues to fire in irregular, involuntary patterns.[116] These aftershocks may be triggered by memory, silence, routine, or nothing identifiable at all. Just as seismic plates keep shifting long after an earthquake, the heart continues to convulse with fresh waves of sorrow even when the external crisis is over. This experience is not regression; it is the body and soul recalibrating under the pressure of profound rupture. Emotional aftershocks are normal, involuntary, and often necessary for integrating trauma into conscious reality without collapsing under its weight.

The Science of Shock and Numbness

When death strikes, the human mind often enters a state that feels unreal, detached, and strangely insulated from full emotional impact. This is not weakness; it is **neurological protection**. God designs the brain with mechanisms that shield us from experiences that would overwhelm us if felt all at once.[117] This early response is commonly called **psychic**

numbness or **traumatic shock**, and it represents one of the most immediate and universal reactions to significant loss.[118]

At the center of this response is the **amygdala**, the brain's alarm system.[119] Under sudden emotional threat, such as the news of a death, the amygdala signals a surge of stress hormones, preparing the body to respond to a crisis. At the same time, the **prefrontal cortex**, responsible for reasoning, sequencing, and emotional evaluation, becomes temporarily impaired.[120] These two reactions create a split sensation: *the body recognizes danger while the mind struggles to interpret what has happened*. As a result, grievers report feeling stunned, disoriented, or strangely calm in moments that should feel unbearable.

This protective shutdown is part of God's design. Scripture demonstrates that shock is a natural and even expected response to devastating news. When Job learned of the sudden deaths of his children, *"Job arose and tore his robe and shaved his head and fell on the ground and worshiped"* (Job 1:20 ESV). His actions reflect both anguish and stunned disbelief. It's a picture of a mind absorbing a blow too great to process immediately. Similarly, in Luke 24:37, when the disciples encountered the risen Christ, they *"were startled and frightened"*. This was a physiological reaction that mirrors what modern neuroscience describes.

Modern psychology refers to this as **dissociation**, an automatic buffering state in which the mind distances itself from reality long enough for the body and emotions to stabilize. People experiencing shock often describe themselves as "watching from outside," "functioning automatically," or "feeling nothing at all." These descriptions align with what trauma specialists call **peritraumatic dissociation**, a temporary suspension of normal emotional processing to prevent psychological overload.[121]

Shock is therefore not an enemy; it is a **grace-filled pause**, allowing the bereaved to endure the first hours or days following loss without collapsing under the full weight of grief. During this stage, many people perform necessary tasks such as answering calls, contacting relatives, and giving instructions to funeral homes without remembering how they accomplished them. The mind protects itself by its focus on the simplest actions required for survival.

Understanding this stage brings two important comforts. First, **numbness is not a sign of spiritual weakness**. Even Jesus' followers experienced shock at moments of intense emotion (John 20:19–20). Second, numbness will not last forever. As the brain gradually re-engages and the cortex regains its full function, emotions that were initially muted begin to surface.[122] This is the transition from shock to sorrow. It is an essential movement in the journey through grief.

For now, the important truth is this: your numbness is not a failure of faith. It is the brain doing exactly what God designed it to do. It is **protecting you until you can feel again**.

The Invisible Emergency

During this phase, friends sometimes misread silence as strength or interpret calmness as indifference. In reality, the bereaved are in neurochemical crisis. The adrenaline that once protected them from collapse will later leave them shaking, exhausted, or sleepless. Their bodies are running a marathon inside while sitting motionless outside.

Compassion must therefore begin with patience, not pep talks. Job's friends sat with him seven days before speaking (Job 2:13). That was wisdom. Words penetrate only after shock subsides.

When the Aftershocks Arrive

Shock eventually loosens its grip, and when it does, the emotional landscape shifts abruptly. Feelings that were previously muted begin to surface with force and unpredictability. Tears erupt without warning in the supermarket, in the car, or in the middle of routine tasks that once felt ordinary. A familiar scent, a favorite song, a sudden memory can trigger an emotional surge powerful enough to take the griever by surprise. This is not regression. It is the nervous system releasing what could not be accessed during the initial freeze response.[123] Aftershocks are the mind's way of metabolizing grief in tolerable fragments. Each wave, though painful, clears internal debris and creates space for healing processes that cannot occur during the numbness of shock.

The Spiritual Dimension of Shock

Shock can unsettle a believer's sense of God's presence, not because faith has failed, but because the nervous system is overwhelmed.[124] Some experience a hollow stillness in prayer; others feel abandoned or disconnected from the spiritual instincts that once came naturally. Even Jesus endured a form of physiological shock in Gethsemane. Luke records that His sweat became "like drops of blood" (Luke 22:44), a description consistent with hematidrosis. This is a rare stress response in which fragile capillaries rupture under extreme pressure.[125] Christ's anguish was not symbolic. His body entered the same crisis state that human bodies experience under traumatic load. Our Savior did not bypass the biology of distress; He entered it fully so that no griever would walk the path of shock alone.[126]

When numbness extends beyond the initial hours, the answer is not self-rebuke but restoration of safety. The body must be re-oriented before the spirit can meaningfully engage hope. Simple practices such as steady breathing, slow walking, nourishing meals, restorative sleep, and trusted voices speaking truth aloud all help the nervous system leave crisis mode. Only as the body regains equilibrium can the soul begin to perceive God's nearness again. This is not a failure of spirituality; it is the natural sequence of healing designed by the Creator Himself.

6.2 The Anger Within Grief

Anger often erupts in the wake of loss, surprising even mature believers who assume such intensity is incompatible with faith. Yet this surging protest is a deeply human and deeply theological response. Grief instinctively declares, *This is not how it was meant to be,* and Scripture affirms that instinct. Death is an intruder, not part of God's original design, entering the world through sin (Romans 5:12). Anger becomes the soul's witness to the fracture of creation, a visceral recognition that something precious has been violated. When expressed honestly and without sin, it can serve as a doorway to lament, helping the griever name the injustice of loss and engage the God who invites His people to pour out every burden before Him (Psalm 62:8).

Recognizing the Energy of Anger

Anger is concentrated emotional energy demanding that something be made right. If pushed inward, it collapses the spirit into despair or depression; if expelled recklessly, it harms the innocent and deepens sorrow. But when honestly acknowledged and wisely directed, anger becomes a catalyst for transformation. In seasons of grief, this energy often lashes out at physicians, circumstances, loved ones, or even God Himself. Scripture does not sanitize these confrontations. The Psalmists cried, "How long, O Lord? Will You forget me forever?" (Psalm 13:1 NIV), voicing rage, confusion, and protest before the throne. God preserved these prayers to show that holy anger is not rebellion but relationship. They are a fierce, honest engagement that opens the door to healing rather than shutting it through denial.

The Body's Reaction

Anger ignites a cascade of physiological reactions that are both rapid and intense. Adrenaline floods the bloodstream, heart rate accelerates, blood pressure rises, and major muscle groups contract in preparation for action. This is the classic *fight response*: a survival mechanism hardwired into the nervous system. When these surges recur without resolution, the body remains in a heightened state of arousal, often resulting in tension headaches, digestive irritation, sleep disruption, or sustained hypertension. Scripture's counsel, "Do not let the sun go down while you are still angry" (Ephesians 4:26 NIV), is more than moral instruction; it reflects biological truth. The body cannot enter restorative rest while stress hormones are still circulating. Unprocessed anger keeps the system on alert, draining physical reserves and impeding the healing God intends for grief-worn hearts and bodies.

Sanctifying the Fire

The path to peace is not the suppression of anger but its sanctification. When anger is purified rather than quenched, it becomes passion for righteousness, compassion toward the suffering, and motivation to act redemptively. Scripture gives us both sides of this truth: Moses' unrestrained fury shattered the tablets in Exodus, yet later, his purified anger fueled courageous leadership that helped deliver a nation. The difference was not personality but surrender. Anger placed in God's hands becomes an instrument of justice rather than destruction.

Practical disciplines help transform the raw energy of anger into constructive expression. Physical movement releases tension stored in the body; honest journaling organizes chaotic emotion into language; and praying Psalms of lament aloud aligns human protest with biblical truth.

Naming the emotion drains its toxicity. Writing, "I am furious that my loved one is gone," allows the chaos to take form, and once a feeling is given words, healing can begin to shape it.

When Anger Targets God

Many believers feel a shock of guilt when they realize their anger has turned toward God. They fear judgment for even thinking: "Why did you let this happen?" Yet Scripture consistently shows that God invites honest lament rather than superficial reverence. Jeremiah cried out, "You deceived me, Lord, and I was deceived!" (Jeremiah 20:7 NIV), voicing anguish that many would consider irreverent. God did not rebuke him. Instead, He remained present, allowing the prophet to articulate pain that could not be held in silence.

Divine relationship is not fragile. Like a parent who continues to embrace a grieving child, striking his chest in confusion, God absorbs the force of our anguish without withdrawing His love. As the surge of anger exhausts itself, the soul often finds a quieter posture, not because the questions disappear, but because the heart discovers that God has been holding it all along.

Anger Turned Inward

When anger lacks a safe or permissible outlet, it often turns inward, masquerading as guilt. Many grieving individuals who declare, "I feel guilty," are in fact carrying anger at themselves, at circumstances, at medical outcomes, or even at people they deeply love. But because their conscience, culture, or spiritual upbringing condemns open expression, that anger folds in on the self. Counselors call this masked anger, a condition that distorts emotion and slows healing. Scripture bears witness to this internal corrosion: *"When I kept silent, my bones wasted away"* (Psalm 32:3 NIV). Suppressed anger depletes the body and burdens the soul, but acknowledged anger releases its grip. Confession does not magnify the emotion; it purifies it, allowing healing to begin where honesty is finally permitted to speak.

6.3 Guilt That Isn't Yours to Bear

After the fires of anger fade, guilt moves in like smoke, lingering in every corner. It asks relentless questions: *Could I have done more? Did I miss a sign? Why didn't I pray harder?* These questions give the illusion of control, as if regret could rewrite history.

Understanding False Guilt

Psychologists distinguish **moral guilt** from **survivor's guilt**. Moral guilt arises from genuine wrongdoing and can be resolved through repentance. Survivor's guilt is irrational sorrow for merely being alive when another is not.[127] In grief, the latter dominates. The bereaved punish themselves for circumstances they never commanded.

Scripture differentiates conviction from condemnation. Conviction comes from the Holy Spirit and leads to confession and peace (1 John 1:9). Condemnation comes from the accuser and leads to despair. One restores; the other ruins. Many grievers unknowingly side with the wrong voice.

The Cognitive Trap

Neuroscience explains guilt's persistence. The human brain craves cause-and-effect. When death defies logic, the mind invents reasons to restore order. "If I had driven slower." "If I had insisted on another test." These thoughts are attempts at mental coping, not moral failures. Unfortunately, repetition cements them in neural grooves, leading to chronic rumination. Romans 8:1 speaks directly to that circuitry: *"There is now no condemnation for those who are in Christ Jesus."* Repeating that verse aloud rewires the loop toward grace.

Forgiveness as Neurological Healing

Studies from Stanford University show that genuine forgiveness lowers cortisol and increases parasympathetic calm.[128] To forgive others or oneself is therefore both a spiritual act of obedience and a form of biological medicine. When Peter wept after denying Christ, his tears contained the chemistry of release.

Much later, Peter himself illustrated this crisis of compassion in the encounter beside the sea after Jesus' resurrection. When Jesus asked him repeatedly, "Do you love me?" He used the Greek word **ἀγαπάω** (*agapaō*), referring to divine, unconditional love. Peter, still tender and uncertain, replied each time, "Yes, Lord, you know that I love you," employing the Greek word **φιλέω** (*phileō*), which signifies brotherly affection.

On the third exchange, Jesus met Peter where he was, adopting Peter's own word—**φιλέω** (*phileō*). It was as if Jesus said, "Peter, do you even love Me as a friend?" Grieved, Peter replied, "Lord, You know everything; You know that I love You." Jesus' gentle concession from **ἀγαπάω** (*agapaō*) to **φιλέω** (*phileō*) revealed not divine disappointment, but divine compassion, accepting imperfect love and transforming it into strength for future faithfulness.

Restoration required articulation; guilt cannot dissolve in silence.

Symbolic Acts of Release

Writing a farewell letter, planting a tree, or donating in memory all externalize closure. They embody the soul's unseen reconciliation. In the Old Testament, mourners placed ashes on their heads; modern mourners place flowers on graves. Both actions say, "I accept reality, but I still honor love."

When Guilt and Faith Collide

Some equate continued sorrow with a lack of faith. They imagine that trusting God should eliminate sadness. But Jesus wept even knowing resurrection was minutes away (John 11:35). Perfect faith and perfect feeling coexisted in the same moment. Grief without guilt honors both love and sovereignty.

Transforming: Guilt into Grace

When guilt finally meets grace, the earthquake subsides. The trembling heart learns that responsibility ends where human limitation begins. God alone carries omnipotence. The mourner can then echo Psalm 31:14-15: *"But I trust in You, Lord; I say, 'You are my God. My times are in Your hands.'"* That sentence re-centers the soul. Control is released; peace returns.

6.4 Learning to Feel Again

Grief silences the heart before it teaches it to sing again. After shock and guilt have spent their fury, the survivor faces the hardest task of all - *to feel again without fear.* Many confuse numbness with strength, but numbness is the anesthesia of pain, not its cure. It is the body's emergency brake, useful for a time but deadly if never released.

When Numbness Becomes Prison

At first, numbness protects. It allows the mourner to plan a funeral, answer condolence calls, and complete paperwork. But over time, emotional deadness can imprison the soul. The bereaved begin to sense distance from God, from others, even from themselves. They may say, "I feel hollow," or "I can't cry anymore." The nervous system, worn down by cortisol, shuts down responsiveness as a form of self-preservation.

Prolonged numbness can mimic depression and produce loss of appetite, exhaustion, indifference, and detachment. Yet its roots differ. Depression despairs of life; numbness refuses to rejoin it. One mourns what was lost; the other fears what remains.

To awaken feeling safely, one must invite emotion back into a body that has forgotten how to welcome it. That requires space, time, and compassion toward oneself. The goal is not to resume old happiness but to rediscover the capacity for authentic emotion, and that is joy, sadness, gratitude, and love without self-censorship.

Tears as Theology

Tears are more than water and salt; they are a divine design. Scientists have found that emotional tears contain stress-related toxins not found in reflex tears (such as from onions). Crying literally cleanses.[129] Scripture affirms this chemistry of compassion: *"You have kept count of my tossings; put my tears in your bottle"* (Psalm 56:8 ESV). God records each tear because each is an offering of trust.

To weep is not weakness but worship. Tears bridge spirit and body; they are sacramental evidence that we remain alive enough to love. When Jesus wept at Lazarus's tomb, He validated every tear shed at a graveside since Eden.

Reclaiming Permission to Feel

Many grieving people were taught that maturity means stoicism. Men in particular fear emotion as a loss of control. Yet emotional suppression contradicts both Scripture and science. David, a warrior-king, poured his soul into the Psalms of Anguish. Jeremiah was called "the weeping prophet." Paul confessed, *"We were under great pressure, far beyond our ability to endure, so that we despaired of life itself"* (2 Corinthians 1:8 NIV). Emotion did not disqualify their faith; it displayed its authenticity.

Permission to feel often begins with physical cues: breathing deeply, unclenching fists, noticing one's heartbeat. These simple acts tell the body, "You are safe now." Safety reactivates the parasympathetic system, allowing tears or laughter to return naturally.

How Feeling Becomes Healing

Emotion is energy in motion. When suppressed, it stagnates; when expressed, it integrates. A study at UCLA showed that naming emotions, that is, literally putting them into words, reduces amygdala activity and increases prefrontal calm.[130] In plain terms, *talking about pain tames it.*

This is why counseling, prayer, or trusted friendship brings relief. Spoken truth orders chaos. It converts unprocessed emotion into narrative, and narrative is the architecture of healing. God began creation with words; we begin re-creation the same way.

When Joy Feels Like Betrayal

As life resumes, mourners sometimes experience guilt for laughing or enjoying themselves. They whisper, "If I smile, it means I've forgotten." But joy does not erase love; it honors it. The same heart that can ache can also remember. Ecclesiastes 3 declares a time for mourning *and* a time for dancing. Both can coexist because love never demanded perpetual sorrow.

When laughter returns, it is resurrection rehearsed. It is proof that death could not confiscate all delight. God designed the human spirit to bend, not break. Isaiah's promise is fulfilled: *"To comfort all who mourn... to give them beauty for ashes"* (Isaiah 61:2–3 KJV).

Faith Window 6

"My Flesh and My Heart May Fail, But God Is the Strength of My Heart" (Psalm 73:26)

This verse captures the paradox of grief: the failure of the human system and the sufficiency of divine strength. "My flesh and my heart may fail". That is physiology and psychology. "But God is the strength of my heart." That is pneumatology, the science of the spirit.

When the Body and Heart Fail

The body weakens under the weight of loss: appetite declines, immunity falters, and sleep becomes elusive. The Psalmist admits this breakdown openly. There is no shame in exhaustion; it is the natural endpoint of over-extended compassion. Even Jesus, after ministry and sorrow, withdrew to solitary places to rest (Luke 5:16). The human system was not built for uninterrupted grief.

When the heart faints, it is not rebellion. It is depletion. Emotional fatigue signals that we have reached the end of our own resources. At that precise moment, divine energy begins its quiet work.

The Transfer of Strength

God does not merely refill human tanks; He exchanges them. *"Those who wait on the Lord shall renew their strength"* (Isaiah 40:31 KJV). The Hebrew word for "renew" literally means *exchange.* We trade our weakness for His endurance. The mechanism of that transfer is faith expressed through surrender.

Surrender is not giving up; it is giving over. When we release control over outcomes, timelines, and explanations, we create space for grace to fill the void. In that exchange, grief loses its dominion.

The Portion Forever

"Asaph ends his lament with, 'God is my portion forever.'" In ancient Israel, a *portion* referred to one's inheritance, one's allotment of land or sustenance. The Psalmist, stripped of comfort, declares that God Himself is his inheritance. The theology of grief matures here: when all else fails, presence remains.

This redefines recovery. Healing is not the return of what was lost; it is the discovery that God is enough even without it. Out of that revelation emerges peace that does not depend on circumstances but communion.

How Divine Strength Manifests

Strength may appear as endurance rather than ecstasy. It may whisper instead of shout. For some, it comes in the ability to rise, shower, and eat breakfast; for others, in the ability to sing again in worship. Each small act of continuation testifies that grace is at work beneath consciousness.

The apostle Paul called it "the power of Christ resting upon me" (2 Corinthians 12:9). The verb *resting* means to *pitch a tent over.* Divine strength doesn't always remove pain. It shelters us inside it.

From Earthquake to Equilibrium

By the time the grieving reaches this point, the emotional landscape has changed. Shock has quieted, anger has found language, guilt has met grace, and numbness has begun to thaw. The same ground that quaked now holds new contours or cracks, yes, but also fertile soil. Out of those fissures grow compassion, patience, and deeper faith.

Grief has not been wasted; it has been transformed. What once felt like the end becomes a threshold. The believer can finally say, "My flesh and my heart did fail; but God became the rhythm that kept me breathing."

Chapter 6 Endnotes

116 Hopper, J. W., Frewen, P. A., van der Kolk, B. A., & Lanius, R. A. (2007). Neural correlates of reexperiencing in PTSD. Journal of Traumatic Stress, 20(2), 107-118.

117 v.an der Kolk, B. A. (2014). The body keeps the score: Brain, mind, and body in the healing of trauma. Viking.

118 Bonanno, G. A., & Burton, C. L. (2013). Regulatory flexibility. Perspectives on Psychological Science, 8(6), 591-612.

119 Lindquist, K. A., Wager, T. D., Kober, H., Bliss-Moreau, E., & Barrett, L. F. (2012). The brain basis of emotion. Behavioral and Brain Sciences, 35(3), 121-143.

120 Arnsten, A. F. T. (2009). Stress signalling pathways that impair prefrontal cortex. Nature Reviews Neuroscience, 10(6), 410-422.

121 Marmar, C. R., Weiss, D. S., & Metzler, T. J. (1997). The Peritraumatic Dissociative Experiences Questionnaire. In J. P. Wilson & T. M. Keane (Eds.), Assessing psychological trauma and PTSD (pp. 412-428). Guilford Press.

122 Hopper, J. W., Frewen, P. A., van der Kolk, B. A., & Lanius, R. A. (2007). Neural correlates of reexperiencing in PTSD. Journal of Traumatic Stress, 20(2), 107-118.

123 Porges, S. W. (2021). Polyvagal theory: A biobehavioral journey to sociality. Comprehensive Psychoneuroendocrinology, 7, 100069.

124 Exline, J. J., Park, C. L., Smyth, J. M., & Carey, M. P. (2011). Anger toward God. Journal of Personality and Social Psychology, 100(1), 129-148.

125 Templin, C., Ghadri, J. R., Diekmann, J., et al. (2015). Clinical features and outcomes of Takotsubo cardiomyopathy. New England Journal of Medicine, 373(10), 929-938.

126 Kapic, K. M. (2018). Embodied hope. IVP Academic.

127 Kubany, E. S., & Manke, F. P. (1995). Cognitive therapy for trauma-related guilt: Conceptual bases and treatment outlines. Cognitive and Behavioral Practice, 2(1), 27-61.

128 Worthington, E. L., Witvliet, C. V. O., Pietrini, P., & Miller, A. J. (2007). Forgiveness, health, and well-being: A review of evidence for emotional versus decisional forgiveness, dispositional forgivingness, and reduced unforgiveness. Journal of Behavioral Medicine.

129 Vingerhoets, A. J. J. M. (2013). Why only humans weep: Unraveling the mysteries of tears. Oxford University Press.

130 Lieberman, M. D., Eisenberger, N. I., Crockett, M. J., Tom, S. M., Pfeifer, J. H., & Way, B. M. (2007). Putting feelings into words: Affect labeling disrupts amygdala activity in response to affective stimuli. Psychological Science, 18(5), 421-428.

Chapter 7

The Seasons of Sorrow

7.1 Winter - The Season of Numbness

Grief's first language is silence. It comes like frost - thin, hard, and everywhere. You move through rooms as if borrowed from yourself. You answer questions, but do not hear your voice. This is winter. It is not failure. It is the body's way of keeping the soul from breaking all at once.

The Body's Hibernation

When bad news lands, the nervous system throws a switch. Adrenaline and cortisol surge. The prefrontal cortex, the planning center, dims so the survival centers can lead.[131] Heart rate climbs. Digestion slows. Sleep breaks into pieces. Appetite fades. Memory stutters. None of this is sin. It is design. God made dust with a built-in brace.

Think of trees in January. Sap pulls inward. Branches look dead, yet life hides at the core. Early grief is like that. On the outside, you may seem still. On the inside, your whole being is working to stay alive. Tears, shaking, even sudden yawns are part of that work. They release pressure.[132] They finish chemical cycles your body started the moment the phone rang, the monitor went flat, or the chair went empty.

What Shock Does to Thought

Shock narrows attention. You can sign forms and miss the meaning of every line. Hours vanish. People later ask, "Do you remember what I said?" Often, you do not. The brain was filing only what kept you moving.[133] That is why simple written notes help: who called, which appointment, and where the keys are.[134] Writing is not weakness; it is wisdom for a brain doing crisis **triage.**[135]

How Winter Feels in the Soul

Faith does not vanish in winter; feeling does. You may sit in worship and sense nothing. You may try to pray and find only a sigh. That sigh counts. Romans 8:26 says the Spirit translates groans.

Paul writes that "**the Spirit Himself intercedes** (*hyperentynchanei*, a compound verb intensifying 'to intercede,' used only here in the NT) **for us with groanings** (*stenagmois*, from *stenazō*, to sigh or groan under pressure) **too deep for words** (*alalētois*, literally "unspoken," "wordless," "inexpressible")." Verse 23 says **'we ourselves groan** (*stenazomen*)' while verse 26 emphasizes **'the Spirit Himself** *(auto to Pneuma)*', suggesting both human and divine groaning. The ambiguity may be intentional. Paul describes intercession so intimate that distinguishing 'His groans' from 'our groans' becomes impossible."

The one "**who searches hearts**" *(ho eraunōn tas kardias* - present active participle, continually examining) **knows "the mind of the Spirit"** (*to phronēma tou Pneumatos),* **the Spirit's intent, disposition**. In Romans 12:15, Paul shifts from vertical intercession to horizontal solidarity: "Rejoice with (*chairein meta*) those rejoicing, weep with (*klaiein meta*) those weeping." Both verbs are present infinitives, ongoing, continual action.

The preposition *meta* (with) implies accompaniment rather than observation. You enter their emotional space. Paul uses *klaiō* (to wail, weep loudly), and not *dakryō* (to shed quiet tears). This is visible, audible grief. The command doesn't say "cheer them up" or "explain their suffering"; it says join them in the valley. This is one of Scripture's hardest demands: to sit in another's pain without the rescue of being useful.

In winter, trust looks like letting others pray out loud while you sit. It looks like borrowing a hymn and letting the words carry you. It looks like getting out of bed when nothing inside wants to rise. Winter faith is quiet, but it is still faith.

The Mercy of Stillness

Modern life rewards motion. Winter demands stillness. The best help a friend can offer these days is presence, not speeches. Bring water. Warm a meal. Sit without turning the silence into a lecture. Job's friends were perfect for seven days. Then they started talking. Do not rush to thaw with hot words. Quiet companionship lowers the heart's alarm and lets the body stand down.

Practices for Surviving Winter

Breathe on purpose. Inhale through the nose, hold for a count of two; exhale slowly through the mouth. Do that five times. It tells your heart there is no tiger in the room.

Wear the day in small pieces. Say: *Now I bathe. Now I dress. Now I drink water.* Three completed tasks are a win.

Anchor to gentle rhythms. Light a candle at dusk and blow it out at bedtime. Read one Psalm aloud each morning. Small rituals build rails for the day to run on.

Accept help without apology. Let others drive, shop, or handle calls. Dependence is not failure. It is how God made bodies to heal in community.

Protect sleep. Lower lights earlier. Keep the room cool. If tears come at night, sit up, breathe, write a sentence of truth. *I am safe right now*, so I can lie down again.

Hydrate and eat. It could be broth, fruit, toast, or eggs. The goal is fuel, not fine dining.

Boundaries That Keep You Safe

Say no to new projects, big purchases, and major moves. Delay life-changing decisions until your mind returns to full size. Put a "quiet filter" on your calendar: funerals, medical meetings, worship, and very little else. If someone presses you for an answer, use this sentence: *"I will decide after the first year."* That line buys time and removes pressure.

How to Handle People in Your Winter

Some will speak clichés because silence scares them. You can answer gently: *"Thank you for caring. I am not ready for explanations. Sitting with me helps most."* Others will want details you do not wish to share. It is fine to say, *"I am keeping that part close."* You do not owe your pain to anyone's curiosity.

If a friend insists on cheering you up, invite them to a task instead: fold laundry, pick up prescriptions, or drive you to an appointment. Doing turns their energy into mercy, sparing you the burden of managing their mood.

When the Body Surprises You

You may laugh at something small and feel guilty. Winter hearts often do. Remember: laughter is not betrayal. It is breath. You may also cry in places you did not plan to: the grocery line, in traffic, at church. Tears in public are not shameful; they are human. Keep tissues handy. If you need to leave, leave. You are not responsible for staging a neat grief.

Faith Window 7 Part 1

In Winter

Do not try to force big revelations. Keep one clear sentence near: *"The Lord is my shepherd."* Or *"God is our refuge and strength."* Or *"My times are in Your hands."* Read it morning and night. Tape it to the mirror. Place it by the kettle. Let a single verse do the heavy lifting while your heart rests underneath.

If you can manage a very short prayer, try this: *"Jesus, keep me."*

The whole gospel fits inside those two words. He knows how.

What Not to Do

Do not sign away property in a haze of sorrow. Do not numb yourself with alcohol or endless screens. Do not measure your grief by someone else's calendar. Do not punish yourself for the body's limits. Winter is supposed to be slower. Let it be slow. Healing is not a race; it is a season.

How Winter Begins to End

Winter ends by inches. You notice the sun through a window and want to stand there a little longer. You hear a song and do not break. You taste food and think, *This is good.* You remember a story and smile before you cry. These are not signs of forgetting. They are proof that love is strong enough to carry memory without crushing you.

When that first thin warmth arrives, do not sprint. Walk. Keep your simple rhythms. Add one small step, perhaps a short stroll outside or a call to a trusted friend. The ground is still thawing. Move gently. Questions will soon wake, as spring always wakes after winter.

If Winter Returns

It will. Anniversaries, holidays, and surprise triggers can pull cold air back into the room. Do not panic. You are not back at the start. You now know the path - breath, water, ritual, rest, help. Walk it again. Each return visit will be shorter. You are not weak for revisiting winter; you are wise for recognizing it and responding early.

And so, the first season of sorrow becomes its own mercy rather than a failure. The silence, the stillness, the numbness, all of it was grace in disguise. Winter did not end our strength; it preserved it. It permitted us to pause until our hearts remembered how to beat without breaking. What felt like paralysis was protection, and what looked like emptiness was space for renewal. We lived through the cold because God was there, even when we could not feel Him keeping vigil in the quiet, guarding the breath beneath the frost.

A Blessing for the Cold

May the Lord guard your breath and grant you sleep. May He place safe hands around your day. May He keep watch when you cannot, and carry what you should not. And when the light lengthens, may He lead you gently into spring.

7.2 Spring - The Season of Questions

Spring breaks the silence with sound, sometimes praise, sometimes protest. The same heart that whispered *"Help me survive"* in winter now murmurs, *"Help me understand."* Curiosity returns before confidence does. The thaw is messy, but it's holy.

When Faith Learns to Ask

As the body stabilizes, the mind wakes. The mourner replays scenes, searching for a pattern that makes sense. Questions form because consciousness itself is healing. Even Jesus, in His agony, asked *"Why?"* (Matthew 27:46). If the sinless Son could question without sinning, then our questions can be sanctified too.

Lament is not rebellion. It is worship in raw form. The Psalmists cried, *"How long, Lord?"* more often than they sang *"Praise the Lord."* God preserved those laments in Scripture because He prefers honest noise to polite silence.

Spring is the mind's rebellion against resignation. It refuses to believe that pain has the final word. The believer begins to reason again, not to replace faith, but to refine it.

How Meaning Grows

Meaning rarely arrives as revelation; it is cultivated like soil. The mourner tills grief through conversation, prayer, and memory until hope begins to germinate. Job's story shows this process: questions multiplied, but so did revelation. By the end, Job no longer needed explanations. He had encountered Presence.

The same happens for us. The storm outside may still rage, but the interior climate changes. The soul that once asked, *"Where are You, God?"* begins to sense, *"You are here."* That shift is not intellectual. It's relational. It may not announce its arrival, but you will know.

Avoiding False Spring

Beware of premature conclusions. Grief sometimes mimics spring by producing quick, shallow answers. The soil may look ready, but frost lingers beneath. People who rush to *"Everything happens for a reason"* or

"They're in a better place" plant brittle theology. Real faith can survive another cold snap; false certainty cannot.

Better to pray, *"Lord, teach me what this pain can reveal, not what it must excuse."* That is honest discipleship, learning without forcing logic.

Practices for the Questioning Heart

Journal honestly. Writing grounds emotions and reveals growth over time.

Pray the lament Psalms. Psalm 13's four verses move from despair to trust; follow its rhythm daily.

Find one safe listener. Processing aloud with someone unafraid of silence helps reframe memories.

Study creation. Observe a seed's paradox: life begins with burial. That is theology in dirt.

Limit advice intake. Too many explanations can drown discernment. One Word, God's Word is enough.

When Reason Becomes Revelation

Eventually, reasoning reaches its ceiling. The mind runs out of lines to draw, and that's where revelation enters. Like the disciples on the Emmaus road, we may walk beside Christ unaware until He breaks bread, and our hearts recognize what our intellect could not (Luke 24:30–31).

Understanding is not salvation; relationship is. The lesson of spring is that mystery can coexist with meaning. Faith does not erase confusion. It holds hands with it until peace arrives.

And when the thaw finally came, it did not bring answers so much as honesty. Questions grew like wildflowers in loosened ground, each one reaching upward, searching for light. Spring taught us that God does not silence our confusion; He sanctifies it. Lament became language, complaint became communion, and little by little, faith learned to breathe again. We stopped asking for explanations and began listening for Presence. The same soil that once held our sorrow now held our trust, and in that trust, new roots of hope began to take hold.

7.3 Summer - The Season of Renewal

Summer begins quietly. The world outside looks the same, but inside, the air is warmer. Appetite returns. Sleep lengthens. You laugh and notice you didn't feel guilty afterward. This is resurrection in miniature.

Physiology of Renewal

After months of adrenaline, the nervous system recalibrates.[136] Cortisol subsides, dopamine levels rise, and oxytocin, our bonding hormone, returns through contact, touch, and community. What feels like a spiritual awakening is also a biological reset designed by God. Healing is not only miraculous; it is molecular.[137]

Rediscovering Joy

Joy reappears shyly, like a bird testing the wind. Some days it perches; some days it flies away. Don't chase it. Create space for it. Joy is nourished by gratitude and service. Paul told the Philippians, *"Rejoice in the Lord always"* (Philippians 4:4), not as a command to feel happy, but as an act of defiance against despair. Each time we choose gratitude, we announce that death has not won.

When Love Turns Outward

Grief initially folds inward. Summer turns it outward. The energy once spent on mourning begins to power compassion. Helping others does not dilute sorrow. It sanctifies it. Paul wrote, *"He comforts us... so that we can comfort those in any trouble"* (2 Corinthians 1:4 NIV). Healing multiplies by being shared.

This is why support groups, ministries, or even a single listening conversation can accelerate recovery. The same empathy that once hurt now heals. You become what woundedness taught you to be: a safe place.

The Gift of Ordinary Days

You notice the sacred in small routines, the hiss of a kettle, the smell of bread, a child's laughter. Ecclesiastes 3:13 calls this *"God's gift."* Mundane moments become altars. The life you feared was over begins to pulse with meaning. This is not pretending the loss never happened; it is proof that love is large enough to include joy again.

The Fear of Moving Forward

Many mourners hesitate to smile, fearing it will be seen as betrayal. But healing does not erase love; it extends it. The relationship changes form, not existence. The dead do not need our misery; they are safe in God's mercy. What honors them most is a life lived fully.

When you laugh again, you fulfill Christ's promise: *"I have come that they may have life, and have it abundantly"* (John 10:10). Abundance after grief is not indulgence; it is obedience.

Faith as Photosynthesis

Summer faith absorbs light. Exposure matters. Avoiding hope to prevent disappointment darkens the soul. Stand again in sunlight, literally and spiritually. Let prayer, worship, and beauty fill you with divine warmth.[138] Practice Philippians 4:8 - "Finally, brothers, whatever is true, whatever is honorable, whatever is just, whatever is pure, whatever is lovely, whatever is commendable, if there is any excellence, if there is anything worthy of praise, think about these things." Over time, you will feel what Psalm 30:11 celebrates: *"You turned my mourning into dancing."*

Practices for Renewal

Serve deliberately. Help someone newer to grief; shared pain breeds solidarity.

Record nightly gratitude. One endurance gained, one kindness received, one beauty noticed.

Rebuild connections. Attend worship, rejoin a hobby, reconnect with friends.

Revisit memories safely. Look at photos not as punishment but as a celebration.

Plan forward. A garden, a trip, a project: hope needs direction to survive.

By the time summer spread across the heart's landscape, we had learned that healing does not mean forgetting. It means learning to live with memory as light instead of weight. The ordinary became sacred: the sound of laughter, the smell of bread, the sight of morning light through curtains. Gratitude replaced guilt, and service became our song. Joy stopped asking permission to exist; it simply began to rise. God's restoration did not erase the ache. It repurposed it, weaving strength where sorrow once lived. The Shepherd who led us through shadow was still leading us through sunlight, teaching us how to dwell among the living again.

Faith Window 7 Part 2

"He Restores My Soul" (Psalm 23:3)

This verse belongs to summer. It does not say *He replaced my soul,* but *He restores it.* Restoration presumes damage. God does not discard the broken heart; He rebuilds it stronger at the fracture.

The Hebrew verb *shuv* means "to bring back." Restoration is not a reset but a return to peace, to purpose, to praise. David, who wrote Psalm 23, had buried both friends and a son. His testimony proves that divine restoration is not theory; it is personal history.

God restores through process. He sends sunlight through Scripture, nourishment through fellowship, and strength through service. Restoration is cumulative grace. It is the daily exchange of exhaustion for endurance. It is what happens when worship replaces weeping, when gratitude outlives guilt, when faith begins to hum beneath ordinary days.

And so, the shepherd of Psalm 23 leads the mourner through summer's fields, not to forget the valley of shadow, but to prove that the shadow was never sovereign.

7.4 Autumn - The Season of Surrender

Autumn follows renewal as evening follows day. The colors are richer now. Some reds and golds come only after the green of summer fades. This is the mature season of grief: acceptance without indifference, peace without forgetfulness. The heart still remembers, but it no longer resists remembering.

The Wisdom of Release

By autumn, the mourner understands that healing is not a straight road but a spiral. The same memories that once cut now carve meaning. You can think of the loved one without losing breath. You can revisit the hospital, the photograph, the anniversary, and stay steady. That steadiness is not detachment; it is resurrection power at work inside you.

The trees teach the lesson perfectly. Leaves fall not because they die but because the tree must live through winter. Letting go is not failure; it is survival. Jesus modeled this rhythm in Gethsemane: *"Not my will but Yours be done."* Release precedes renewal.

Autumn faith recognizes limits. We cannot change yesterday, but we can bless it. We cannot erase sorrow, but we can transform it into wisdom. Like Joseph, we learn to say, *"You meant it for evil, but God meant it for good"* (Genesis 50:20). Acceptance is not passive. It is participation in God's larger redemption.

Living with the Absence

Absence never fully disappears; it changes shape. Sometimes it sits quietly like furniture you stop noticing. Other times, it walks into a room uninvited. The goal of grief is not to remove absence but to make peace with its company.

Set a chair for memory. Speak aloud the stories you once avoided. Tell the next generation who they were, what they taught, and how they loved. In doing so, you declare that death did not erase the relationship; it relocated it. The communion of the saints bridges two dimensions of the same Kingdom.

The Rhythm of Reflection

Autumn invites gratitude for what was and humility for what remains. This is when many find new callings, such as writing, mentoring, and serving. Pain becomes pedagogy. You start teaching lessons you learned the hard way, and others listen because truth spoken from scars carries authority.

Theological maturity arrives here. You see that God never wastes anything, neither the sleepless nights nor the trembling prayers. Romans 8:28 becomes more than a quotation; it becomes muscle memory. You no longer *believe* it because you read it; you believe it because you lived it.

The Spiritual Discipline of Remembering

Memory sanctified is memory redeemed. Israel built altars after every crossing, stones that said, *"God met us here."* Build your own altars: a framed note, a journal entry, a verse underlined because it carried you. Every reminder is a protest against forgetfulness and a celebration of survival.

If tears come, let them. Even in autumn, rain still falls. But now the rain waters gratitude instead of guilt. Each tear says, *"Love still matters."*

How to Recognize Autumn's Arrival

You know you are in autumn when you can listen to someone else's grief without your own re-breaking. You can comfort rather than compare. You can thank God for memories without demanding their return. You can rest in unfinished stories because you trust the Author.

And when autumn arrived, it did not come as an ending but as understanding. The colors deepened, the air slowed, and the heart at last accepted that every letting go is also a kind of faith. We learned to bless the past without being bound by it, to remember without reliving, and to walk calmly through the garden of what remains. Loss had not left us empty. It had enlarged us. Gratitude became our equilibrium; peace, our harvest. And as the final leaves drifted earthward, we sensed that even in surrender, God was preparing the soil for another beginning.

Autumn ends the frantic search for meaning. It replaces *"Why?"* with *"Thank You."* It ends bargaining prayers and begins blessing prayers. You start saying, *"Lord, make my pain useful."* That is surrender, not surrender to loss, but surrender to love's endurance.

Faith Window 7 Part 3

"Those Who Sow in Tears Shall Reap with Joy" (Psalm 126:5)

This is the promise of autumn: sowing sorrow into the soil of faith and waiting for joy to rise. The Psalmist does not say joy cancels tears; it grows from them. The same field that received grief becomes the field that produces gladness. God wastes nothing, not even our weeping.

Tears are seeds. They soften the soil of the soul so that compassion can grow. Every act of kindness done in memory of the one you lost is a harvest from that seed. The weeping sower is not punished but prepared.

Biblically, joy is not an emotion; it is fruition. It means God's purpose has ripened. When Jesus promised that sorrow would turn to joy (John 16:20), He used childbirth as the metaphor: pain transformed, not deleted. The child proves the agony was not in vain.

The harvest of joy may come as peace after prayer, laughter shared at a memorial, or courage to mentor someone else in loss. Each fruit bears the same signature: redemption through remembrance. In Christ, every autumn becomes a prelude to spring again.

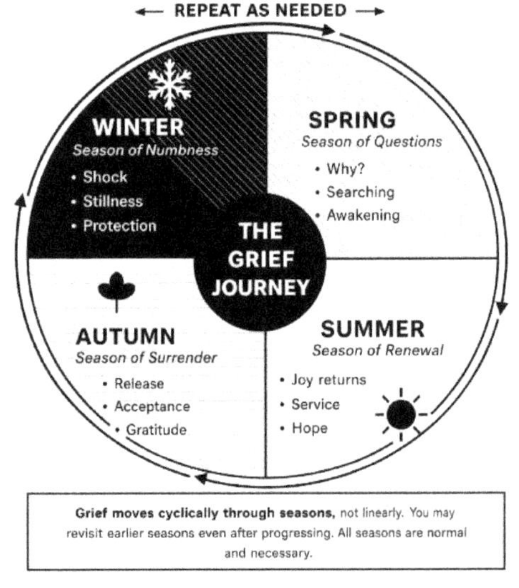

Grief moves cyclically through seasons, not linearly. You may revisit earlier seasons even after progressing. All seasons are normal and necessary.

7.5 The Unbroken Circle

The seasons of grief do not replace one another; they revolve. After many years, you may revisit winter for a day or two, feel the cold breath of loss, then return quickly to summer's warmth. The circle is evidence of life, not regression. Healing is not linear because love is not linear. It remains alive, and living things move in cycles.

The final posture is not forgetting but faithfulness. The believer learns to carry memory like light rather than weight. You do not get over love; you grow around it. The wound becomes a window. Through it, you see eternity more clearly.

And the God who was there in the winter silence, who tolerated your spring questions, who smiled through your summer laughter, who walked with you through autumn surrender—that same God will meet you again in every season yet to come.

Chapter 7 Endnotes

131 Godoy, L. D., Rossignoli, M. T., Delfino-Pereira, P., Garcia-Cairasco, N., & de Lima Umeoka, E. H. (2018). A comprehensive overview on stress neurobiology: Basic concepts and clinical implications. Frontiers in Behavioral Neuroscience, 12, 127.

132 Bylsma, L. M., Croon, M. A., Vingerhoets, A. J. J. M., & Rottenberg, J. (2020). When and for whom does crying improve mood? A daily diary study. Emotion, 20(7), 1280-1295. https://doi.org/10.1037/emo0000633

133 Diamond, D. M., Campbell, A. M., Park, C. R., et al. (2007). The temporal dynamics model of emotional memory processing. Neural Plasticity, 2007, 60803.

134 Shields, G. S., Sazma, M. A., & Yonelinas, A. P. (2016). The effects of acute stress on core executive functions. Neuroscience & Biobehavioral Reviews, 68, 651-668.

135 Pennebaker, J. W., & Smyth, J. M. (2016). Opening up by writing it down (3rd ed.). Guilford Press.

136 McEwen, B. S., & Akil, H. (2020). Revisiting the stress concept. Journal of Neuroscience, 40(1), 12-21.

137 Russell, G., & Lightman, S. (2019). The human stress response. Nature Reviews Endocrinology, 15(9), 525-534.

138 Newberg, A. B., & Waldman, M. R. (2009). How God changes your brain. Ballantine Books.

Chapter 8

When Faith Feels Far Away

8.1 The Silence of God

Grief can make the world go quiet. Voices you relied on feel faint. Prayers that once flowed now stall in your throat. You are not faithless; you are wounded. The Psalmists knew this ache: "How long, O Lord? Will you forget me forever?" (Psalm 13:1). Scripture gives honest room for this question, not a rebuke for asking it.

David opens with the interrogative *"ʿaḏ-ʾānāh"* (how long), repeated four times in verses 1-2. It is a rhetorical pounding that refuses to be ignored. The verb *"šāḵaḥ"* (forget) doesn't mean God has memory loss; in Hebrew thought, to "forget" someone means to withdraw active care, to act as though they don't exist. The adverb *neṣaḥ* (forever) means "to completion, perpetually". David is not asking for information ("when will this end?") but expressing the subjective experience of abandonment that feels endless. Yet notice the Psalm's structure: verses 1-2 (lament), verse 3 (petition), verse 4 (reason), verses 5-6 (trust and praise).

David doesn't move from lament to praise by skipping the lament. He moves through it. The final verse declares, "I will sing (*ʾāšîrāh*—cohortative, expressing determination) to the Lord, for He has dealt bountifully (*gāmal*—rewarded, recompensed) with me." This is not a denial of verses 1-2; it's hope spoken over unresolved pain. The structure teaches: you can bring your darkest questions to God, sustain them honestly, and still choose trust, not because the questions are answered, but because God receives those who question Him.

Two things often happen at once in early grief. First, the nervous system is on high alert.[139] Sleep breaks. Appetite shifts. Attention narrows to survival details. In that state, even ordinary spiritual practices feel hard. Your brain is not broken; it is protecting you. Second, meaning feels unstable. The God you knew on good days seems far away on hard nights. That gap between what you believed and what you now experience is painful and real. Researchers call this a "shattered assumptions" moment, when life no longer fits the old map.[140] The Bible calls it "lament," a faithful cry that brings our confusion to God, not away from him (see Psalm 42; Lamentations 3).

Silence does not mean absence. In grief, God often speaks at a different volume and through different channels. Elijah did not hear God in the wind, earthquake, or fire but in a low whisper (1 Kings 19:11–13). When your inner world is loud with sorrow, a whisper is easy to miss. That is why this Chapter invites you to listen more slowly.

Start with small, doable anchors. One breath prayer, morning and night: "Lord Jesus Christ, have mercy on me." One verse to carry: "The Lord is near to the brokenhearted" (Psalm 34:18). One short walk outside where you name what you see: clouds, trees, light. This is not a denial of sorrow. It is a way to hold a rail while the stairs feel steep.

Lament is not a failure of faith; it is an act of faith. Every "Why?" and "How long?" is still a prayer addressed to God. Grief can thin your words, but you can still come with the words you have. When the prodigal "came to himself," he spoke a single true sentence and walked home (Luke 15:17–20). You can, too.

You may also notice that your body now carries faith differently. Tears come without asking. Hands feel heavy. Fatigue wears you down. Treat your body as an ally. Eat simple foods. Sip water. Go to bed earlier than feels normal. Light a candle during prayer if darkness in the room mirrors the darkness in your heart. The candle does not make God present; it helps you pay attention to the God who is present.

If you cannot sing, let others sing for you. Let recorded Psalms or hymns play while you sit quietly. Consider this a form of "borrowed praise." Israel did not always walk into worship strong; sometimes they limped in and borrowed each other's strength (Psalm 122:1–2). The Church exists for days like yours.

Finally, give language to what hurts. Try this simple, biblical sentence: "Lord, here is my complaint" (Psalm 142:2). Then name three specifics. Keep them concrete and small: "I miss her voice. The house is too quiet. Mornings are the worst." Close with one request: "Stay with me." That one request is enough for today (Psalm 23:4).

The silence of God is not the absence of God. It is often the classroom of deeper trust. Many who pass through it later say, "I did not get all the answers, but I found the One who holds me." That discovery often begins right here, where words are few and groans are many (Romans 8:26–27). In grief, God's silence is often experienced as absence, but Scripture consistently separates the two. Silence may withhold explanation, but it does not withdraw presence.

Practice today:

Light a candle. Pray the Jesus prayer once. Read Psalm 13 slowly. Stop at the last line: "I will sing to the Lord, because he has dealt bountifully with me" (v.6). You may not be ready to sing it yet. Place the words on tomorrow's shelf.

8.2 When Prayers Bounce Off the Ceiling

It can feel like your prayers hit the ceiling and fall back into your lap. You speak, but heaven stays quiet. This sensation is common in grief. It often rises from three overlapping places.

First, overload. When your stress system fires for weeks, concentration frays. You start a prayer and forget where it was going.[141] That is normal under strain. Short prayers and scripted prayers can help. The Lord's Prayer, spoken slowly, gives scaffolding when you have no energy to improvise (Matthew 6:9–13). So can the Psalms, already shaped by people who prayed through disaster (Psalm 61;77;88).

Second, expectations. Before the loss, you may have felt God mainly in strong emotions during worship or in quick answers to requests. Grief changes the register of God's presence from bright to dim, from immediate to patient. The dimness is not God pulling away; it is God meeting you where endurance grows (James 1:2–4). Oak trees are not grown in one storm. They deepen across many.

Third, interpretation. In pain, we often assign hard meanings to silence: "God is displeased with me" or "My faith is defective." The Psalms show another reading: "Why do you hide your face?" is not self-condemnation; it is honest relationship (Psalm 44:24). You can hold two truths at once: "God loves me" and "I do not feel him today." That tension is biblical and safe.

When you say your prayers go nowhere, consider simple changes that honor your limits.

Pray with your body

Kneel if you can. Sit with your feet grounded. Open your hands on your lap as a sign of need. Scripture treats the body as a partner in prayer, not an obstacle (Psalm 95:6). If standing feels like too much, sit. If kneeling aches, bow your head. The point is not posture for its own sake; it is bringing all of you to God.

Pray in sentences, not paragraphs

Give God single, clear lines. "God, keep me through 10 a.m." "Lord, meet me in this paperwork." "Father, hold my family." Jesus commends prayers that are simple and sincere, not verbose (Matthew 6:7–8).

Short prayers repeat well while you drive, fold laundry, or wait in a doctor's office.

Pray by borrowing words

Use Psalm 42 on the days you cannot craft your own sentences: "Why are you cast down, O my soul, and why are you in turmoil within me? Hope in God" (v.5). Let the Psalmist argue with his own despair while you stand beside him. It is not cheating to use a script. It is wisdom. The Church has prayed this way for centuries.

Pray with one friend

If possible, invite a trusted person to sit with you for ten minutes a week. No speeches. One Psalm aloud. One minute of silence. One short prayer each. Jesus promised a unique nearness to those who gather in His name (Matthew 18:20). In grief, that promise is a lifeline. Community does not remove loss; it shares the weight.

If prayer still feels blocked, name the block to God: "Lord, prayer feels pointless today." That sentence is itself a prayer. God is not fragile. He can hold your honesty. The Psalmist's pattern is frankness followed by "yet": "Yet I will remember you" (Psalm 42:6). Your "yet" may be small today. It counts.

Over time, many discover that "bounced prayers" were not wasted. They were stored. They made room in the soul where deeper trust could grow. The harvest is usually slow. But slow is not empty. Seed waits in the dark before it breaks the soil (Mark 4:26–29).

Practice today**:** Set a three-minute timer. Sit with feet grounded, hands open. Pray the Lord's Prayer once, out loud. Then say, "Lord, stay with me." When the timer ends, stop. Let that be enough.

8.3 When the Bible Feels Closed

Grief can make Scripture feel distant or opaque. Words you once loved now seem flat. Pages that used to speak now whisper nothing. This is more common than most believers admit. You are not doing anything wrong; you are carrying a wound that changes how your mind, attention, and spirit process information.

Trauma research notes that loss disrupts the brain's capacity for sustained attention and emotional integration.[142] Linear reading becomes hard. Memory feels unreliable. Even simple texts can trigger frustration. None of this is a spiritual failure. It is physiology, psychology, and sorrow interacting at once. This is why God repeatedly meets hurting people with gentle words like "Fear not," "Take heart," and "Do not be afraid." He knows what it feels like to have shaken minds.

Scripture itself acknowledges seasons when the Word feels silent. Psalm 119, the longest Chapter in the Bible, is written by someone who keeps crying out for understanding: "My soul clings to the dust; give me life according to your word!" (v.25). That is the voice of someone who wants to read but feels spiritually fogged. You are in good company.

Instead of forcing yourself to "read like before," consider approaches that honor where you are right now. Reading the Bible in grief is not about volume; it is about oxygen. One small breath at a time is enough.

Begin with narrative, not instruction

Narrative is easier for the grieving mind to absorb than long instruction sections. When the heart is heavy, stories carry truth more gently. Return to the narratives that show God meeting people in their valleys: Joseph in prison (Genesis 39), Hannah in anguish (1 Samuel 1), Elijah in burnout (1 Kings 19), Mary at the tomb (John 20). These stories act as mirrors. Your tears do not disqualify you from hearing God; they position you alongside many of God's people.

Read shorter passages with longer pauses

Most grieving readers benefit from short passages and spacious silence. Try one paragraph per day at most. Read it slowly. Then sit for one minute. Do not force application. Let one phrase rise naturally. If nothing rises, that is fine. You showed up. God is not giving grades.

Jesus said the Word is seed (Mark 4:14). Seeds begin their work underground. Growth is invisible before it becomes visible. Trust that something good is happening beneath your fatigue.

Read aloud instead of silently

Silent reading can feel empty when inner noise is loud. Reading aloud slows you down, engages your breath, and widens your awareness. It also bypasses the "numbness filter" that often sits between your eyes and your heart in grief.

Try reading Psalm 23, Isaiah 41, John 14, or Romans 8 aloud. Let the sound of your own voice carry truth to your own ears. You hear Scripture differently when you speak it.

Stay with the Psalms of lament

When the Bible feels closed, the Psalms that match your emotional reality often reopen it. Psalms 6, 13 ,22, 31, 42, 77, and 88 give language to sorrow, confusion, anger, and tired hope. They do not rush to resolution. Many end on unresolved tension. That is why grieving hearts understand them.

Lament Psalms teach us how to bring the worst days into the presence of the best God. They permit honesty while aiming toward trust.

Write down one sentence, not notes

If you write anything, let it be a single sentence per reading: "Here is what stands out today..." Or "Here is what I wish God would do..." Or "Here is my fear right now..."

This is not a Bible study journal. It is a grief survival journal. One sentence is enough to anchor the moment.

Bring Scripture into ordinary tasks

If sitting still to read is hard, integrate Scripture into simple moments. Play an audio Bible while brushing your teeth. Listen to one Psalm while washing dishes. Place a verse on your refrigerator. God can meet you in quiet domestic rhythms. He has done so for many people over the centuries.

Do not judge your spiritual temperature

Grief distorts perception. You may feel spiritually cold when, in fact, you are being held closer than ever. Jesus draws near to the brokenhearted (Psalm 34:18), whether or not they feel His nearness. Faith is not measured by emotional warmth but by returning to God with whatever you have that day.

What to expect over time

For most people, Scripture slowly reopens. Verses regain color. Stories gain meaning. Promises land deeper than before. You begin to notice things you missed in years past. This is not because grief made you spiritually weak; it is because grief made you spiritually honest. The Word meets you now not on the mountaintop, but in the valley, and it is just as true there.

***Practice today*:**

Read Psalm 23 aloud. Stop at the phrase "He restores my soul." Repeat it once. Let it be enough.

Under Emotional Fog

Grief creates an internal weather system. Even on a sunny day, the soul can feel overcast. You might wake up with a heaviness you cannot name. You might sit in church and feel as if the service is happening underwater. Some describe it as numbness. Others call it exhaustion. Scripture often calls it "the faint heart" (Psalm 61:2). Whatever name you choose, the experience is real and shared by millions who walk through loss.

This emotional fog is not a sign of spiritual regression. It is the mind and heart working overtime to process a reality they did not ask for. Strong Christians, lifelong believers, pastors, and theologians all report the same sensation after loss. If faith feels muted, blurry, or inconsistent, it does not mean you have lost it. It means you are grieving.

Your emotions are not theological statements

One of the most important truths to grasp in grief is this: emotions are signals, not verdicts. Feeling abandoned does not mean God has abandoned you. Feeling numb does not mean you are faithless. Feeling low does not mean something is spiritually wrong with you.

Jesus Himself endured emotional agony so intense that His sweat became "like great drops of blood" (Luke 22:44). That level of distress did not reflect a lack of trust; it revealed the depth of His humanity. If Jesus could feel that level of emotional overwhelm without sinning, then you, too, can feel deeply without shame.

Your mind is working behind the scenes

During grief, the brain goes into a complicated mode. Stress hormones remain elevated. Memory retrieval becomes harder. Concentration weakens. Emotions swing, often without warning. All of this can create the feeling that faith has somehow evaporated. Yet faith often survives these changes quietly, like a pilot light that stays lit even when the room goes dark.

The Bible never equates faith with emotional stability. Instead, it frames faith as a trust that endures pressure, even when feelings contradict it. Abraham believed God "in hope against hope" (Romans 4:18). David cried, complained, and pleaded throughout the Psalms, yet still returned to trust (Psalm 56:3–4). Faith is not the absence of turmoil. It is a direction you keep turning toward.

You can trust while trembling

Grief makes you tremble. Sometimes literally. Sometimes inwardly. But trembling is not failure. Scripture shows many examples of faithful trembling:

Daniel trembled before receiving divine comfort (Daniel 10:8–12). • Paul confessed he ministered "in weakness and in fear and much trembling" (1 Corinthians 2:3). • The women at the empty tomb fled "with trembling and astonishment" (Mark 16:8).

Notice something: trembling did not disqualify any of them. In every case, God moved toward the trembling person, not away.

Build tiny habits of faithfulness

When grief fogs your emotions, big spiritual goals feel impossible. But small practices slip past the fog and still feed your spirit.

Take one Scripture into your day

Not a Chapter. Not a paragraph. Just one verse. Place it in your pocket. Set it as your phone wallpaper. Let it sit with you. The goal is not insight; the goal is oxygen.

Pray a two-sentence prayer

"God, hold me today. Keep me from despair." Or "Lord, I am tired. Stay near." These short prayers build a gentle rhythm of turning your face toward God.

Keep a five-minute Sabbath each day

Sit still. No agenda. No performance. Grief needs room to breathe. This tiny Sabbath reminds you that God holds the world even when you can't.

Anchor yourself in what does not change

When emotions swing wildly, you need truths that do not. Scripture offers anchors that stay put when everything else feels unstable:

God's character does not change (Malachi 3:6). • God's love is steadfast even when yours feels weak (Psalm 136). • God is near to the brokenhearted (Psalm 34:18). • God keeps every tear (Psalm 56:8). • God finishes what He starts (Philippians 1:6).

These are not motivational slogans. They are theological bedrock. Even if you feel nothing when you read them, they are still true. Faith during grief often looks like whispering these truths into the fog until the fog thins.

Borrow faith when yours feels faint

Sometimes your faith will feel too small to stand on. Borrow someone else's for a while. That is what the Body of Christ is for.

Let a friend pray for you. Let a worship song carry you. Let a church service surround you, even if you cannot sing. You don't have to feel strong to be carried by the strength of others. God built community precisely for seasons like this.

Expect the fog to shift over time

The fog rarely lifts all at once. It thins. Then thickens. Then thins again. Eventually, you begin to notice clarity returning in small patches. Scripture starts speaking again. Prayer regains meaning. Spiritual energy returns in whispers before it returns in full.

This is how most believers recover: slowly, quietly, faithfully. You are not behind. You are healing.

***Practice today*:** Choose one truth from the anchor list above. Speak it aloud once in the morning and once before bed. Let it stand guard over your emotions.

8.4 When Worship Feels Impossible

There comes a moment in grief when the idea of worship feels almost foreign. You walk into church, and the songs sound too bright, too fast, too certain. People lift their hands while you can barely lift your head. Someone says, "Just praise your way through," and you want to disappear. If this is you, breathe. You are not the problem. You are not spiritually defective. You are grieving.

Worship is not a performance for God; it is a meeting place. And meeting places can feel fragile after loss. In Scripture, worship is not always loud. Sometimes it is a whisper. Sometimes it is a groan. Sometimes it is the sound of someone sitting silently in ashes (Job 2:13). God receives them all.

Why worship feels heavy in grief

Loss creates dissonance between your inner and outer worlds. Your heart is aching, while the worship environment may feel celebratory. This mismatch can make you feel out of place, or worse, inadequate. But in the Bible, worship consistently makes room for sorrow:

Israel worshipped at the edge of the Red Sea *while still wet with fear.* • David worshipped after an unbearable loss, not because he felt triumphant but because he turned toward God with empty hands. • Jesus called the mourning blessed, not because mourning feels holy, but because God draws near to the mourner (Matthew 5:4).

Your grief is not in the way of worship. Your grief *is* the offering.

God does not demand an emotional soundtrack

Many believers think worship must be joyful, grateful, and energetic. But Scripture paints a broader picture. Worship includes lament, questions, tears, trembling, silence, and stillness.

Worship can be a tear

A single tear shed in God's direction is worship. Psalm 39:12 says, "Hold my tears in Your hands." Tears are not interruptions; they are prayers with no words.

Worship can be a sigh

Romans 8:26 says the Spirit intercedes "with groanings too deep for words." The sigh you breathe when you walk into church and do not know how you will make it through the service… God hears that as worship.

Worship can be a whisper

Saying "Lord, help me" during a song you cannot sing is still worship. It is a declaration of need. God honors need.

When you cannot sing, let the room sing for you

During grief, your voice may feel locked. Lyrics may feel heavy. But in Scripture, people often survive on *borrowed worship*:

Israel leaned on Moses' faith when they had none. • Paul and Silas sang while others simply listened (Acts 16:25). • The early church "devoted themselves" together so that weak believers could lean on strong ones (Acts 2:42–47).

Worship is communal by design. When you cannot sing, let the congregation carry you. Let the choir lift what you cannot. Let recorded hymns fill the silence. You are not cheating; you are participating.

Worship through the body when the heart feels numb

Your emotions may be quiet, but your body can still worship. Scripture frequently uses the body to express truth when the heart feels flat.

Stand if you can

Standing during worship, even in weariness, is a simple embodied prayer: "I am still here."

Place a hand on your chest

This small gesture reconnects your awareness to your breath and your God. It is grounding, steadying, human.

Sit in silence with open hands

Open hands say, "I need You." No words required.

Find the worship posture that matches your grief

Not every worship environment feels safe when you are raw. That is not immaturity; it is discernment. Consider experimenting with different forms of worship in this season:

Quiet, reflective worship

Soft hymns, instrumental Psalms, or gentle acoustic versions of songs can hold you without overwhelming your senses.

Scripture-soaked worship

Instead of singing, listen to the Psalms spoken aloud. Psalm 27, 46, 62, 91, 121, and 130 minister deeply to grieving hearts.

Private worship

You may need to worship at home for a while. A candle. A chair. A Psalm. A single whispered prayer. God is just as present there as in the sanctuary.

The goal is not happy worship; it is honest worship

Grief purifies worship. It removes pretense. It strips away clichés. It presses your soul toward what is real. You discover quickly that the only worship worth offering is the kind that comes from the truth of your condition, not the strength of your emotion.

Honest worship says:

"God, I don't understand, but I am still Yours." "God, my heart is heavy, but I turn to You." "God, I cannot lift my hands, but I lift my eyes."

This is worship heaven treasures.

Over time, worship slowly reopens

Most grieving believers find that worship returns in stages:

First, you endure worship.

Then, you listen to worship. • Then, you participate in pieces. • Then, you whisper along. • Then one day, unexpectedly, your voice returns.

That moment doesn't erase the grief, but it reminds you that you are healing. You did not lose your faith. You were walking through fire, and God walked there with you.

***Practice today*:** Play one gentle worship song or Psalm. Sit with open hands. You don't need to sing. Just breathe the pain and presence of God in the same space.

8.5 When You Cannot Feel God at All

There is a particular kind of grief that goes beyond sorrow, confusion, or exhaustion. It is the grief that makes you say, "I feel nothing." Not numbness alone. Not sadness alone. Nothing. It is as if your spiritual senses have shut down to preserve what little strength you have left.

If this describes your season, hear this clearly: you are not alone, you are not broken, and God has not withdrawn.

The experience of feeling nothing in the presence of God is as ancient as Scripture. It is the cry of Job. The ache of David. The silence of Elijah. The lament of Jeremiah. The bewilderment of Mary Magdalene before the risen Christ spoke her name. The Bible is brutally honest about this human phenomenon because God understands it better than we do.

The emotional blackout is protective, not punitive

Your brain is trying to reduce overload. When the emotional system burns too hot for too long, it can shut down certain pathways to preserve vital functioning.[143] Neurologists refer to this as "protective dissociation." Psychologists describe it as "temporary emotional flattening."

But Scripture names it more tenderly: *"The spirit grows faint."* (Psalm 142:3)

Your lack of felt experience is not rebellion. It is injury. And God responds to injury with gentleness, not judgment.

Biblical giants walked this same valley

The idea that only "weak Christians" feel nothing is false. Consider:

David: "My soul refuses to be comforted… I am so troubled I cannot speak" (Psalm 77:2–4).

• **Job:** "Behold, I go forward, but He is not there" (Job 23:8–9).

• **Jeremiah:** "He has walled me about so that I cannot escape… my soul is bereft of peace" (Lamentations 3:7,17).

• **Even Jesus:** "My God, why have You forsaken Me?" (Matthew 27:46), not because He doubted the Father, but because His human frame entered a depth of suffering that veiled His felt sense of the Father's nearness.

If Scripture preserved their emotional emptiness with such transparency, then your emptiness is not outside the boundaries of faith. It is inside the very story of faith.

Feeling nothing is still a feeling

Silence is still an experience. Blankness is still a signal. It simply means your inner world is overwhelmed. God does not ask you to manufacture emotion. He asks you to bring Him what you *do* have, not what you wish you had.

Bring Him your emptiness

"Here I am, Lord. I feel nothing. But I am here." This is prayer. This is worship. This is faith.

Bring Him your questions

"What are you doing with me in this silence?" This, too, is prayer.

Bring Him your fatigue

"God, I'm tired."

This is a confession, not a failure.

God is closest when He is least felt

This truth is counterintuitive but biblically consistent.

Psalm 34:18 does not say, "The Lord is near to the joyful." It says, "The Lord is near to the brokenhearted."

Nearness in Scripture is not measured by sensation. It is measured by promise. And God has never, not even once, broken a promise.

When you cannot feel God, His nearness is not reduced. Your receptors are simply exhausted.

When the emotions shut down, switch to practices that require none

Your relationship with God does not depend on emotional intensity. It depends on truth, presence, and the steady choices you make in the dark.

Sit before God in silence

No agenda. No expectation. Just presence.

This is the oldest spiritual practice in the Christian tradition, and it is tailor-made for grief.

Use anchor verses rather than long readings

Choose one:

Psalm 23:4 • Isaiah 41:10 • Matthew 11:28 • Romans 8:26–28 Repeat it slowly once or twice a day. Let truth drip, not rush.

Let your body signify what your heart cannot feel

Light a candle.

Place your hand on your chest. Keep your Bible open nearby. These are signs of availability, not performance.

Practice quiet companionship

Sometimes the only thing that helps is sitting with someone who says nothing. Jesus healed people this way more often than we realize. Presence heals what explanations cannot.

Eventually, the spiritual senses return

Most grieving believers describe a day, sometimes months later, when a phrase in Scripture suddenly feels warm again. A worship lyric suddenly lands. A prayer suddenly feels real. A tear finally comes.

That moment does not mean the pain is gone. It means your spirit is reawakening.

God did not leave you in the silence. He was rebuilding you within it.

***Practice today*:** Sit in silence for 3 minutes. No prayer words. No goals. Just breathe and let your presence stand before God. Whisper one line at the end: "Here I am."

Faith Window 8

Silence, Absence, and the Felt Withdrawal of God

Scripture does not deny the experience of God's silence. Some of the most faithful voices in the Bible describe seasons in which God feels distant, hidden, or entirely absent. Job cries out and hears nothing in return. David asks why God seems far away in times of trouble. Even Jesus, at the height of suffering, gives voice to abandonment rather than reassurance.

The absence of felt comfort is not evidence of spiritual failure. It is a documented part of the human encounter with suffering. Faith, in these moments, is not sustained by clarity or consolation, but by endurance—by continuing to speak to God even when no response is perceived. Silence is not rejection; it is often the space in which faith is tested rather than explained.

Chapter 8 Endnotes

139 Pitman, R. K., Rasmusson, A. M., Koenen, K. C., et al. (2012). Biological studies of PTSD. Nature Reviews Neuroscience, 13(11), 769-787.

140 Milman, E., Neimeyer, R. A., Fitzpatrick, M., MacKinnon, C. J., Muis, K. R., & Cohen, S. R. (2019). Prolonged grief and the disruption of meaning. European Journal of Psychotraumatology, 10(1), 1652126.

141 Shields, G. S., Sazma, M. A., & Yonelinas, A. P. (2016). The effects of acute stress on core executive functions: A meta-analysis. Neuroscience & Biobehavioral Reviews, 68, 651-668.

Arnsten, A. F. (2009). Stress signalling pathways that impair prefrontal cortex structure and function. Nature Reviews Neuroscience, 10(6), 410-422.

142 Palitsky, D., Mota, N., Afifi, T. O., Downs, A. C., & Sareen, J. (2013). The association between adult attachment style, mental disorders, and suicidality. Journal of Nervous and Mental Disease, 201(7), 579-586.

143 Maier, S. F., & Watkins, L. R. (2010). Role of the medial prefrontal cortex in coping and resilience. Brain Research, 1355, 52-60.

Chapter 9

Finding Your Way Back

9.1 When Faith Feels Weak but Love for God Remains

There is a strange and sacred tension many grieving people experience. They say something like: "My faith feels weak… but I still love God." This tension is not a contradiction. It is actually one of the clearest indicators that genuine faith is still alive.

Love for God is not the same as the *feeling* of God. Love for God persists even when the emotional winds shift, even when prayers feel flat, even when Scripture feels distant, even when worship feels beyond reach. Love for God is not loud or dramatic in grief. It often whispers through cracked places.

If you still want God, even quietly, even minimally, you are already being held by Him.

Weak faith is still real faith

The Bible never teaches that faith must be strong to count. Jesus said faith the size of a mustard seed, which was the smallest seed His audience knew, is enough to move mountains (Matthew 17:20). He never said faith must be intense, emotional, or confident. He simply said faith must be *real*. The mustard seed (*kokkos sinapeos*) was proverbially tiny (1-2mm) and was used in rabbinic literature to represent the smallest measurable amount. But Jesus isn't establishing a minimum threshold ("get your faith up to this size"); He's demolishing the entire measurement paradigm. Later rabbinic teaching distinguished between "little faith" and "great faith," but Jesus collapses that distinction: living faith, however small, has divine potency.

The problem isn't insufficient faith; it's substituting measurement for connection. A mustard seed doesn't strain to grow larger. It simply stays alive, rooted, and the life within it does the rest. Faith isn't a spiritual muscle you pump up through exertion; it's a living connection you maintain through trust, and God is responsible for the outcomes.

In Matthew 17:20, Jesus identifies the problem, not as the absence of great faith, or the presence of little faith, but the presence of no faith or unbelief (*apistia)*. Finally, Jesus implies that there is an inherent life principle even in the smallest of seeds that causes its influence to grow and spread. And in the adjoining parable of the yeast spreading through the entire batch of dough, the principle is confirmed.

Weak faith is not fraudulent faith. Weak faith is weary faith. And weary faith is honored by God.

Faith is measured by direction, not intensity

In grief, your faith may not feel like a fire. It may feel like a flickering wick (Isaiah 42:3). Yet Scripture says God will not snuff out a faintly burning wick. He protects it. He shields it from the wind. He tends it until it burns again.

This imagery comes from Isaiah 42:3, part of the first Servant Song describing the Messiah: "A bruised reed He will not break, and a faintly burning wick (*pištâ k̂ēhāh*) He will not quench (*yək̂abbennâ*)." The adjective *k̂ēhāh* means dim, faint, failing, and on the verge of going out. The verb *k̂ābâ* means to extinguish, snuff out.

Isaiah juxtaposes two images: the bruised reed (*qāneh rāṣûṣ* - a bent, cracked papyrus stalk, useless for construction or writing) and the smoking wick (a lamp whose oil has nearly run out, giving more smoke than light). Ancient practice would discard both as worthless. But the Servant Matthew explicitly applies this to Jesus, and refuses to discard what others consider finished (Matthew 12:18-21). The promise isn't that God tolerates weakness; it's that He actively protects fragile faith until it strengthens. The Hebrew phrase *ʾĕmeṯ yôṣîʾ mišpāṭ* (He will faithfully bring forth justice) means His commitment to the weak is not sentimental but covenantal. He has bound Himself to preserve the flickering flame. If your faith feels more like smoke than fire, you are not disqualified. You are under divine protection until the oil is replenished and the flame burns steadily again.

You may be whispering "yes" to God through tears. That whisper is louder in heaven than the shouts of a stadium full of "undistressed" believers.

Love for God can survive emotional collapse

Your emotions may shut down. Your strength may collapse. Your energy may drain. And yet, you still find yourself saying:

"I want to trust Him."

"I believe He is good… even when I don't feel it." "I am hurt, but I have nowhere safer to go."

This is not denial. This is covenant love.

Peter said to Jesus, "Lord, to whom shall we go? You have the words of eternal life" (John 6:68). That was not the statement of a man who understood everything. It was the statement of a man whose love for Christ survived his confusion.

Love for God is deeper than emotional clarity

Love for God survives unanswered questions.

It survives broken hearts. It survives theological fog. It survives numbness. It survives anger. It survives silence.

Love for God is not the same as perfect peace. It is the deep, stubborn, unexplainable desire to stay with Him even when you don't understand Him.

Learn to bless God in the dark

Job, at the height of his confusion, said, "Though He slay me, yet will I trust Him" (Job 13:15). This was not naïve optimism. It was the declaration of someone who had lost nearly everything except his love for God.

Many grieving believers find themselves speaking similar words: "I don't know why this happened… but I still want God." "I am hurting deeply… but I can't walk away." These statements come from a place beyond circumstances. They are love speaking from the soul's foundation.

Blessing God does not require feeling blessed

You can bless God while wounded.

You can bless God while confused. You can bless God while numb. You can bless God through tears. And God receives that blessing with tenderness, not demand.

Blessing God in the dark is not pretending. It is trusting that the God you once knew is still the God who holds you now.

Take small steps to keep love alive

Grief tries to shut down everything. But you do not have to let the shutdown reach your love for God. You can nurture that love gently, without pressure.

Recall one memory of God's faithfulness

Just one. Not a long list. Not a testimony speech. One moment where you saw God help you. Remembrance strengthens love.

Speak one sentence of love each day

"God, I still love You."

"Father, I want You near." "Lord, You matter to me." These sentences rebuild the bridge from your pain to His presence.

Keep one symbol of His love visible

A Bible open to a comforting passage. A cross necklace. A Psalm taped to your mirror. These symbols remind your grief that your story did not end with the loss.

God honors even the smallest flame

If your faith feels like smoke instead of fire, know this: smoke is the evidence of a flame that still exists. And God never despises weak flames.

Psalm 103:14 says, "He knows our frame; He remembers that we are dust." God is not disappointed with your weakness. He accounted for it before the foundation of the world. His love for you does not waver with your strength.

Weak faith plus strong love is still worship. Still trust. Still devotion. Still relationship. Still covenant. Still victory.

Your love for God is the seed of your healing.

***Practice today*:** Whisper one sentence to God, any sentence of love or desire, even if you feel nothing. Your whisper is welcome. Your whisper is enough.

9.2 When You Feel Guilty for Struggling Spiritually

Grief is hard enough on its own. But many people carry a second burden that makes the journey even heavier: **spiritual guilt.** You might find yourself thinking:

"I should be stronger than this."

"I've walked with God for years. Why am I falling apart now?" "I should be praying more." "I shouldn't feel angry." "I shouldn't feel numb." "If I really trusted God, I wouldn't be like this."

These thoughts do not come from wisdom. They come from pain, fatigue, and a sincere heart that does not want to disappoint God. But guilt in grief is almost always misplaced, misinformed, and unnecessarily cruel.

Let's walk through this honestly and biblically.

Guilt is the uninvited companion of sorrow. When something catastrophic happens, the mind looks for explanations. It tries to assign meaning. It searches for cause and effect. This is the brain's attempt to regain control.

Psychologists call it "survivor's guilt," "intrusive responsibility," or "adaptive self-blame." Scripture describes it differently but no less truthfully: *"My iniquities have overtaken me, though they are more than the hairs of my head"* (Psalm 40:12).

David was not listing actual sins. He was describing emotional overwhelm that *felt* like guilt.

Grief blurs the lines between real guilt and false guilt. Most spiritual guilt after loss falls into that second category.

You are not disappointing God by grieving

Many believers fear that God expects them to be unfazed, unshaken, perpetually strong, and spiritually composed. But Scripture shows the opposite.

God invites emotional honesty

Abraham questioned Him.

Moses argued with Him. David cried to Him. Jeremiah complained to Him. Jesus wept before Him.

Not once did God call their grief "disobedience."

God never commands emotional denial

There is no verse that says:

"Thou shalt not feel overwhelmed." "Thou shalt not question." "Thou shalt not ache." "Thou shalt not tremble."

Instead, Scripture says:

"*Cast all your anxieties on Him*" (1 Peter 5:7). "*Pour out your heart before Him*" (Psalm 62:8). "*Come to Me, all who labor and are heavy laden*" (Matthew 11:28).

These are invitations to honesty, not perfection.

Feeling spiritually weak does not mean being spiritually wrong

In grief, weakness is not sin. Weariness is not sin. Numbness is not sin. Confusion is not sin.

Job tore his robe, cursed his birth, questioned God, and vented his anguish. Scripture says in the same breath, "In all this Job did not sin" (Job 1:22).

This is one of the most liberating truths in the entire Bible.

Job's emotional collapse was not spiritual rebellion. It was human pain. But God did not punish him. God comforted him.

You can stop punishing yourself.

When guilt whispers lies, counter it with truth

False guilt speaks in absolutes:

"You failed." "You are not spiritual enough." "You are falling behind." "God is disappointed."

Truth speaks differently:

"The Lord is compassionate and gracious, slow to anger, abounding in steadfast love" (Psalm 103:8). "He knows our frame; He remembers that we are dust" (Psalm 103:14). "There is therefore now no condemnation for those who are in Christ Jesus" (Romans 8:1).

These verses were not written for believers on their best days. They were written for believers at their worst.

Separate conviction from condemnation

Conviction is God's loving nudge toward life. Condemnation is the enemy's attempt to bury you under shame.

Here is the difference:

Conviction is specific: "Make peace with this person," "forgive," "return to prayer." • **Condemnation is vague**: "You are not enough," "you are failing," "God must be tired of you." • **Conviction leads to hope. • Condemnation leads to despair. • Conviction makes you want God. • Condemnation makes you hide from God.**

If what you are hearing leads you away from God, it is not His voice.

Guilt often rises from unrealistic expectations of yourself

People who love God deeply often expect far more of themselves than God expects. You may hold yourself to standards God never wrote.

- You expect spiritual strength.
- God expects you to lean on Him.
- You expect emotional stability
- God expects honesty.
- You expect immediate healing
- God expects a journey.
- You expect unbroken confidence
- God expects dependence.
- You are not failing. You are grieving.
- Release the guilt you were never meant to carry

God is not standing above you with a clipboard. He is standing beside you with compassion. Jesus described His own heart as "gentle and lowly" (Matthew 11:29). That is the heart closest to you right now.

Every tear that falls is seen (Psalm 56:8). Every sigh is heard (Psalm 38:9). Every weakness is understood (Hebrews 4:15).

You do not need to fix your spiritual life before God will draw near. He draws near *because* your spiritual life feels fragile.

***Practice today*:** Place your hand over your heart and say aloud, "God is not disappointed in me." Repeat it once more. Let the truth push back against the guilt.

9.3 Rebuilding a Spiritual Life at a Sustainable Pace

There will come a day, slowly, quietly, without fanfare, when you begin to sense that your spiritual life wants to grow again. Not the way it used to. Not on the same schedule. Not with the same emotional texture. But something inside you begins to move. You feel a gentle tug toward prayer. Toward Scripture. Toward worship. Toward God.

This is the moment many grieving believers miss because they expect the return of spiritual strength to feel dramatic. But real spiritual rebuilding doesn't begin with fireworks. It begins with a flicker. But that flicker deserves room to breathe.

Rebuilding spiritually after grief is less like constructing a house and more like recovering from an injury. Healing is slow, layered, uneven. Some days look strong. Other days feel like setbacks. But as long as you keep moving gently forward, you are rebuilding.

Rebuilding is not returning to "how you were."

Many people try to return to the prayer life they had before the loss, the worship rhythms they once maintained, or the Scripture habits they once kept. But grief is transformative. It reshapes the inner landscape. The point is not to return to what was; the point is to grow into what *is now possible.*

You are not going back. You are going forward — even if forward looks small.

Start with the simplest spiritual practices.

Your spiritual muscles have been under strain. Do not run before you can walk. Rebuilding spiritually after grief works best in tiny, life-giving steps.

One breath prayer each day

Pick a line that steadies your soul: "Lord, be near." "Jesus, stay with me." "Father, hold me."

Your nervous system responds well to repetition. Your spirit responds well to honesty. A breath prayer marries both.

One Psalm a week

Not a Chapter a day. Not a reading plan. Not a regimen. Just let one Psalm live with you for seven days. Psalm 23. Psalm 27. Psalm 46. Psalm 62. Psalm 121. Let the Psalm become a companion instead of an assignment.

One moment of gratitude

You're not aiming for a gratitude journal. Just one acknowledgment: "God, thank You for that phone call." "Thank You for that hour of peace." "Thank you for that sunrise."

Small gratitude softens the soil for spiritual renewal.

Re-engage the community slowly and honestly.

You do not need to jump back into full spiritual activity. In fact, doing too much too soon often sets people back. Instead, re-enter gently.

Choose one spiritual gathering.

A Sunday service.

A small group. A prayer meeting. A Bible study. Just one. Not five.

Let yourself arrive as you are, whether you're silent, sad, anxious, or hopeful.

Allow others to carry part of your weight.

Real community involves shared strength. When you feel weary in prayer, sit near someone who prays. When you feel quiet, sit among those who sing. When you feel unsure, sit with those who believe. It is holy to let the faith of others hold you while your own faith regains shape.

Honor your new spiritual capacities.

Grief creates permanent shifts. You may find:

You pray fewer words but more honest ones • You read less Scripture but absorb it more deeply • You worship more quietly but more sincerely • You see God in everyday moments more than dramatic ones

This is not spiritual decline. This is spiritual maturity born from pain.

Expect a deeper form of faith.

Many believers eventually realize that grief carved out more room for God, not less. What felt like collapsing was actually the soil being turned for new growth. Your spiritual life after loss may become:

Quieter, but more anchored

Simpler, but more authentic • Less emotional, but more stable • Less hurried, but more meaningful • Less performative, but more surrendered

Allow God to lead you instead of forcing yourself forward

Rebuilding spiritually is not a self-directed project. It is a responsive journey. Your role is not to manufacture spiritual momentum. Your role is to stay available to the small invitations God places in your path.

Notice the gentle nudges.

You may feel:

A small desire to pray • A quiet urge to read • an impulse to worship • A longing to reconnect with believers

Do not rush. Do not force. Just respond. One step. One moment. One yes at a time.

Celebrate spiritual progress without comparing it

Your progress may look different from others. That is fine. You are not racing anyone. You are recovering your soul.

Celebrate the small wins:

You prayed one sentence.

You felt one verse resonate. • You survived one church service. • You sensed God's presence for three seconds. • You cried during a worship song — not from pain this time, but from recognition.

Heaven sees these as victories.

Let spiritual life return through joy, not pressure

When the time is right, something surprising emerges: joy begins to return. Slowly. Carefully. But genuinely.

It's not the joy of denial. It's not the joy of pretending. It is the joy of someone who has walked through darkness and discovered that God was still there even when you could not feel Him.

This joy is not loud. It is steady. It grows quietly, like dawn.

***Practice today*:** Choose one tiny spiritual step — a breath prayer, a short Scripture, or five quiet minutes. Let today's faith be enough for today.

9.4 The Long View: Grief and Your Spiritual Identity

Grief Changes Your Spiritual Identity - Not Destroys It

There is a point in the grief journey where you begin to look at yourself and ask, "Who am I now?" The loss has changed your routines, your emotions, your priorities, your capacity, your relationships, and yes, your spiritual life. What you once relied on feels different. What you once assumed feels uncertain. What you once practiced with ease now requires effort.

This identity shift is not a spiritual collapse. It is a spiritual transformation.

Loss reshapes the soul. It strips, exposes, reveals, and rebuilds. It takes away things you once stood on and replaces them with things that can actually hold your weight. Grief does not destroy spiritual identity. It refines it.

You are not who you were — and that is not a failure

Most people expect their spiritual life to "return to normal." But grief creates a new normal. The person you were before the loss is not the person you are now. But that difference is not a deficit. It is part of the human journey; God Himself walks with you.

Abraham did not return to who he was after Isaac was born. Moses did not return to who he was after the burning bush. David did not return to who he was after his years of running. Job did not return to who he was after his suffering. Peter did not return to who he was after the resurrection.

Great sorrow and great encounters with God change people. They always have.

Grief deepens the soul.

There are things you can learn about God only in deep waters. Not because God withholds insight during peaceful seasons, but because the soul opens differently when it is wounded.

Deep sorrow creates:

•Deeper compassion •Deeper humility •Deeper reliance
•Deeper honesty •Deeper maturity

These are not punishments. They are the fruits of being held by God when you had nothing left to hold.

You gain a truer sense of spiritual priorities.

When grief strips away illusions, distractions, and false securities, your spiritual life becomes more focused. You discover:

What truly matters

What you can release • What strengthens you • What drains you • What draws you closer to God

Before the loss, you may have carried spiritual obligations that God never required. After the loss, you begin to see clearly that God values sincerity over routine, presence over performance, depth over speed.

You become more honest before God

Grief removes the mask.

It removes the filters. It removes the pressure to appear "strong."

Your prayers become clearer. Your conversations with God become truer. You stop trying to impress Him, and finally begin to trust Him with your full humanity.

God has always welcomed honesty over eloquence. The Psalms prove that. Jesus' anguish in Gethsemane proves that. When you come to God now, you come as you truly are — and that is a spiritual gift.

You discover new ways God speaks

When one spiritual channel feels muted, God often opens another:

A Scripture that suddenly becomes alive • A hymn that feels like a hand on your shoulder • A phrase that stays with you for days • A moment of stillness that steadies you • A quiet sense of being guided • A person whose words arrive at the exact right moment

This is not imagination. It is divine accommodation. When grief makes one path difficult, God clears another.

Your faith becomes gentler and less brittle

Before grief, many believers carry subtle assumptions:

"Life should be predictable."

"Good people should be protected." "Faithful Christians should avoid deep suffering." "God should intervene quickly."

Grief dismantles these assumptions. But what replaces them is not cynicism. It is resilience.

Your faith becomes:

Humble instead of presumptuous

Realistic instead of idealistic • Curious instead of rigid • Open-handed instead of demanding • Anchored instead of anxious

This is what Scripture calls "tested faith," more valuable than gold (1 Peter 1:6–7).

You learn that God's presence is deeper than God's felt presence

One of the most important long-view truths is this: **God is present even when you are not aware of Him.**

Your awareness fluctuates. God's presence does not.

This recognition frees you from chasing spiritual sensations and anchors you in God's unchanging character. It is maturity born of sorrow.

You become a companion to others who grieve.

People who have walked through darkness carry a compassion others cannot fake. You will notice it in yourself over time:

You listen differently. You speak more gently • You withhold quick judgments • You understand unspoken pain • You make room for others' confusion • You reflect God's comfort in ways you could not before

Grief does not just change you. It equips you. You become a safe place for others because you survived what you once thought you wouldn't.

You begin to trust God in ways you never trusted Him before

Not with naive optimism.

Not with emotional certainty. But with surrendered steadiness.

This is the kind of trust built in fire. The kind of trust that circumstances cannot shake. The kind of trust God grows through hardship, not ease.

You do not merely believe that God is good. You learn that God is good *even here.*

Grief rarely moves in straight lines. Even as faith deepens, moments of clarity can coexist with sudden returns of confusion, longing, or silence. This uneven movement is not regression; it is how the soul integrates loss over time. Growth in grief does not replace earlier pain. It carries it forward with new understanding. What feels like repetition is often refinement.

Practice today: Write one sentence about how grief has changed you spiritually, not negatively, but honestly. Then write one sentence about what part of that change might actually be a sign of growth.

Many people try to make sense of this non-linear experience by forcing grief into stages—a move that often creates more confusion, guilt, and spiritual strain than clarity, a misconception examined in detail in Chapter 10.

Faith Window 9 Part 1

When God Seems Silent, His Love Is Not

There are seasons when the soul reaches for God and feels only air. Seasons when prayer tastes like dust, Scripture feels closed, worship feels distant, and faith feels threadbare. These moments do not mean God has stepped away. They mean you are walking through a valley where spiritual senses dim long before spiritual reality does.

Scripture shows again and again that God is nearest when His people feel Him least.

"The Lord is near to the brokenhearted and saves the crushed in spirit." **Psalm 34:18 (ESV)**

Your emotions do not measure nearness. His covenant love measures it.

Throughout the Bible, God does His deepest work in silence. Joseph found Him in a prison. Moses found Him in the wilderness. Elijah found Him in a whisper. David found Him in tears. Paul found Him in weakness. Mary Magdalene found Him at a tomb she thought was filled only with death.

Silence in Scripture is not abandonment. It is preparation.

When you cannot feel God, the Spirit is still praying for you:

"The Spirit Himself intercedes for us with groanings too deep for words." **Romans 8:26 (ESV)**

When you cannot hold on, Christ holds you:

"My sheep hear My voice… no one will snatch them out of My hand." — **John 10:27–28 (ESV)**

When you cannot see the path, God guides you one step at a time:

"I will counsel you with My eye upon you." **Psalm 32:8 (ESV)**

But when you feel spiritually empty, God's gentleness meets you:

"A bruised reed He will not break, and a faintly burning wick He will not quench." **Isaiah 42:3 (ESV)**

Grief does not push God away; it pulls Him close. Your weakness is not a barrier to His presence. It is the very place where His presence becomes most tender.

As you move forward, do not measure your spiritual life by how much you feel. Measure it by this: *You are still turning toward God.* Even quietly. Even slowly. Even trembling. That turning is faith. That turning is worship. That turning is life.

Your spiritual senses will return. Your hunger for God will revive. Your joy will rise again. Not because you force it, but because the God who began a good work in you will finish it.

"He who calls you is faithful; He will surely do it." —**1 Thessalonians 5:24 (ESV)**

This is your window of faith: God is faithful in the silence, gentle in your weakness, and closer than your breath, even when you cannot feel Him at all.

Faith Window 9 Part 2

Reconstruction, Trust, and the Return of Meaning

Scripture also testifies that faith can survive rupture and return altered but intact. Those who once questioned God's nearness later discover that trust does not require constant emotional assurance. The Psalms frequently move from lament to quiet confidence without resolving every question in between.

Rebuilding faith after loss rarely means returning to what once was. Instead, it involves learning to trust God without demanding certainty, comfort, or immediate understanding. This quieter faith, less triumphant, more resilient, often proves stronger than the one that preceded grief. What emerges is not naïve belief restored, but mature trust forged through loss.

Chapter 10

Grief's Hidden Companions

Anxiety, Depression, and Loneliness

10.1 The Five Stages of Grief: Origin, Limits, and Misuse

Few ideas about grief are as widely known, or as widely misunderstood, as the so-called *Five Stages of Grief*: denial, anger, bargaining, depression, and acceptance. Many grieving people encounter these "stages" early, often through books, articles, well-meaning friends, or even professionals. They are frequently presented as a roadmap: a predictable emotional sequence that every grieving person must pass through to heal.

This presentation is not only inaccurate; for many people, it becomes quietly harmful.[144]

To understand why, it is important to clarify where the model came from, what it was originally intended to describe, and how it has been misapplied in popular grief culture.

Where the Five Stages Came From

The Five Stages were first articulated by psychiatrist **Elisabeth Kübler-Ross** in 1969 in her work with **terminally ill patients**, not bereaved survivors.[145] Her observations emerged from conversations with individuals who were facing their own impending death, not from a systematic study of people grieving the loss of someone else.

This distinction matters.

Kübler-Ross herself later clarified that the stages were **never meant to be linear**, universal, or prescriptive. They were descriptive observations of common emotional responses among some patients confronting mortality. Over time, however, the model escaped its original context and became simplified, systematized, and exported into bereavement care—often without nuance or warning labels.

What began as a compassionate attempt to understand emotional responses to dying gradually hardened into an implied formula for grieving.

How the Model Is Commonly Misused

In popular culture, the Five Stages are often taught as:

A required sequence

A timeline

A benchmark of progress

A way to determine whether someone is "stuck" or "doing grief wrong."

This misuse creates several problems.

First, it suggests that grief is **predictable** when in reality it is profoundly individual. People may experience some of these emotions, all of them, none of them, or many others that do not appear on the list. They may feel anger before denial, acceptance before depression, or move back and forth between states repeatedly.

Second, it implies that *acceptance* is the end goal—and that once achieved, grief should largely resolve. This framing does not align with lived experience or contemporary grief research. Most people do not "accept" loss in a final, emotional sense. They learn to **integrate** it, **carry it**, and **live alongside it**. Love does not progress neatly toward closure.

Third, the model can unintentionally burden the grieving with **self-monitoring**:

"Am I in the right stage?"
"Why haven't I moved on yet?"
"What's wrong with me?"

These questions do not heal. They increase anxiety, guilt, and confusion at a time when the nervous system is already under strain.

What Modern Grief Research Shows Instead

Contemporary grief psychology has largely moved away from stage-based models. Research now emphasizes that grief is:

Non-linear

Oscillatory

Context-dependent

Influenced by attachment, meaning, trauma, and biology

People move **back and forth** between states of engagement and withdrawal, sorrow and functioning, longing and stabilization.[146] This movement is not regression; it is regulation. The nervous system alternates between processing pain and restoring balance.

One influential framework describes grief as a **dual process**, involving:

Periods of loss-oriented focus (yearning, remembering, sorrow)

Periods of restoration-oriented focus (daily tasks, distraction, re-engagement)

Healthy grieving involves moving between these states over time—not progressing through emotional checkpoints.

This understanding aligns with what you have already seen throughout this book: grief unfolds in waves, not steps.

Why the Stages Persist (Despite the Evidence)

The Five Stages endure because they offer **simplicity** amid chaos. When loss feels overwhelming, people reach for structure. A numbered list feels reassuring. It promises order where there is none.

But grief does not heal through simplification. It heals through **truth**, **patience**, and **companionship**.

The danger is not that the stages exist as emotional possibilities. The danger is when they are treated as **rules** rather than **responses**.

A More Accurate Way to Understand Grief Emotions

Instead of stages, it is more faithful to science, Scripture, and lived experience to think in terms of **grief responses**:

Emotions arise and recede in response to triggers, memory, fatigue, support, and safety.

Multiple emotions can coexist without contradiction.

Calm does not mean healing is complete.

Pain returning does not mean healing has failed.

Anger, sadness, numbness, relief, gratitude, fear, love, confusion, and even moments of joy can appear on the same day. None of these invalidates the others.

This is why the Psalms move fluidly between lament and trust, sometimes within the same breath. Scripture never portrays grief as a staircase. It portrays it as a journey, often winding, often slow, always relational.

If You Have Been Measuring Yourself by the Stages

If you were taught to expect grief to follow a set order, and your experience does not match that expectation, hear this clearly:

- You are not behind.
- You are not resistant.
- You are not failing.
- You are grieving like a human being.

Let go of the pressure to locate yourself on a chart. Healing is not about reaching a final stage; it is about **learning how to live truthfully in the presence of loss**—with support, with meaning, and with compassion for your own limits.

The work you are doing in the chapters of this book, regulating the nervous system, gently rebuilding faith, honoring silence, receiving community, and allowing growth to emerge, is far better aligned with how grief actually heals than any stage model could ever be.

Grief is not something you pass through and leave behind. It is something you learn to carry with greater steadiness over time.

And that learning does not follow a linear path. It follows relationship, truth, and patience.

10.2 When Grief Becomes Anxiety

Grief often brings companions you did not invite. Anxiety is usually the first to arrive. It creeps in quietly during the early days of loss, then rises sharply as the shock wears off. Many bereaved people describe feeling as if their heart is constantly racing, their thoughts running ahead of them, and their body vibrating with a fear that has no clear source.

The brain's threat-detection system (explored in Chapter 2) remains hyperactive during grief, affecting your daily experience.

A grieving woman once said, "My husband died, and now my body acts like everything is a threat. Even the microwave ding makes me jump." Her description is painfully accurate. Anxiety during grief is not a sign of spiritual weakness. It is the nervous system's survival response, attempting to shield you from a world that suddenly feels unsafe.[147]

The Hidden Physiology of Grief

Researchers have shown that acute grief can mimic traumatic stress.[148] Sleeplessness, racing thoughts, chest pressure, trembling hands, digestive upset, and difficulty concentrating are common. They are not signs of "losing control," but signals that the nervous system is struggling to recalibrate.[149]

Many grieving people visit emergency rooms thinking they're having cardiac events. Doctors run tests, find nothing physically wrong, and say, "You're under stress." But grief-induced anxiety is more than stress.[150] It is a profound biological shock.

Your body is not betraying you. It is trying, however imperfectly, to protect you.

A Contemporary Example: The Fear That Came Out of Nowhere

A 39-year-old accountant lost his mother unexpectedly to a medical complication. For three weeks, he functioned "normally"—handling paperwork, greeting visitors, and making arrangements. But one afternoon at work, he experienced a sudden wave of dizziness and a pounding heart. He thought he was dying. Paramedics found nothing wrong. The diagnosis: a panic attack triggered by grief.

He later shared, "I didn't feel sad that day. I felt fine. But I guess my body needed to say what my mouth wouldn't." That is how anxiety often works. It expresses the emotional truth you have been too overwhelmed to articulate.

Nature's Mirror: The Hyperalert Deer

In the natural world, a deer that senses danger freezes. Its ears rotate like radar dishes. Its muscles tighten. Its breath shortens. Even after the predator disappears, the deer may remain alert for hours.

Grief places people in a state of hypervigilance. The physiological stress response discussed in Chapter 2 continues to shape your experience of grief. Your mind may scan for threats even in safe spaces. Sudden noises feel amplified. Crowds feel overwhelming. You may avoid places that remind you of the person you lost because your nervous system interprets those memories as threats to your stability.[151]

Just as the deer slowly relaxes when the environment becomes predictable again, you too will gradually ease out of hyper-alertness as your life stabilizes.

Practices for Calming the Anxious Heart

- **Name the fear.**

David said, "When I am afraid, I put my trust in You" (Psalm 56:3). Naming fear disrupts its power.

- **Ground your body.**

Breathing out slowly activates the parasympathetic nervous system. Try: inhale for 4, hold for 2, exhale for 6. Repeat five times.

- **Narrow the time window.**

Grief anxiety tries to make you solve the next year. Wisdom asks you to steward the next hour.

- **Borrow calm from others.**

Sitting with a steady friend for ten minutes can physiologically lower stress hormones as your body co-regulates with theirs.[152]

- **Anchor your senses.**

When overwhelmed, identify five things you can see, four you can touch, three you can hear, two you can smell, one you can taste. This pulls you back to the present.

- **Pray small, honest prayers.**

"Lord, help me survive this moment." "Lord, slow my breathing." "Lord, hold me steady."

Anxiety is not the enemy. It is a messenger. And its message is simple: **You are hurting. You need comfort. You need compassion. You need care.**

10.3 The Shadow of Depression

Depression often follows grief like dusk follows sunset. Not immediately, not all at once, but gradually dimming the emotional landscape until everything feels muted and gray. You are not broken. You are grieving.

Depression during grief is not a moral failure or a spiritual shortcoming. It is a natural, neurochemical, and emotional response to devastating loss.

Why Depression Happens in Grief

Your brain's reward system, consisting of dopamine, serotonin, and oxytocin pathways, depends heavily on relational connection.[153] When the person you loved dies, those circuits take a blow. Activities you once enjoyed feel flat. Motivation disappears. Energy drains. Life becomes heavy. It becomes difficult to imagine the future, let alone move toward it.

A grieving father said, "I'm not choosing sadness. My sadness is choosing me." This is depression in grief, not hopelessness, but depletion.

The Weight of Absence

Depression here is not only about sorrow. It is about **absence**. The absence of your spouse's voice. The absence of your child's laughter. The absence of your mother's wisdom. The absence of your father's strength. The absence of your friend's companionship.

Your heart is not only grieving what was lost, but adjusting to what will never be again. That adjustment demands energy—and the emotional cost is enormous.

A Real-World Story of Grief and Depression

A 28-year-old teacher lost her younger brother in a tragic accident. After the funeral crowds disappeared, she described the following weeks as "moving through fog." She struggled to complete basic tasks such as laundry, cooking, and lesson planning. She stopped returning calls. She slept twelve hours but woke exhausted. Her pastor gently suggested a grief counselor. After several sessions, she understood that she wasn't "weak." She was grieving. Her body had lowered her emotional temperature to survive the shock.

Grief depression does not mean you are broken. It is evidence of your deep love.

Nature's Wisdom: Trees in Winter

When winter arrives, trees shed their leaves not because they are dying but because they are conserving strength. Their energy pulls inward. Their movement slows. They remain alive, rooted, waiting for the warmth of spring.

This mirrors grief and depression.

Your emotional system withdraws to preserve strength. You are not failing. You are conserving.

And like the tree, you will feel green again—but not before the season completes its necessary work.

Finding God in the Shadowed Places

People of faith often feel confused when depression settles over grief. Questions arise:

"Where is God?"

"Why can't I feel His comfort?" "Why does prayer feel empty?"

Scripture gives permission for this struggle.

Jeremiah said, "*My soul is downcast within me*" (Lamentations 3:20). The Psalmist cried, "*How long, O Lord?*" (Psalm 13:1). Even Jesus experienced sorrow so intense that His soul was "overwhelmed to the point of death" (Matthew 26:38).

The Hebrew verb *šôaḥ* (downcast, bowed down) conveys being bent over, humiliated, crushed by weight. Jeremiah's soul is physically bowed within him. Yet this verse sits at the center of Lamentations, a five-chapter acrostic lament over Jerusalem's destruction. Chapters 1-2 detail the catastrophe; Chapter 3 (the theological apex) is Jeremiah's personal lament; Chapters 4-5 return to communal grief.

The structure itself embodies the isolation of suffering - Jeremiah alone in the middle, surrounded by collective devastation. But verses 21-23 contain Scripture's most unexpected pivot: "**This I recall** (*ʾāšîḇ ʾel-libbî* - I return to my heart/mind) **and therefore I have hope**: **the steadfast love** (*ḥesed*—covenant loyalty) **of the Lord never ceases; His mercies** (*raḥămîm*, from *reḥem*, womb—motherly compassions) **are new every morning**."

Notice: Jeremiah doesn't say the grief disappeared. He says, "This I recall to mind. It is a volitional cognitive act. He chooses to remember God's covenant character while grief remains. The promise isn't that morning erases night, but that God's mercies are renewed (*ḥădāšîm*—fresh, not used up) each dawn. The grammar is present tense: they are being new, continuously. Hope in Lamentations isn't the absence of darkness. It's finding small, renewable light within it. Morning doesn't solve night; it offers enough clarity for one more step.

God is not offended by your heaviness. He meets you in it.

Small, Faithful Movements

When depression sits heavily upon grief, healing often begins with very small acts:

Drink a glass of water.

Sit outside for five minutes. • Read one verse aloud. • Make your bed. • Take a warm shower. • Tell someone, "Today is hard."

These tiny steps signal to your brain that you are still moving, still living, still choosing light even when surrounded by darkness.

And if depression does not lift after many weeks, or sinks into despair, seek compassionate professional care. Elijah, overwhelmed and exhausted, needed rest, nourishment, an angelic touch, and a renewed word from God (1 Kings 19:5–8). Grief is no different. Support is not a sign of defeat. It is a tool God uses to restore strength.

10.4 The Deep Ache of Loneliness

Loneliness is grief's most persistent companion. It is not just the absence of people. It is the absence of a **particular person** whose presence shaped your world.

You can sit in a room full of family and still feel unbearably alone. Because loneliness in grief is not about company. **It is about irreplaceability.**

Why Grief and Loneliness Hurt So Much

Neuroscientists have discovered that the brain processes deep relational loss using the same circuits as it does for physical pain.[154] That's why loneliness feels sharp, heavy, or physically painful.

Your loved one's absence is not merely emotional. It is neurological, sensory, and embodied.

Their voice. Their footsteps. Their scent. Their laughter. Their routines. Their energy. Their touch.

All of these were woven into your nervous system. Removing them creates an ache that feels as real as an injury.

Three Forms of Loneliness After Loss

- **Relational Loneliness** - missing the specific person you lost.
- **Identity Loneliness** - missing the version of *you* that existed with them.
- **Social Loneliness** - feeling out of sync with people whose lives have not changed.

These forms intertwine, creating a profound sense of disconnection.

A Real-World Story of the Empty Chair

A widower said the loneliest sound in the world was the click of his front door locking at night. "That used to mean I was safe inside. Now it means I'll never walk through it again."

Loneliness is not simply sadness. It is the ongoing reminder that what once filled your life with warmth is no longer here to shape your days.

Nature's Lesson: Emperor Penguins

In Antarctica, emperor penguins huddle together during brutal winters. They rotate positions so that each penguin spends time at the center, shielded from the wind. No penguin survives alone.

Grieving hearts function the same way. You need warmth, emotional, spiritual, and relational. You need safe people and shared silence. You need companionship, not explanations. You need presence, not pressure.

Loneliness as Invitation

Loneliness is painful, but it is also revealing. It invites you to honor the love you lost. It invites you to seek new forms of connection. It invites you to let others in slowly, gently, safely. It invites you to rediscover belonging one step at a time.

And above all, it invites you to receive the truth of Psalm 68:6: **"God sets the lonely in families."**

You are not meant to remain in isolation. God is already forming a circle of care around you.

10.5 The Role of Community in Recovery

Grief may feel like a solitary experience, but healing is profoundly communal. Human beings are created for connection, physiologically, spiritually, and emotionally. When someone you love dies, your world contracts. The routines you shared fracture. The emotional balance you once carried collapses. The mind retreats inward. The body stiffens in protection. The soul grows weary.

And yet, it is precisely here at the intersection of pain and isolation that community becomes essential. **Essential,** and not optional. **A lifeline,** and not an accessory.

Community is the environment in which God often wraps His comfort, His wisdom, and His presence. Scripture consistently shows God's people recovering through the support of others: Naomi through Ruth, Elijah through the angel and the widow, David through Jonathan, the early church through shared meals, prayers, and generosity.

Modern psychology affirms the same truth: connection is medicine. When safe people surround a grieving person, the nervous system stabilizes, meaning returns, and hope begins to sprout again.[155]

Community fulfills four indispensable roles in the aftermath of loss: **stability, witness, shared strength, and spiritual renewal**.

Stability: A Foundation When Everything Feels Unsteady

Grief destabilizes routines, appetites, sleep cycles, and daily rhythms. You wake up confused. You feel unsure about decisions that once felt simple. You may lose track of time, skip meals, or forget appointments. This shaking is normal—but it is exhausting.

Stability returns through predictable relational touchpoints.

A family member checking in each evening. A church friend who brings groceries every Thursday. A neighbor who walks with you on Saturday mornings. A small group that reserves a seat next to you.

These rhythms work like emotional scaffolding. They hold you upright while you regain your balance. Neuroscientists note that predictable interpersonal contact helps regulate the hypothalamic-pituitary-adrenal axis, the system responsible for stress and emotional response.[156]

One grieving mother described it this way: "Every Tuesday, my friend Marcia took me to lunch. I didn't need the food. I needed the *Tuesday*."

Predictability is power when everything else feels unpredictable.

Witness: The Healing of Being Seen and Heard

Grief demands storytelling. You need to talk about your loved one. You need to repeat memories, describe moments, articulate regrets, voice confusion, and share the painful details of the final days. Every retelling is a step toward integration, and is your heart learning to make sense of what happened.

But storytelling requires witnesses.

People who are not afraid of your tears. People who do not rush you. People who do not say "you should be over this by now." People who simply sit, listen, nod, and hold space for your truth.

God Himself models witnessing: "I have seen the misery of My people… I have heard their cry" (Exodus 3:7). To be seen and heard is healing.

A contemporary example: A newly widowed man said, "My brother didn't fix anything. He didn't preach. He just said, 'Tell me about her.' So, I talked. And talked. He saved my life without knowing it."

Your story deserves witnesses.

Your grief deserves compassion. Your heart deserves room to speak.

Shared Strength: Carrying What You Cannot Carry Alone

When grief becomes unbearable, strength does not come from within; it comes from those around you. Scripture illustrates this vividly with Moses on the mountain. When he grew too weary to keep his arms raised,

Aaron and Hur stood beside him, one on each side, holding him up until the victory was won.

That is the template for grief support.

Community lifts you when you cannot lift yourself. They pray when you cannot pray. They intercede when you cannot speak. They drive you to appointments when you cannot drive. They sit with you in silence when you cannot talk.

Shared strength does not remove grief; it redistributes its weight.

A contemporary story: A church group of twelve women created a rotating schedule to accompany a grieving widow to her evening walks. "If I walked alone," she said, "I felt the emptiness. But when someone walked with me, I felt God again."

Strength grows through others.

Hope returns through others. Courage rekindles through others.

Nature's Testimony: The Redwood Forest

Redwoods are among the tallest and oldest trees on Earth. They depend not on deep roots, but on interconnected roots. Beneath the forest floor, their roots stretch out and intertwine with those of neighboring trees. When strong winds or storms strike, the entire forest stands as a single living unit.

A redwood alone cannot survive.

A redwood, together with other redwoods, can withstand centuries.

Likewise, grief can knock you off balance, but the interconnectedness of community keeps you from falling.

You do not need to be strong alone. You need strong people beside you.

Spiritual Renewal: Reconnecting the Soul to Meaning and Transcendence

Loss not only wounds the heart and mind; it disrupts the soul's orientation toward meaning, purpose, and God. Spiritual renewal occurs when the community gently reopens space for transcendence through shared prayer, worship, Scripture, ritual, and reverent silence without forcing answers or minimizing pain. In grief, faith is often fragile, questioned, or exhausted; community carries belief on your behalf until you can hold it again.

Paul writes, "Bear one another's burdens" (Galatians 6:2). This is a command that includes spiritual burdens. Renewal is not the removal of doubt but the restoration of trust over time, as grief is held within a larger story of hope, presence, and redemption. When others pray for you, sing with you, or simply sit before God alongside you, the soul slowly remembers that it is not abandoned—and meaning, though altered, can live again.

When Community Feels Overwhelming or Unsafe

Not everyone can rejoin the community immediately after a loss. The emotional bandwidth required to talk, socialize, or even smile may feel beyond reach. You may fear crying in public. You may feel embarrassed by the rawness of your emotions. You may worry about being a burden.

These fears are normal, but they must not trap you.

Gentle reentry is the goal: not forced, not pressured. Here are steps that honor your limits:

Start with one person. You do not need a crowd. You need one safe, steady presence.

Choose predictable interactions. Short visits. Short calls. Small gatherings. Familiar faces.

Be honest about your capacity. "It is good to see you, but I may only last fifteen minutes."

Allow yourself to leave early. Permission reduces anxiety. Anxiety reduces overwhelm.

Use silence. You do not have to talk. Sitting beside someone who will not rush you can be profoundly healing. Let others carry the conversation if needed. Your presence is enough.

Remember: Jesus Himself withdrew when overwhelmed (Matthew 14:13), yet always returned to community. Withdrawal is natural; return is essential.

The 30-Day Community Reconnection Blueprint

This blueprint is designed for grieving hearts—not as a burden, but as a gentle guide.

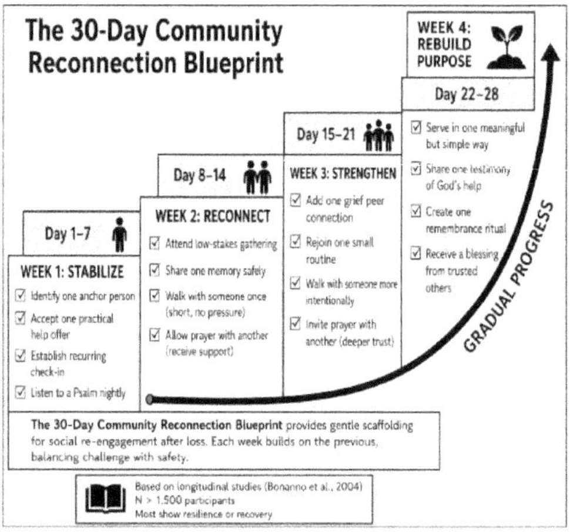

Week 1 - Stabilize

Identify one "anchor person." Accept one practical help. • Establish one recurring check-in time. • Listen to a Psalm aloud each night.

Week 2 - Reconnect

Attend one low-stakes gathering (prayer circle, small group, short visit). • Share one memory of your loved one with a safe person. • Walk with someone once this week. • Allow one person to pray with you.

Week 3 - Strengthen

Add one peer with a similar grief experience. • Rejoin one small routine (choir practice, Bible study, lunch tradition). • Accept one household assistance offer. • Name one small hope each day.

Week 4 - Rebuild Purpose

Serve in one meaningful but simple way (ushering, setup, greeting). • Share one testimony of God's help. • Create one remembrance ritual. • Receive a blessing circle comprised of two or three friends speaking Scripture over you.

This blueprint is not a test. It is a path toward reconnection.

Boundaries That Protect Without Isolating

Boundaries in grief are holy. You are allowed to say:

"I can stay for twenty minutes."

"I need to step outside." "I prefer not to answer that." "Please don't compare my grief with someone else's."

Boundaries protect your heart from unnecessary pain while allowing you to receive the support you need. Jesus modeled boundaries throughout His ministry: withdrawing to pray, limiting His inner circle, and choosing solitude when needed.

Boundaries are not walls. They are doors with hinges. They open and close to protect your healing.

How Community Rebuilds the Spirit

Community not only supports your emotions; it strengthens your faith.

Shared worship reignites hope. Hearing others sing truth strengthens you when your voice trembles.

Shared Scripture reorients your soul. A friend reading Psalm 23 aloud is sometimes more healing than reading it alone.

Shared prayer surrounds you. When you cannot pray, others will pray for you, holding up your arms, as Aaron and Hur did.

Shared compassion restores dignity. Simple acts such as sharing meals, visits, and quiet presence become living reminders of God's love.

In community, the heart relearns trust.

In community, the soul regains strength. In community, faith breathes again.

10.6 When Grief Needs Professional Help

Most grief is painful but healthy. It crushes you and then, slowly, lets you breathe again. But sometimes grief locks onto the nervous system like a vise and won't let go. When that happens, seeking professional help is not a failure of faith; it is wisdom.

Please reach out to a doctor, counselor, or emergency service immediately if any of the following are true for you or someone you love:

Thoughts of wanting to die, wishing you would not wake up, or planning to harm yourself.

You are using alcohol, prescriptions, or street drugs just to get through the day, and you feel out of control.

Panic attacks, terror, or nightmares that do not ease over several weeks and keep you from sleeping or working.

You cannot perform basic tasks (eating, bathing, getting out of bed) for days at a time, and nothing seems to improve.

You hear voices others do not hear, or you feel completely detached from reality and fear you are "losing your mind."

Friends and family repeatedly tell you they are very worried about your safety.

God often answers prayer through trained people. Inviting a wise counselor or physician into your story is one way to receive His care, not replace it.

Faith Window 10

"He Sets the Lonely in Families" (Psalm 68:6)

Take a slow breath. Place your hand over your heart. Feel its rhythm. Now hear this truth softly, gently, personally:

You were never meant to walk through grief alone.

God sees your loneliness.

God understands your ache. And God answers loneliness with community.

Pray quietly:

"Lord, gather me into the family You are forming around me. Give me courage to reach toward others, and grace to receive their love."

Now imagine a table prepared for you. A seat with your name on it. People around it: friends, mentors, siblings in Christ, each placed by God to walk with you.

Carry this promise today:

"He sets the lonely in families." This is not poetic language. It is God's commitment to your healing. You are not abandoned. You are not unseen. You are not forgotten. You are being placed, gently, intentionally, compassionately, into a community where your heart can breathe again.

Chapter 10 Endnotes

[144] Bonanno, G. A. (2009). *The other side of sadness: What the new science of bereavement tells us about life after loss*. New York, NY: Basic Books.

[145] Kübler-Ross, E. (1969). *On death and dying*. New York, NY: Macmillan.

[146] Stroebe, M., & Schut, H. (1999). *The dual process model of coping with bereavement: Rationale and description.* **Death Studies, 23**(3), 197–224. https://doi.org/10.1080/074811899201046

147 Eisma, M. C., & Stroebe, M. S. (2021). Rumination following bereavement. Clinical Psychology Review, 85, 102000. https://doi.org/10.1016/j.cpr.2021.102000

148 Simon, N. M., Shear, K. M., Thompson, E. H., Zalta, A. K., Perlman, C., Reynolds, C. F., & Silowash, R. (2007). The prevalence and correlates of psychiatric comorbidity in individuals with complicated grief. Comprehensive Psychiatry, 48(5), 395-399.

149 Porges, S. W. (2021). Polyvagal theory. Comprehensive Psychoneuroendocrinology, 7, 100069.

150 Henningsen, P., Zipfel, S., & Herzog, W. (2007). Management of functional somatic syndromes. The Lancet, 369(9565), 946-955.

151 Shear, M. K., Wang, Y., Skritskaya, N., et al. (2014). Treatment of complicated grief in elderly persons. JAMA Psychiatry, 71(11), 1287-1295.

152 Sbarra, D. A., & Hazan, C. (2008). Coregulation, dysregulation, self-regulation: An integrative analysis and empirical agenda for understanding adult attachment. Personality and Social Psychology Review, 12(2), 141-167.

153 O'Connor, M. F., Wellisch, D. K., Stanton, A. L., Eisenberger, N. I., Irwin, M. R., & Lieberman, M. D. (2008). Craving love? Enduring grief activates brain's reward center. NeuroImage, 42(2), 969-972.

154 Eisenberger, N. I. (2012). The pain of social disconnection: Examining the shared neural underpinnings of physical and social pain. Nature Reviews Neuroscience, 13(6), 421-434.

155 Coan, J. A., Schaefer, H. S., & Davidson, R. J. (2006). Lending a hand: Social regulation of the neural response to threat. Psychological Science, 17(12), 1032-1039.

156 Coan, J. A., & Sbarra, D. A. (2015). Social baseline theory: The social regulation of risk and effort. Current Opinion in Psychology, 1, 87-91.

Chapter 11

The Healing Journey: Growth Through Pain

11.1 Growing After Loss

Understanding Post-Traumatic Growth

Loss has a way of reshaping the inner world. It interrupts routines, shifts identity, and alters the landscape of daily life in ways that are often invisible to others but painfully clear to the one grieving. In the aftermath, many people long to "feel normal again," but grief does not return us to what once was. Instead, grief moves us toward a different kind of becoming. This gradual reshaping, emotional, relational, and spiritual, is often referred to as **post-traumatic growth**, or PTG.

PTG does not mean the loss was good. It does not mean the trauma was beneficial. It reflects something far more nuanced: that in the wake of profound disruption, many people discover capacities, insights, and strengths they did not know they possessed. In psychological research, PTG consistently appears across five areas: greater appreciation of life, deeper relationships, increased personal strength, new possibilities that emerge after loss, and spiritual or existential deepening.[157] These changes do not replace grief. They grow beside it.

Grief and growth often unfold together. Weeping and wisdom can live in the same heart. Exhaustion and resilience can coexist. Some days feel like steps forward; others feel like emotional landslides. Researchers observing people after significant loss describe three broad, overlapping patterns: stability through the storm, recovery after disruption, and transformation marked by new meaning and clearer values.[158] None of these patterns is better than the others. They are simply different ways humans adapt after being unmoored.

A helpful way to understand PTG is to see it not as a destination but as a **deepening**. It is less about "becoming strong" and more about becoming honest, grounded, and unafraid of one's own emotional truth. Growth shows up quietly - sometimes in how a person listens more attentively, or how they cherish relationships more consciously. At other times, it emerges through a shift in priorities or an unexpected sense of clarity about what matters and what no longer does.

Over time, silence does more than frustrate understanding; it reshapes the inner posture of the grieving person. What begins as absence often becomes formation—training the heart to live without constant reassurance.

Maria's Story

Maria and her husband had been married for forty-one years. When he died, the silence in the house felt unbearable. Simple decisions drained her. Holidays stung. Conversations with friends felt shallow. She moved through her days with the heaviness of someone carrying too much memory in too small a space.

Months later, her granddaughter asked her to teach an old family recipe. That request became a small Sunday tradition, one bowl of soup each week, one moment of togetherness at a time. Eventually, neighbors joined. There were tears, laughter, long pauses, and shared stories. One afternoon, Maria said quietly, "I don't feel better. I feel deeper." That sentence captures the essence of PTG: not the erasure of sorrow but the expansion of the soul.

Remember Dem Bones

Bones that endure a fracture and heal properly often grow stronger at the exact site where they once broke. This biological principle, known as Wolff's Law, reflects the body's remarkable ability to respond to stress by reinforcing its structure.[159] The break is not good, but the healing process can produce unexpected strength. In similar ways, the human spirit may discover resilience and wisdom in places once defined only by pain.

How Growth Takes Root

Studies on PTG highlight four recurring elements that support growth after loss:[160]

- Honest acknowledgment of the pain
- Telling one's story in a safe relationship
- Searching for meaning without forcing quick answers
- Taking small, purposeful steps aligned with new clarity

These four processes mirror how many people naturally rebuild their inner world after trauma.

Each element invites reflection rather than performance. They do not demand positivity. They simply offer ways to navigate grief with gentleness and intention.

Let's Reflect

Set aside a quiet moment today.

Write down three ways your loss has shifted what you value, how you see relationships, or how you view your own inner strength. There are no right answers. Let the truth be simple and unforced.

What Growth Is Not

Growth is not a verdict on your faith or character. It is not a scoreboard where "more growth" means "less love for the one you lost." It is not a straight line. It does not demand positivity or constant productivity. Growth allows tears at a birthday, quiet laughter at an old joke, and a full stop on a hard morning. It gives you permission to be human while you heal.

Five Subtle Signs You're Growing

- You notice small good things without arguing against them.
- You ask for help sooner instead of waiting until you're exhausted.
- You tell the truth about hard days without feeling like you've failed.
- You treat your body with more kindness, not less.
- You can hold a cherished memory without needing to escape it.

When Waves Hit Again

Waves recur. That is not regression; it is how memory and love work. Three responses can help:

Name it: "This is a wave." Naming shrinks confusion.

Narrow it: "For the next ten minutes, I will breathe, walk, or sip water." Time-boxing restores a sense of agency.

Normalize it: "Love leaves echoes. Echoes are not enemies." The wave will pass. You do not have to pass every test to keep the growth you've gained.

Let's Reflect

Write a few sentences that begin with "Since the loss, I value…" Do this without editing. Read it aloud once. Keep the page. You're allowed to change your mind later; this is simply today's truth.

11.2 Remembering Without Reliving

How to Carry Your Memories Differently

Memories after loss behave in unpredictable ways. Some return softly, almost like a gentle visitation of love. Others arrive sharply, uninvited, reopening emotional wounds without warning. Many grieving people describe feeling ambushed by their own minds in moments when everyday sights, smells, dates, or sounds suddenly unleash a surge of emotion far more intense than expected. This experience is common, and it does not mean you are "going backward." It means the brain's memory networks are still reorganizing.[161] [162]

When a person experiences deep loss, the brain begins to work to integrate the experience into existing memory systems.[163] But memories linked with high emotion, sensory detail, or trauma are stored differently. They often feel active, vivid, and intrusive because the brain is still labeling them as "important, unresolved, pay attention." Neuroscientists explain that emotionally intense memories can trigger strong physiological responses even when the danger is long gone.[164] This is why certain moments bring tears, a rapid heartbeat, or a tightening of the chest.

The goal is not to erase these memories. It is to carry them differently; to remember without reliving. Over time, and with gentle intention, the brain can relearn how to revisit memories without treating them as emergencies.[165] The shift is subtle but powerful: the memory remains real, but the emotional charge softens.

Jordan's Turning Point

Jordan lost his sister in a sudden accident. For months, he avoided anything that reminded him of her—their favorite song, certain roads, even a particular aisle in the grocery store. His therapist encouraged him to take small, structured steps toward reclaiming these avoided spaces. He began listening to their song for just one minute a day, then two. He slowly walked the aisle he had avoided, controlling his breathing. Eventually, he realized he could encounter memories with less fear. The memories still carried weight, but they no longer crushed him.

This gradual exposure to safe reminders is supported by research showing that controlled, gentle, repeated engagement with difficult memories helps the brain re-categorize them as non-threatening.[166] This reduces avoidance and emotional reactivity.[167] In time, the emotional intensity decreases, and the person regains a sense of agency.

Meaningfully Manage Your Memories

Choose one memory connected to your loss. Something meaningful but not overwhelming.

Set a timer for three minutes.

Sit comfortably. Breathe naturally.

Recall the memory intentionally.

Picture it like watching a scene from a distance.

Narrate the memory in one or two sentences. Out loud or silently. Keep it simple and truthful.

Shift attention to the present moment.

Notice your breath, your surroundings, the chair beneath you.

End with one grounding sentence.

"This memory is part of my story, not the whole of it."

This practice is not about forcing closure. It is about helping your mind learn that memories can be visited without being feared.

A Lesson from Nature

Some seeds require disturbance before they can begin to grow. In forests where wildfires occur, certain pine cones only release their seeds when exposed to intense heat, a process that opens them so new life can emerge. The fire is not good, but the design allows growth to follow disruption. In a similar way, difficult memories can eventually become places of insight or tenderness rather than only pain.

Your Next Gentle Step

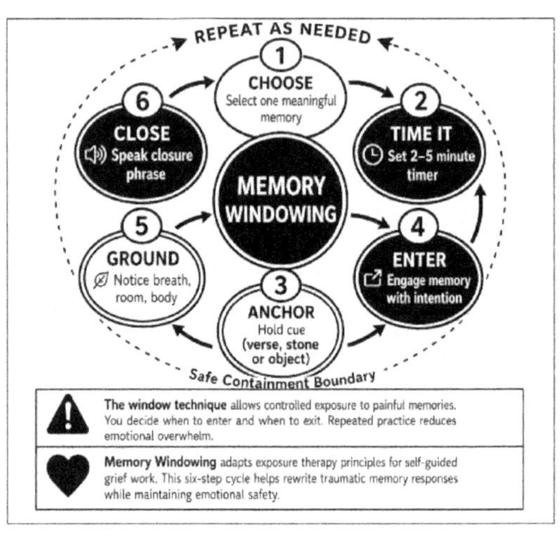

Choose one difficult memory.

Sit with it for a few quiet minutes using the six-step process above. End with the grounding sentence. If tears come, let them. If clarity comes, welcome it. Either response is valid.

Map Your Triggers

Make a simple two-column list headed **Cues** and **Conditions**. Under Cues, note specific sights, sounds, places, dates, and smells that spike your emotion. Under Conditions, note what makes you more vulnerable (fatigue, hunger, anniversaries, conflict, being rushed). Triggers often multiply when conditions stack. When you can see the pattern, you can plan for it.

Windowing

Instead of trying to conquer a memory, **visit it through a window**:

Choose a photograph, object, or location tied to the memory.

Decide the **window length** (two to five minutes).

Place an **anchor** (a verse on a card, a smooth stone to hold, or a short prayer).

Visit, notice, and then close the window on purpose. Repeated windowing teaches your mind that you decide when to enter and when to step back.

Three Anchors for Public Moments

When emotion surges in a store, at work, or in church:

Feet: press both feet flat to the floor and feel it.

Eyes: find one steady object and study it for ten seconds.

Words: silently speak one sentence of truth: "I am safe; this is a memory." These anchors are discreet, fast, and effective when you need composure without shutting down your feelings.

Your Next Gentle Step

Circle one cue from your map. Plan a two-minute window with an anchor. Do it once this week. You're not trying to be brave; you're training your nervous system to trust you.[168]

11.3 The Freedom of Forgiveness

Releasing What Holds You Down

Forgiveness becomes complicated in seasons of grief. Loss can surface old wounds, unspoken tensions, disappointments, broken promises, and painful memories involving people who are still alive, and even people who are not. There may be anger toward those who failed to help, toward those who made mistakes, toward oneself for words unspoken, or even toward God for not intervening. These inner conflicts are heavy. They unintentionally accumulate in the heart.

Forgiveness is not forgetting. It is not excusing. It is not pretending things never happened. And it certainly is not reconciliation with someone who remains unsafe or unchanged. Forgiveness is the decision to release the tight emotional grip that keeps you tied to what hurt you. It does not erase the memory; it changes your relationship to the memory. It is a gift you give yourself, not a reward you give someone else.

Researchers studying the emotional and physiological effects of forgiveness consistently report benefits, including reduced anger, improved cardiovascular health, and lower stress levels. The release of resentment literally allows the body to relax and the mind to recalibrate. Forgiveness is both emotional liberation and physical relief.

Elaine's Turning Point

Elaine struggled with resentment toward a relative whose lack of presence during her mother's final days had felt like a betrayal. She replayed the hurt repeatedly—on the drive to work, while lying in bed, even while cooking dinner. One day, she realized the pain was becoming part of her routine. She decided to try something different: she wrote a short statement naming what hurt her and placed it in a small box on her dresser. Every morning, she touched the box and said, "I release this today." Over time, she found the emotional tightness loosening. She forgave, not because the person deserved it, but because her heart needed the space.

The distinction between forgiveness and reconciliation is important. Reconciliation requires two people, mutual honesty, and genuine change. Forgiveness requires only one willing heart and the courage to let go of bitterness. Studies show that people who practice forgiveness, even privately and without re-engagement, demonstrate higher emotional resilience and lower stress markers.[169]

Think of a Clenched Fist

When a fist remains clenched for too long, the muscles stiffen, blood flow is restricted, and the hand loses strength. But when the hand is opened slowly and deliberately, circulation returns, and the fingers regain flexibility. The emotional state of chronic resentment is much like a clenched fist. It restricts the flow of emotions, keeping the heart in a state of tension. Forgiveness gently opens the hand.

The Four-Step Release

Name the hurt honestly.

Write a sentence describing what happened and how it affected you.

Release your grip.

Whisper, "I let go of what holds me."

Affirm your boundaries.

Forgiveness does not mean welcoming harmful patterns back into your life.

Invite spaciousness.

Say, “I welcome peace into this part of my heart.”

This sequence is a practice, not a one-time event. Repetition lightens the load.

Try This Next

Choose one name or one moment connected to unresolved pain. Write it down. Then write the sentence: “I am willing to release this.” Keep the paper in a place where you can revisit it. Let the release deepen over days, not minutes.

Self-Forgiveness

Grief exposes the “if onlys”: If only I had called sooner. If only we had tried another doctor. If only my last words were softer. Self-forgiveness begins with accuracy: Were you acting with the knowledge and resources you had then? Hindsight carries information you did not possess at the time. Hold yourself to the truth, not to an idealized version of the past. Speak this sentence aloud: **“I was limited, not loveless.”** Repeat it when the mind re-indicts you.

Boundary Scripts

Forgiveness can coexist with sturdy boundaries. Practice short scripts so your body has language ready:

“I’m not available for that conversation today.”

“I’m choosing distance for a while.”

“I forgive you, and I’m not ready to meet.”

“That topic is off-limits; let’s talk about something else.” Scripts are not walls; they are doors you open and close with wisdom.

Repair, When Possible

If restoration is wise and safe, focus on **specific repair**, not global apologies:

- Name the behavior.
- Name its impact.
- Name the change you will practice.

Ask one question: "Is there something reasonable that would help rebuild trust?" Repair is measured in consistency, not speeches.

Try This Next

Write two boundary scripts that fit your life. Keep them on your phone. Use one within the next week. Note how your body feels before and after you speak it.

11.4 Gratitude That Strengthens

Finding Light in Difficult Days

Gratitude does not cancel grief. It does not demand that you feel good about painful events or pretend everything is fine. Instead, gratitude makes room for perspective in the midst of sorrow. It shifts the focus from what was taken to what remains, from what hurts to what still gives life meaning. This gentle widening of awareness can offer emotional steadiness on days when the world feels dim.

Psychological research shows that intentional gratitude practices help counterbalance the brain's "negativity bias," the natural tendency to notice and remember painful events more vividly than positive ones. Intentional gratitude practices help rewire attention away from loss-focused rumination toward appreciation.[170] Regular expressions of gratitude improve mood, enhance sleep quality, and reduce emotional distress. These benefits do not diminish grief but support the heart as it navigates it.

Aisha's Ritual

After losing her son, Aisha began a brief nighttime ritual. Each evening, she sat in the same chair and whispered three 'thank-yous': one about God's character, one about a person, and one about a small kindness she observed during the day. Most nights, she cried. Yet over time, she noticed that naming these small moments did not remove her pain. It made the emotional space around her pain less suffocating. Gratitude helped her breathe again.

Sunflowers Seek Light

Sunflowers turn their faces toward the light throughout the day. They do not create the light; they simply orient toward it. Gratitude works the same way. It does not erase the darkness, but it keeps you facing the direction where light enters. This orientation supports emotional balance and strengthens a person's ability to cope with difficult experiences.

A Fourteen-Day Rhythm

Days 1 – 3: Notice

Write three specific things you appreciate each evening.

Days 4 – 6: Share

Tell one person per day something you appreciate about them.

Days 7 – 9: Savor

Pick one daily activity - tea, a walk, a moment of rest - and slow down to fully experience it.

Days 10 –12: Serve

Do one quiet act of kindness each day.

Days 13 –14: Remember

Read a Psalm or a meaningful passage slowly, underlining lines that speak hope.

Each small act strengthens the heart's capacity for balance.

Moving Forward

Tonight, pause for one minute.

Place your hand over your heart. Name one thing, just one that brought comfort or steadiness today. Let that awareness settle gently within you.

Faith Window 11

"I Will Turn Their Mourning Into Joy"

There are moments in grief when the heart feels too heavy to lift and the mind too tired to make sense of anything. In such times, a gentle return to Scripture can offer a small anchor - something steady and trustworthy when everything else feels fragile. The words of Jeremiah 31:13 speak directly to this tender space: *"I will turn their mourning into joy; I will comfort them, and give them gladness for sorrow."*

This promise is found in Jeremiah's "Book of Consolation" (Chapters 30-33), written during Jerusalem's final siege. Yet two Chapters earlier comes perhaps Scripture's most misapplied verse: "**For I know the plans** (*maḥăšāḇôṯ* - thoughts, intentions) **I have for you, declares the Lord, plans for welfare** (*šālôm* - peace, wholeness) **and not for evil** (*rāʿâ* - calamity), **to give you a future and a hope** (*tiqwâ*)" (Jeremiah 29:11).

This is not a prosperity promise for individuals. It's a corporate word to exiles facing seventy years in Babylon (29:10). The "you" is plural; the "plans" include exile, captivity, and a lifetime of waiting. The verb *yāḏaʿ* (I know) implies intimate knowledge and purposeful design—God hasn't lost control.

But in its original context, the timeline is generational, not immediate. The exiles who heard this word would die in Babylon; their grandchildren would return. The promise isn't "God will fix this now"; it's "God's purposes are not defeated, even by catastrophe."

As you endure a period of grief and mourning, the arc of recovery is much shorter than the seventy years of exile experienced by the Israelites. But the principle applies. God's default posture is blessing, good, prosperity, and abundance— all triggered by our obedience. How much more so when the burden of the grief we endure is not the result of our disobedience. We can find comfort in the assurance that weeping may endure for a night, but joy comes in the morning.

This promise does not demand emotional readiness. It simply invites openness, an inner posture that makes room for comfort to enter slowly.

A Gentle Practice

- Sit comfortably
- Settle into a position where your body feels supported.
- Breathe softly
- Inhale for four counts, pause briefly, exhale for six.
- Read the verse slowly
- Let one word rise naturally: *turn*, *comfort*, or *gladness*.
- Name your sorrow
- Whisper: "Today I bring You…" and finish the sentence honestly.
- Welcome a small turning
- Ask for one gentle shift in your heart today, nothing more.
- Rest in the moment
- Allow stillness to hold you for a few breaths.

A Lesson from Nature

Just before sunrise, the world begins brightening long before the sun clears the horizon. This early light is subtle, barely noticeable, but it signals the coming day. Scientists call this "first light," a stage when the sky brightens though the sun is still hidden. In a similar way, small moments of comfort can appear before clarity arrives. They are early signs of hope.

A Quiet Conversation with God

"Father, You know the places in me that still ache. You see the memories that return without warning, and the moments when my strength feels thin. Stay near me. Turn my mourning little by little into joy. Give me comfort in the places I carry sorrow, and let gladness find its way back to me in time. Hold me gently as I continue this journey. Amen."

Chapter 11 Endnotes

157 Tedeschi, R. G., & Calhoun, L. G. (2004). Posttraumatic growth: Conceptual foundations and empirical evidence. Psychological Inquiry, 15(1), 1-18.

158 Bonanno, G. A. (2004). Loss, trauma, and human resilience. American Psychologist, 59(1), 20-28.

159 Frost, H. M. (2003). Bone's mechanostat: A 2003 update. The Anatomical Record Part A, 275(2), 1081-1101.

160 Tedeschi, R. G., & Calhoun, L. G. (2004). Posttraumatic growth: Conceptual foundations and empirical evidence. Psychological Inquiry, 15(1), 1-18.

161 Nader, K., & Hardt, O. (2009). A single standard for memory: The case for reconsolidation. *Nature Reviews Neuroscience, 10*(3), 224-234.

162 Bonanno, G. A., Wortman, C. B., & Nesse, R. M. (2004). Prospective patterns of resilience during widowhood. Psychology and Aging, 19(2), 260-271.

163 O'Connor, M. F. (2019). Grief: A brief history of research. Psychosomatic Medicine, 81(8), 731-738.

164 LaBar, K. S., & Cabeza, R. (2006). Cognitive neuroscience of emotional memory. Nature Reviews Neuroscience, 7(1), 54-64.

165 Bryant, R. A., Creamer, M., O'Donnell, M., et al. (2017). Acute and chronic PTSD symptoms. JAMA Psychiatry, 74(2), 135-142.

166 Boelen, P. A., de Keijser, J., van den Hout, M. A., & van den Bout, J. (2007). Treatment of complicated grief. Journal of Consulting and Clinical Psychology, 75(2), 277-284.

167 Shear, M. K., Wang, Y., Skritskaya, N., Duan, N., Mauro, C., & Ghesquiere, A. (2014). Treatment of complicated grief in elderly persons. JAMA Psychiatry, 71(11), 1287-1295.

168 Porges, S. W. (2021). Polyvagal theory. Comprehensive Psychoneuroendocrinology, 7, 100069.

169 Toussaint, L. L., Shields, G. S., & Slavich, G. M. (2016). Forgiveness, stress, and health: A 5-week dynamic parallel process study. Annals of Behavioral Medicine, 50(5), 727-735.

170 Kini, P., Wong, J., McInnis, S., Gabana, N., & Brown, J. W. (2016). The effects of gratitude expression on neural activity. NeuroImage, 128, 1-10.

Wood, A. M., Froh, J. J., & Geraghty, A. W. (2010). Gratitude and well-being: A revew and theoretical integration. Clinical Psychology Review, 30(7), 890-905.

Chapter 12

The Role of Faith and Science in Healing

Before continuing, it bears repeating what this book does not ask of you. You are not required to move on quickly, to explain your grief, or to spiritualize your pain into silence. There is no correct pace, no emotional checklist, and no faith test you must pass here. This book exists to walk with you, not to hurry you.

12.1 How Therapy Works with Grief

Good therapy does not erase love or rush you past your loss. It helps your brain and body process what happened in a tolerable, safe way. Different approaches use different tools, but many of them share the same goals: calming the nervous system, untangling painful thoughts, and rebuilding connection.

Some therapies gently revisit the story of the loss so that memories can be remembered without reliving the trauma every time.

Others focus on the thoughts that keep you stuck: "It was all my fault," "I should have saved them", and help you replace them with truer, kinder beliefs.

Still others teach skills for breathing, grounding, and noticing God's presence amid panic.

None of these methods are enemies of faith. They are ways of cooperating with how God designed the brain to heal - through repeated, honest, supported contact with the truth.

In practice, these supports may take different forms.

Cognitive Behavioral Therapy (CBT) helps identify and soften thought patterns that intensify distress.

Eye Movement Desensitization and Reprocessing (EMDR) is often used when grief is complicated by trauma and intrusive memories.

Acceptance and Commitment Therapy (ACT) emphasizes making space for pain while continuing to live in line with deeply held values.

Somatic and body-based therapies attend to how grief is stored and released through the nervous system.

For some, Complicated Grief Therapy provides structured support when mourning remains stalled or overwhelming.

These approaches differ in method, but they share a common aim: helping the grieving person regain steadiness without erasing love.

12.2 How Belief Affects Biology

When grief upends your world, the body does not stand at a distance. It listens to every thought, flinch, and whisper of fear. You may notice shallow breathing, a tight jaw, or a chest that won't quite open. None of this means you are "weak." It means your biology is registering loss. The encouraging truth is that what you believe and how you make meaning after loss can also speak back to the body. Belief can increase pain or ease it, slow your recovery or gently nudge it forward. Learning to notice and shape this dialogue between mind and body is not denial; it is stewardship.

Modern research shows that expectations change physiology. When a person expects relief, the brain often releases its own pain-modulating chemicals, dampening discomfort; when a person expects harm, the body can heighten pain and stress responses. Scientists call these the placebo and nocebo effects. They do so not because the pain is "imagined," but because expectation recruits real neurochemical pathways, including endogenous opioids and dopamine circuits, which alter perception and even immune activity.[171] This is one reason why encouragement from trusted voices can reduce pain, and why frightening medical language can worsen it. In grief, ominous inner sentences such as "I will never sleep again," "I'm broken beyond repair"—function like nocebos. They aren't moral failures; they are understandable reflexes. But they can be softened, updated, and retrained.

A simple illustration: imagine a concert hall at night. At first, every instrument is being tuned loudly and painfully. The conductor steps up and raises a hand. The noise doesn't disappear; it reshapes. Belief works like a conductor's hand. Your nervous system contains many "instruments" (sympathetic arousal, pain amplification, cortisol rhythms). Meaning-making and expectation do not mute them all at once, but they can coax a healthier arrangement over time.

Contemporary example

After losing her spouse, Mara began waking at 3:00 a.m. with racing thoughts and a hard thudding in her chest. She assumed, "My heart is failing." A full workup was normal. Her clinician reframed it: "Your heart is grieving. We can teach it a calmer rhythm." Together, they practiced slow-exhale breathing at bedtime, paired with a statement she could believe: "My body knows how to downshift." Within two weeks, Mara still woke some nights, but the pounding subsided. She had not erased grief; she had changed the meaning of her sensations. Expectation shifted her physiology: slower respiratory rate, increased heart rate variability, and a quieter stress axis.

Nature/science illustration.

Consider the immune system as a border of sentry trees along a river. During drought (chronic stress), the trees thin and their leaves shrink. With steady water and nutrients (healthier sleep, safer thoughts, supportive connection), the leaves return. Belief is not water by itself, but it opens the irrigation gate. Studies in psychoneuroimmunology show that perceived safety and a sense of supportive meaning are associated with more balanced inflammatory signaling and improved antibody responses. Again, this is not instant magic; it is a quiet rebalancing that accrues with practice.

None of this denies the starkness of grief. It honors it. The point is not to "think happy thoughts," but to plant true thoughts that the body can safely lean on: "I am devastated, and I am breathing; both are true." That sentence becomes an instruction to your nervous system: stay here, and soften where you can. Over time, those instructions write new patterns in the brain.

12.3 Hope and Neuroplasticity

Hope is not a mood you either have or lack. It is a cognitive-emotional skill, made of two elements: pathways (seeing plausible routes forward) and agency (believing you can take the next step).[172] Even in sorrow, hope can be trained. And because the brain can change its wiring through neuroplasticity, small, repeated acts of hope can physically remodel the circuits that regulate attention, emotion, and stress responses.[173]

Early neuroimaging studies showed measurable brain changes after relatively short periods of focused training. People who learned a new skill, for example, juggling, showed small but significant increases in gray matter in motion-related areas, which receded when practice stopped.[174] Mind-body practices and contemplative attention have been associated with structural and functional alterations in regions tied to attention regulation and emotion processing, such as the anterior cingulate and insula. While not a cure-all, these findings suggest that what we practice, we become. For the grieving heart, this means micro-practices of attention and meaning can gradually repattern reactivity.

Contemporary example.

Malik lost his sister in a sudden accident. Driving past the intersection where it happened triggered a flood of images and a spike of panic. His first goal was not to "feel nothing," but to create one pathway of choice in the moment. He practiced a brief sequence: name five blue things in the environment, lengthen the exhale for six breaths, touch the center console, and say, "I'm here." After six weeks, he still felt the ache, but the spike of panic softened sooner. The practice rewired a cue-response loop: traumatic reminder → orienting attention outward → parasympathetic nudge → anchored statement. That is neuroplasticity at the human scale.

Nature/science illustration.

Picture a meadow after a storm. Water carves channels through the grass. If more rain falls quickly, it follows the grooves, deepening them. But if the meadow has time to recover and water is redirected slowly along different routes, new rivulets form. The brain behaves similarly. After loss, certain pathways (catastrophic prediction, hypervigilance) become "storm channels." Gentle, repetitive redirection, such as orienting to the room, softening the jaw, speaking one truthful hope, encourages new tracks. Imaging and longitudinal studies suggest that repeated attentional training and meaning-making are associated with durable changes in connectivity and stress biomarkers.[175]

Hope does not mean certainty. It means identifying the next wise step when certainty is impossible: drink water; text a friend; finish one task; visit the grave; write a sentence that begins, "I miss you and I will…" These are not small psychologically; they are synaptic. Each subsequent step builds a tiny bridge. Bridges accumulate sequentially.

There is also a grief-specific nuance: some days, "hope" looks like creating room for sorrow without drowning in it. Allowing tears and then grounding the body is not backsliding. It is paired learning. The brain notices: "I can cry and still settle." Over weeks, the "still settle" pathway grows more available. This is not stoicism. It is the hard work of rewiring the nervous system toward gentler baselines.

12.4 The Convergence of Prayer, Medicine, and Mindfulness

We often treat these three domains as if they compete for the same seat. In practice, they complement one another. Medicine can stabilize physiology and treat conditions that require targeted interventions. Mindfulness, by which we simply mean steady, non-judging attention, helps you stay with the truth of the moment without getting thrown by every wave. Prayer carries the language of trust, lament, gratitude, and presence. Together, these approaches can support a grieving body-mind in ways none of them could accomplish alone.

Research on prayer and health is complex and mixed. Some controlled trials of intercessory prayer have not shown measurable benefits on specific medical outcomes, while others suggest modest associations between religious/spiritual practice and markers of well-being, reduced depressive symptoms, and longer-term mortality benefit in observational cohorts.[176] Importantly, many benefits likely flow through behavioral, social, and meaning pathways: supportive community, reduced harmful coping, more consistent health behaviors, and a broadened frame for suffering.

Neuroimaging studies of prayer and meditation point to activity in attention and emotion-related networks, overlapping with circuits that mindfulness also engages.[177] Rather than pitting them against each other, it is more honest to say: each can offer a doorway to calm attention, strengthened meaning, and renewed agency.

Mindfulness is not the absence of faith; it is the practice of present-tense noticing. For a grieving person, that might sound like: “Tears are here; I feel heat in my throat; my hands can soften on my lap.” That noticing can be paired with prayer: “God, hold me here.” When used together, prayer may supply the felt relationship and values framework, while mindfulness trains the skill of staying with experience without bracing. Both can be integrated with medical care, including sleep support, pain management, treatment for anxiety or depression, so that body and soul receive consistent, compassionate input.

Contemporary example.

After a complicated hospitalization for a cardiac event, Juanita’s grief resurfaced with fear: “If I fall asleep, I may not wake.” Her cardiology team optimized medications and reassured her about the numbers. A counselor gave her a 10-minute evening practice: breathe slowly, scan from the forehead to the toes, and end with a brief prayer of yielding. She also set a simple cue. When she reached for the lamp, she whispered, “Safe enough for now.” Within a month, her sleep extended by 45 minutes on average before her first awakening. The team did not assign credit to one method. They measured success by “total load lowered”: medication stabilized the heart, mindfulness eased arousal, and prayer softened anticipatory fear. Together, the load dropped.

Nature/science illustration.

Think of a tripod under a camera on uneven ground. One leg is medicine, one is mindfulness, one is prayer. On their own, each can steady the picture somewhat, but the frame still wobbles. With all three, the camera stabilizes enough to capture a truer image. You still see the ache, the empty chair, the anniversaries, but the picture is no longer a blur. Physiologically, that stability often shows up as steadier respiratory patterns, improved heart rate variability, and clearer day-night cortisol rhythms—none of which cancel sadness, all of which increase resilience.

If you have tried to pray and felt nothing, you are not failing. Numbness is common in grief. If you have tried mindfulness and felt more anxious, you are also not failing; some practices need gentler pacing, shorter sets, or anchor points outside the body (like sound or sight) to avoid overfocusing on painful sensations. If medication feels like an admission of defeat, consider this: using the tool that helps you engage love, memory, and meaning is not defeat. It is devotion to what matters most. The test is not purity of method; it is whether you are being helped to love well, grieve honestly, and remain present to life.

Scripture also shows that silence is not always permanent. Job heard God after long silence (Job 38), Elijah after despair (1 Kings 19), and Zechariah after enforced muteness (Luke 1). In the biblical pattern, silence is often preparatory rather than punitive, and makes room for discernment, healing, and eventual integration. Of these three, Job's account is by far the most detailed.

After 35 Chapters of Job's protest and his friends' failed theodicy, God speaks "out of the whirlwind" (*mittôk hassə'ārâ*—from within the storm, 38:1). But He doesn't answer Job's questions. Instead, He asks seventy of His own, beginning with: "Where were you when I laid the foundation of the earth? Tell me, if you have understanding" (38:4). The verb *yāsad* (laid foundation) is used of establishing buildings or nations—God pictures creation as architectural work. The interrogative *'êpōh* (where) implies not spatial location but participation: "Were you present? Did you contribute?" Job had demanded answers (Chapters 23-24, 31); God responds not with explanation but with reorientation. The divine questions span cosmology (38:4-38), meteorology (38:22-38), and zoology (38:39-39:30; 40:15-41:34), systematically dwarfing human understanding.

The cumulative effect: you cannot comprehend the governance of the physical world; how then presume to judge the moral governance of the universe? Yet this is not mockery. The Hebrew grammar uses second-person singular direct address throughout. God is engaging Job personally, inviting him into wonder, rather than explaining his suffering. Job's response (40:4-5; 42:1-6) is not "I understand now," but "I repent in dust and ashes." The repentance isn't for false accusations, as God vindicates Job against his friends (42:7). It's for demanding God fit his categories. Sometimes the answer to "Why?" is not information but encounter: seeing beyond your pain into a larger story where God remains sovereign and good, even when He does not explain Himself.

12.5 Medication and Faith: Enemies or Partners?

Many sincere believers wrestle with the question, "If I trust God, should I really take medication for my mood, sleep, or anxiety?" The fear behind the question is understandable: If I take a pill, am I saying God is not enough?

Scripture never tells us that using wise means is a lack of faith. We gladly thank God for surgeons, antibiotics, and insulin. We do not accuse the diabetic of unbelief for taking insulin or the heart patient for taking blood-pressure medicine. In the same way, there are times when the brain's chemistry is so shaken by grief, trauma, or genetics that temporary medical support is an act of stewardship rather than betrayal.

Medication cannot do the work of mourning, forgiveness, or hope. It cannot replace prayer, community, or the comfort of the Holy Spirit. But it can quiet a panic that will not stop, lift a fog deep enough to make basic tasks impossible, or steady sleep so that therapy and Scripture can actually be heard. Think of it as a tool, not a savior. Christ remains your healer; medicine is one of His instruments.

If you are considering medication, do so in prayer and in conversation with a wise physician who respects your faith. Ask what the medicine can and cannot do, how long it is usually needed, and what other supports it should be paired with, including counseling, exercise, and community interaction. Lean on trusted believers to pray with you for discernment. Using a prescribed medication in this way is not a sign of spiritual failure; it is one more way of saying, "Lord, I am receiving every good gift You provide for my healing."

Faith Window 12

"With God All Things Are Possible" (Matthew 19:26)

The sentence is simple and often quoted, but in grief, it asks for a fresh hearing. "All things are possible" does not promise that what has happened will unhappen. It does not force a silver lining over loss. It opens a different door: that presence and help are possible here, that courage is possible for the next hour, that mercy is possible when anger flares, that meaning is possible even when understanding is not. In that sense, the "all" reaches into places we think are closed: the sleepless night, the silent meal, the day of the firsts.

With God, softness can exist beside sorrow. With God, breath can come back to a tight chest. With God, memories can sting and bless in the same minute. With God, love does not end at the grave, and living does not betray the one you miss. Power is not always the removal of pain; often it is the strength to carry what remains without losing the ability to notice goodness.

God, I am in need. Hold me where I cannot hold myself. Let this hour be enough. Quiet my body, steady my mind, and keep my heart tender. Teach me to live with what I cannot change and to trust Your nearness in what I cannot fix. Amen.

Chapter 12 Endnotes

171 Wager, T. D., & Atlas, L. Y. (2015). The neuroscience of placebo effects: Connecting context, learning and health. Nature Reviews Neuroscience, 16(7), 403-418.

Benedetti, F. (2014). Placebo effects: Understanding the mechanisms in health and disease (2nd ed.). Oxford University Press.

172 Snyder, C. R., Harris, C., Anderson, J. R., Holleran, S. A., Irving, L. M., Sigmon, S. T., & Harney, P. (1991). The will and the ways. Journal of Personality and Social Psychology, 60(4), 570-585.

173 Hölzel, B. K., Carmody, J., Vangel, M., Congleton, C., Yerramsetti, S. M., Gard, T., & Lazar, S. W. (2011). Mindfulness practice leads to increases in regional brain gray matter density. Psychiatry Research: Neuroimaging, 191(1), 36-43.

174 Tang, Y. Y., Hölzel, B. K., & Posner, M. I. (2015). The neuroscience of mindfulness meditation. Nature Reviews Neuroscience, 16(4), 213-225.

175 Jha, A. P., Krompinger, J., & Baime, M. J. (2007). Mindfulness training modifies subsystems of attention. Cognitive, Affective, & Behavioral Neuroscience, 7(2), 109-119.

176 Masters, K. S., Spielmans, G. I., & Goodson, J. T. (2006). Are there demonstrable effects of distant intercessory prayer? Annals of Behavioral Medicine, 32(1), 21-26.

177 Newberg, A. B., Wintering, N. A., Yaden, D. B., Waldman, M. R., Reddin, J., & Alavi, A. (2015). A case series study of the neurophysiological effects of altered states of mind during intense Islamic prayer. Journal of Physiology-Paris, 109(4-6), 214-220.

Chapter 13

Being Present, Listening, and Available

13.1 What to Say (and What Not to Say)

There is a tender quiet that surrounds someone in grief, the kind of quiet that asks for gentleness rather than brilliance. Most people know the feeling of wanting to say the right thing but fearing they will say the wrong thing. After a loss, this pressure intensifies. Words suddenly seem too small, too clumsy, or too fragile for what the grieving heart carries. Yet the need for human presence becomes even more important. This section explores how language can either soothe or wound, and how presence often matters far more than speech.

People tending to the bereaved often fall into a predictable pattern: rushing to fill the space with explanations, advice, or spiritual conclusions. These responses come from a sincere desire to help, but they frequently miss the mark. Studies in bereavement psychology show that grieving individuals register supportive tone and emotional safety far more deeply than content itself.[178] What brings comfort is not the cleverness of a sentence but the sense that someone is willing to stand near them without shrinking from their pain.

A real-world example illustrates this with clarity. A woman named Marissa lost her teenage son in a car accident. In the early days, people offered phrases like "He's in a better place" or "God needed another angel," thinking these words brought comfort. Instead, she felt a sting of alienation, as if her son's absence needed justification rather than acknowledgment. But one friend simply sat beside her during the memorial, placed a hand gently on her back, and whispered, "This is unimaginably hard, and I'm right here." Months later, that was the moment Marissa remembered as her anchor. She said it felt like someone had given her permission to feel exactly what she felt.

Nature offers its own lesson here. When a tree suffers damage to its bark, it does not heal because another tree explains the purpose of storms. It heals because the inner cambium continues its slow work, protected by stillness and the tree's own internal design. Supportive presence works the same way; it does not eliminate the wound, but it shields the heart long enough for its deeper processes to begin.

The heart of this ministry of presence is humility. Instead of reaching for explanations or forcing meaning too early, it offers language that acknowledges the reality of the pain. Simple statements like "I'm so sorry," "I'm here with you," or "This shouldn't have happened" carry truth and kindness without presumption. Silence, too, becomes a gift when it is steady and unafraid. It serves as a reminder that the grieving person does not need to be rescued from grief, only accompanied through it.

When choosing what *not* to say, a good internal guide is to avoid anything that seeks to minimize, compare, or prematurely resolve. The grieving heart needs space more than solutions. Presence opens that space. Presence keeps it safe. Presence dignifies the one who is hurting.

13.2 The Power of Listening

Grief often arrives carrying more emotion than words. People in mourning may not know how to articulate their pain, or they may worry that speaking it aloud will overwhelm others. In such moments, listening becomes one of the most profound acts of compassion. It allows the bereaved to unfold at their own pace and to validate their inner world. Listening is not passive; it is a deliberate, attentive act that communicates, "Your story matters. Your heart matters. I am here to understand, not to direct."

Psychological research on active listening reveals its remarkable effect on emotional regulation. When a grieving person speaks and senses genuine receptivity, the brain's threat response calms. The body settles. The mind finds a bit of clarity. Listening lowers emotional overload, not because it "fixes" anything, but because it makes room for the intensity to be shared rather than carried alone.[179]

Consider the experience of Daniel, who lost his spouse after a long illness. People often asked him how he was doing, but before he could answer, they would quickly pivot to stories of their own hardships or words meant to cheer him up. He felt unseen. But during one late-night conversation, his brother simply said, "Talk as long as you need, and I won't interrupt." Daniel described that night as the first time the grief loosened its grip. With someone listening without judgment, he could finally release what he had been holding inside.

A powerful illustration from nature mirrors this process. When deep-sea divers descend into darker waters, they rely on a technique called "equalization." The pressure increases as they go deeper, and unless they release air through tiny adjustments, the mounting force becomes painful and dangerous. Listening functions like equalization for the grieving soul. As people speak their truth, pressure dissipates. The weight becomes survivable.

True listening requires presence, patience, and quiet courage. It asks the companion to withhold quick conclusions, to avoid shaping the narrative, and to resist the urge to make the grieving person "feel better." Instead, the listener becomes a safe space. A good listener tracks not only the words spoken but also the pauses, hesitations, and shifts in expression. Listening honors the full spectrum of grief: sorrow, confusion, anger, and even moments of unexpected laughter.

This form of presence conveys value in a way no speech can imitate. It reminds the grieving that their voice matters at a time when nothing else feels stable. Listening does not take away grief, but it does prevent grief from becoming isolation.

13.3 The Compassionate Companion

Walking with someone through grief requires a particular kind of companionship: steady, observant, and willing to adapt. Compassionate companionship is the art of being emotionally available without becoming intrusive, supportive without being controlling, and present without overshadowing. It is a posture of tenderness and respect, shaped by the needs of the grieving rather than the comfort of the companion.

Research on grief support shows that what people value most is not the grand gesture but consistent, thoughtful contact.[180] Small actions such as a message check-in, a shared meal, a walk taken together, or a willingness to sit through uncomfortable silence serve as reminders that they are not alone. The compassionate companion provides continuity in a world that suddenly feels ruptured.

A vivid example comes from the story of Anika, who lost her mother unexpectedly. Many friends reached out immediately, but within weeks, most drifted back into their routines. One coworker, Mia, quietly remained present. She didn't overwhelm Anika with calls but consistently left room for connection. Some days she brought lunch. Other days, she simply paused to ask, "What does today feel like?" without expecting an uplifting answer. Mia's presence gave Anika a sense of stability during a season of emotional volatility.

Nature teaches a similar lesson through the migratory behavior of certain birds. In species like the whooping crane, long flights become nearly impossible without formation flying. Each bird benefits from the lift created by the wings of the one in front, conserving energy and preserving endurance over impossible distances. When one bird weakens, another shifts position to help sustain the formation. The journey is communal. Compassionate companionship mirrors this pattern; it offers uplift when grief makes forward motion feel too costly.

Such companionship respects boundaries, understands emotional rhythms, and avoids assuming the role of problem-solver. It also involves a willingness to show vulnerability. The grieving often feel pressure to "be strong," and when a companion slows down, listens carefully, admits uncertainty about what to do, and stays anyway, it normalizes the emotional landscape. It says, without words, "We can move through this together."

Being a compassionate companion means embracing the long arc of grief, not just the immediate shock. It acknowledges that healing is not linear, and it offers a presence that does not evaporate when outward signs of coping appear. Compassion remains attentive to subtle shifts such as fatigue, withdrawal, and emotional spikes, and responds with gentleness rather than impatience.

Companionship of this kind becomes a bridge to resilience. It reinforces the truth that grief is not meant to be survived in isolation, and that caring relationships help soften the hardest seasons of life.

13.4 Becoming a Bridge, Not a Bandage

Grief asks for companionship that honors depth rather than distraction. Many well-meaning supporters try to "bandage" grief with quick encouragements, optimistic reframing, or attempts to shift attention elsewhere. These gestures, though kind in intention, can accidentally send the message that the mourner's experience is too heavy, too upsetting, or too inconvenient to be held in its full weight. The role of a true companion is not to cover the wound but to help build a bridge through it. A bridge allows movement, dignity, and agency. A bandage, when misapplied, can immobilize and suffocate.

This distinction matters because grief is not an infection to be sealed off; it is a profound human response to loss. Studies show that grief metabolizes over time through expression, connection, and shared meaning, not through suppression.[181] When someone becomes a bridge, they do not rush the person across. They walk at the mourner's pace, sometimes stopping, sometimes sitting, sometimes moving forward again. They become a presence that makes traversing the landscape of loss feel possible.

A contemporary example of "bridge behavior" comes from a young man named Trevor, whose father died unexpectedly. Most people in his life avoided the subject, fearing they would trigger pain. But his neighbor, Mr. Alvarez, approached him differently. Every Saturday morning, they met on the porch. Some weeks they spoke about the loss directly. Other weeks, they talked about sports or the weather. What mattered was the consistent presence. Trevor later said, "He never tried to fix me. He just kept showing up, and that's what helped me keep walking."

Nature offers a powerful illustration in the behavior of river stones. When water flows over them day after day, the stones neither resist nor attempt to redirect the current. They simply remain, and over time, the water shapes new paths around them. Bridges in grief work the same way.

They do not force meaning or direct emotion; they create safe passage for whatever the heart needs to feel. The mourner, like the water, finds new channels in the presence of steady support.

Becoming a bridge involves asking gentle, non-intrusive questions: "What would help you today?" "Is this a moment you want quiet or conversation?" It includes responding to emotional spikes with patience rather than judgment. It also requires the humility to avoid becoming the center of the healing narrative. The companion is not the healer but the helper, the witness, the stabilizer.

Bridges honor autonomy. They hold space without controlling it. They welcome tears, silence, anger, and laughter with equal acceptance. Above all, they resist the temptation to hurry grief along. Grief cannot be accelerated. But with a bridge beside them, a grieving person can keep moving, step by step, toward a life that still has meaning, even in the presence of loss.

13.5 Caring Without Burning Out - Self-Care for Helpers

Supporting someone in grief is sacred work, but it can also be draining. Compassion fatigue is real, and even the most well-intentioned supporters can reach a point where emotional reserves run thin. Caring without burnout requires self-awareness, boundaries, and a commitment to replenishing one's inner life. Otherwise, the helper becomes fragile, irritable, or overwhelmed. And all of these are conditions that ultimately make meaningful presence impossible.

Research in caregiver psychology indicates that people who provide long-term emotional support often underestimate their own stress load.[182] They may feel guilty stepping back or worry that taking time out for themselves signals abandonment. Yet the opposite is true: sustained compassion requires sustained restoration. Helpers who nourish themselves become more patient, more attuned, and more resilient.

A contemporary example highlights this reality.

Olivia, a close friend of a grieving widower, spent months checking on him daily, bringing meals, and listening to long, tearful conversations.

Over time, she noticed her own energy dipping. She grew irritable toward coworkers and avoided phone calls because she feared she had nothing left to give. After talking with a mentor, she realized she needed rhythm, moments of presence, and moments of rest. She told her friend, "I care about you deeply, and I'm here, but I also need to keep myself steady." He understood. Their connection strengthened, not weakened, because she honored both hearts in the relationship.

Nature offers another illustration

In forest ecosystems, mycorrhizal networks link trees together, allowing them to share nutrients and signaling chemicals. But the system has limits. When too many trees pull resources without adequate replenishment, the network weakens, destabilizing the entire forest. Healthy forests require balance with intake and output, giving and receiving. Human relationships function similarly. Helpers cannot give endlessly from an unrefreshed reservoir.

Healthy boundaries are not barriers; they are supports. They create clarity about when one is available, what one can realistically offer, and when one needs to pause. This might mean choosing specific days for check-ins, protecting personal time, or engaging in restorative practices such as walking, prayer, journaling, or seeking quiet. Effective companions are honest about their limitations because honesty fosters trust.

Self-care does not diminish compassion; it strengthens it. Helpers who attend to their own emotional health bring a steadier presence to the grieving. They offer empathy without drowning, support without depletion, and love without losing themselves. Caring for oneself ensures that the ministry of presence remains a long-lasting gift rather than a short-lived burst of sympathy.

Faith Window 13

"Rejoice with Those Who Rejoice; Mourn with Those Who Mourn" (Romans 12:15)

The heart that chooses to walk with the grieving steps into a sacred rhythm — one that honors both joy and sorrow. Romans 12:15 invites this balanced way of living. It suggests that authentic love adapts, listens, and aligns with the emotional reality of another person. In times of sorrow, this verse calls for a presence that neither fixes nor avoids but simply shares the weight of the moment. Grief becomes less isolating when another person willingly enters its space.

This passage also hints at the tenderness of shared humanity. When people mourn together, they express a quiet solidarity that does not demand explanations or solutions. It reminds the grieving that their emotions are not too much to bear, and that sorrow can be held in compassionate community. Such companionship echoes the grace of God, who meets people gently in their most vulnerable seasons.

A simple prayer brings these reflections to rest:

Prayer:

God of comfort, teach us how to walk gently with those who mourn. Help us bring presence that is steady, compassionate, and wise. Strengthen our hearts so we can support others without losing ourselves. Guide us to listen deeply, speak kindly, and remain present in both the joy and the sorrow. May our care reflect Your tenderness and bring peace to those who grieve. Amen.

Chapter 13 Endnotes

178 Neimeyer, R. A., & Jordan, J. R. (2002). Disenfranchisement as empathic failure. In K. J. Doka (Ed.), Disenfranchised grief (pp. 97-117). Research Press.

179 Weger Jr, H., Castle Bell, G., Minei, E. M., & Robinson, M. C. (2014). The relative effectiveness of active listening in initial interactions. International Journal of Listening, 28(1), 13-31.

180 Wortman, C. B., & Lehman, D. R. (1985). Reactions to victims of life crises: Support attempts that fail. In I. G. Sarason & B. R. Sarason (Eds.), Social support: Theory, research and applications (pp. 463-489). Springer.

181 Pennebaker, J. W., & Seagal, J. D. (1999). Forming a story: The health benefits of narrative. Journal of Clinical Psychology, 55(10), 1243-1254.

182 Rumpold, T., Schur, S., Amering, M., Kirchheiner, K., Masel, E. K., Watzke, H., & Schrank, B. (2016). Informal caregivers of advanced-stage cancer patients. Supportive Care in Cancer, 24(5), 1975-1982.

Figley, C. R. (2002). Compassion fatigue: Psychotherapists' chronic lack of self care. Journal of Clinical Psychology, 58(11), 1433-1441.

Chapter 14

Living Beyond Loss

When Purpose Returns

14.1 The Call to Meaning

There comes a moment in grief when silence stops echoing quite as loudly. It doesn't mean pain has vanished; only that the mind begins searching for a reason to keep moving. This search is rarely dramatic. For many, it starts with a faint restlessness, a subtle recognition that even in loss, life continues to unfold. Meaning doesn't announce itself with clarity; it whispers. The challenge is learning to listen again.

Psychologists have long observed that the human mind gravitates toward purpose as a stabilizing force. Viktor Frankl argued that people can endure almost any circumstance if they believe their lives carry meaning. Modern clinical studies affirm this idea, showing that individuals who engage in small, purpose-driven activities such as caring for a plant, supporting a neighbor, or volunteering a few hours experience lower physiological stress responses during bereavement[183] . Meaning is not an escape from grief; it is a companion that helps grief become livable.

Contemporary Example

A contemporary example comes from a woman who lost her fiancé unexpectedly six weeks before their wedding. For nearly a year, she avoided the world they had built together. One afternoon, while cleaning out a drawer she had avoided, she found a list of goals he had written. Most were simple: "learn to make homemade pasta," "visit a national park," "improve my photography skills." She folded the list and put it in her pocket. Later that month, she signed up for a photography workshop. She described the experience not as honoring him but as rediscovering a version of herself still capable of curiosity. The shift was small, almost imperceptible at first, but it marked the beginning of her personal return to meaning.

An Illustration from Nature

Nature illustrates this pattern with startling clarity. After a forest fire, certain species of pine release seeds that only open under extreme heat. The devastation activates their growth. Ecologists call these serotinous cones nature's way of ensuring renewal after destruction. The forest is not restored overnight. But the very conditions that feel ruinous become conditions in which new life takes root. Loss, too, has this strange duality: it destroys, yet it also reveals soil where unexpected beginnings can take hold.

As purpose slowly re-enters a grieving life, it often feels fragile. This fragility is normal. Neuroscientific research shows that the brain's reward circuits become sluggish during prolonged grief, especially when routines collapse abruptly.[184] Reintroducing activities that offer even mild satisfaction helps those circuits relearn engagement. This is why purpose rarely begins with grand reinventions. It starts with something like preparing a new recipe, reorganizing a room, or reconnecting with a person who once brought warmth. Smallness does not diminish meaning; it enables it to emerge sustainably.

Meaning is not something grief allows you to manufacture on command. It is something that grows at its own pace, shaped by your values, experiences, and story. What matters most is recognizing the moment when meaning begins knocking again. Sometimes it knocks softly. Sometimes it knocks from the inside.

14.2 Building New Traditions

When the familiar patterns of life are disrupted by loss, the old rituals that once brought comfort can begin to feel hollow. Even joyous occasions such as birthdays, holidays, and anniversaries become emotionally complicated. Many grieving individuals report that rituals that once anchored them now feel like shadows cast by a different life. The challenge is not to eliminate traditions, but to reshape them so they fit the changed landscape of who you are now.

Creating new traditions does not betray what was lost. It allows the present to breathe. One man who had always spent Christmas morning cooking breakfast with his adult son found himself unable to step into the kitchen the following year after his son's sudden passing. Instead of forcing himself through the old routine, he invited a few friends over in the afternoon and served a simple meal, nothing elaborate, nothing sentimental, just a different moment in the day. That single adjustment gave him space. Over time, this new pattern became a gentle annual marker, not of forgetting, but of surviving with honesty.

Traditions Matter

Science gives us an intriguing window into why traditions matter. Anthropologists studying ritual behavior note that structured practices reduce cognitive load, help regulate emotion, and produce predictable physiological calming effects, even when the rituals are newly formed.[185] In other words, the body responds not only to the emotional meaning of a tradition but to the pattern itself. Rhythm creates stability. Familiarity soothes, even newly built familiarity.

An Illustration from Nature

Nature also makes room for the emergence of new rhythms. Consider the migration of monarch butterflies. Their multigenerational journey spans thousands of miles, yet each generation must form new patterns based on its own environment. They rely on genetic instincts, shifting wind currents, and changing temperatures to establish new routes each year. Their survival depends on adaptation, not rigid repetition. Grief often forces a similar biological truth: the old pathway is gone, and the new one must be discovered by moving, sensing, adjusting.

New traditions don't have to be significant or symbolic. They may emerge accidentally. A woman who lost her brother noticed that she began taking quiet walks every evening at dusk—something she had never done before. One day, she realized this habit had become a ritual that marked the transition between day and night. It grounded her rhythm. She later described it as "a conversation with the silence." Nothing ceremonial, nothing dramatic, just a small act that supported her internal balance.

Yet new traditions can also be expressions of creative rebuilding. Families sometimes start lighting a candle on certain nights, not as a shrine to memory but as a marker of continuity. Others choose to begin an activity the loved one enjoyed, such as gardening, reading a particular author, or watching a particular genre of films, not to replicate the past, but to let life expand into the space that grief created. These rituals do not close grief; they accompany it.

The deeper purpose of new traditions is not to replace what was lost but to help life regain flow. Research in behavioral psychology notes that predictable rituals enhance a sense of agency during emotional upheaval. Agency, in turn, strengthens resilience. When the world has changed without your consent, establishing a few small practices that you choose helps restore a sense of orientation. It reminds you that even within grief, there are ways to shape your days.

Building new traditions is not an event. It is a slow unfolding. Some attempts will feel right; others will fall flat. There is no failure in the trying. The work is simply to make room, room for new rhythms, new gestures, new moments that help carry your life forward without asking you to erase what came before.

14.3 How Hope Becomes Habit

Hope rarely arrives as an emotion. More often, it begins as an interruption. Something small shifts: a thought, a moment of relief, a surprising sense of steadiness—and the mind pauses long enough to notice it. That pause is important. Neuroscientists describe hope not as a single feeling but as a cognitive process: the brain recognizes a possible future and begins evaluating the steps required to reach it. Even after deep loss, this mechanism remains available. It may be quiet, but it is not gone.

In grief, early hope can feel untrustworthy. People often report moments of lightness followed by guilt or confusion, as if feeling even slightly better dishonors what they lost. This reaction is common. The nervous system is adjusting to a new emotional environment, and hope competes with the body's memory of distress. As you will recall from Chapter 2, research shows that after prolonged stress or trauma, the amygdala becomes hypersensitive to danger signals while the prefrontal cortex struggles to maintain balance. Small hopeful experiences help recalibrate this system. They teach the brain that not every change is a threat.

A Contemporary Example

A contemporary example comes from a man who lost his mother after a long illness. For months, he lived in a cycle of exhaustion and numbness. One morning, without planning it, he stopped at a coffee shop on his way to work. He sat by the window, sipped slowly, and watched people walk by. Nothing meaningful happened. But he returned the next morning, and the next. Over time, the simple ritual became a thin thread leading him back to himself. He didn't call it healing. He called it "breathing space." Only later did he realize it was the beginning of hope becoming part of his routine.

An Illustration from Nature

Nature displays a similar pattern. Consider the regeneration of coral reefs after damage from storms or temperature shifts. When a reef is stressed, it loses color and structure. But if conditions stabilize, tiny polyps begin rebuilding centimeter by centimeter. The process is slow, sometimes imperceptible to the eye, but measurable over months and years. Recovery is not a single event; it is a habit of growth. In grief, hope behaves the same way. It returns not through dramatic breakthroughs, but through steady, repeated interactions with life.

Engagement

Hope becomes habit through engagement. Psychologists define engagement as intentional contact with meaningful activities, even when motivation is minimal. This might be watering a plant, responding to a message, stretching in the morning, or reading a few pages of a book. These micro-engagements stimulate dopamine pathways associated with reward, anticipation, and resilience. Over time, the body learns to expect the future.

One woman discovered this in an unexpected way. After losing her husband, she struggled with evenings. These were the quiet hours where loss felt especially sharp. Eventually, she began listening to short science podcasts while preparing dinner. The information offered no emotional comfort, yet something in the practice grounded her evenings. Months later, she noticed she was curious again. Her mind had begun reaching outward. She described the shift as "slow oxygen." Each small practice helped hope anchor itself inside her routines.

Habit Formation

Habit formation research helps explain why these patterns matter. Repetition strengthens neural pathways, making an experience easier to access over time.[186] Even hope, which feels abstract, becomes easier to reach when it is reinforced by predictable behaviors. It becomes a companion rather than a visitor.

But hope is not linear. People often experience emotional setbacks that make progress feel undone. These reversals do not negate growth; they reflect the natural oscillation of grief. Physiologically, the body cycles between states of heightened stress and partial restoration as it adapts to the demands of loss. The presence of setbacks does not mean hope has failed. It means the system is still recalibrating.

Rebuilding life after loss requires patience, but not the passive kind. It requires the kind of patience that notices small improvements and gives them space to accumulate. When hope becomes part of daily rhythms, even in modest, almost invisible ways, it reshapes the inner landscape. It enlarges capacity. It teaches the heart that moving forward is possible without erasing what was loved.

Hope, in the end, is less of an emotion and more of a practice. A quiet turning toward life. A willingness to participate again, even with wounds. A gentle agreement with the future.

14.4 7 Small Steps to an Emotional Reset

As hope begins to re-enter a life shaken by loss, routines often feel either too heavy or too hollow. Many grieving people want to regain a sense of steadiness but do not have the capacity for large commitments or structured programs. What they need are small, repeatable touches of care—brief resets that do not demand more than they can offer in any given moment. The following seven steps are designed with that reality in mind. They can be used in any order, at any pace, within any seven-day stretch. None is meant to create pressure. They simply open small spaces in which emotional breathing room can return.

Step 1 - Slower Breathing (3 minutes)

Slow your breathing just a little for three quiet minutes. Not deep. Not controlled. Simply slower than your usual pace. Even this small shift can soften the internal tension grief often builds. You can repeat this as often as you like throughout the day. It is a gentle reset for the body.

Step 2 - One Honest Sentence

Write a single sentence that describes how you feel right now. One is enough. It does not need to be polished or clear. Putting a feeling on paper reduces the strain of holding everything inside. If all you can manage is a fragment, it still counts.

Step 3 - A Small Touch of Order

Select one tiny area - a corner of a desk, a single drawer, or a small section of a shelf- and tidy it for a few minutes. Not as a task to accomplish, but as a way to give your mind a brief sense of steadiness. A little order in a small space can make the inner world feel less crowded.

Step 4 — A Glimpse of Life Outside

Spend a moment looking at something alive: the sky shifting color, a plant by a window, a tree moving in the wind, or a bird crossing your view. You do not have to step outside; even watching through a window helps. Life continues with a patient rhythm, and your mind often finds comfort in matching it.

Step 5 - One Gentle Task

Choose a task that takes under five minutes and carries no emotional weight. Wash one cup. Fold two items of clothing. Reply to a single message. These small completions do not rush healing; they simply remind you that, even in exhaustion, you can still move a little.

Step 6 - A Low-Pressure Connection

Reach out to one person with a simple message. It does not need to explain anything. "Thinking of you today" is enough. Grief can make the world feel smaller. A brief connection widens it again without demanding more than you can comfortably give.

Step 7 - Permission to Feel

Pause for a moment and allow today's feelings to be what they are. Not what others expect, and not what you wish they were—simply what they are. Giving yourself permission to feel is often more healing than attempting to change or suppress anything.

Using These Steps

You can repeat a single step many times or skip others entirely on days when capacity is low. Some days you may use several; other days only one. Both are normal. Emotional reset begins with small, compassionate choices. Healing does not need perfection—only presence, one small step at a time.

These seven steps do not eliminate grief, nor do they ask you to rush what cannot be rushed. They simply make space for hope to settle back into its rightful place. With that gentleness in mind, we turn now to a quieter reflection.

Faith Window 14

"Behold, I Am Making All Things New" (Revelation 21:5)

There are moments in grief when the world feels permanently dimmed, as if joy belongs to another lifetime. In those moments, the words "I am making all things new" do not demand belief; they simply offer room to breathe. They speak to the possibility that life can expand again, even when the heart feels worn thin. Renewal is not a sudden reversal. It is a slow tenderness—a quiet assurance that God's presence holds steady even when you cannot feel where the path leads next.

This promise is not about forgetting what was lost. It is about the gentle unfolding of life around the ache. Newness, in this sense, is not a replacement but a soft restoration of strength. It is the gradual return of color to places that felt beyond repair. Even when the road ahead remains uncertain, this verse reminds us that nothing in God's hands stays frozen in sorrow forever. He works patiently, piece by piece, breath by breath, rebuilding the human spirit from the inside out.

Prayer

Lord, stay close as life slowly reshapes itself around the empty places. Give strength for the small steps, comfort for the heavy hours, and quiet assurance that Your renewing work continues even when we cannot see it. Help the heart welcome gentle hope without fear, and let Your calming presence guide each new beginning. Make room for peace, for purpose, and for moments of unexpected grace. Amen.

Chapter 14 Endnotes

183 Park, C. L. (2010). Making sense of the meaning literature: An integrative review of meaning making and its effects on adjustment to stressful life events. Psychological Bulletin, 136(2), 257-301.

184 O'Connor, M. F., Wellisch, D. K., Stanton, A. L., Eisenberger, N. I., Irwin, M. R., & Lieberman, M. D. (2008). Craving love? Enduring grief activates brain's reward center. NeuroImage, 42(2), 969-972.

185 Norton, M. I., & Gino, F. (2014). Rituals alleviate grieving for loved ones, lovers, and lotteries. Journal of Experimental Psychology: General, 143(1), 266-272.

186 Lally, P., Van Jaarsveld, C. H., Potts, H. W., & Wardle, J. (2010). How are habits formed: Modelling habit formation in the real world. European Journal of Social Psychology, 40(6), 998-1009.

Appendix

When Grief and Justice Collide:

Communal Anger After Violent or Wrongful Loss

"How long, O Lord? Will you forget me forever?" — Psalm 13:1

This book has addressed grief's many companions: anger, guilt, numbness, depression, and loneliness. Most of what has been written addresses the grief that unfolds quietly inside an individual heart. But there is another face of grief that demands its own treatment before these pages close—and that is the grief that erupts in the streets.

In recent years, communities across America and around the world have grieved deaths that felt not only devastating but *preventable* — and that distinction changes everything. A drunk driver who crossed the center line. A pilot whose company ignored its own safety protocols. A government that failed to post a warning sign before a deadly curve. Federal agents, police officers, or armed individuals take the lives of citizens who posed no credible threat. What these losses share is not a category of perpetrator, but a category of wound: the knowledge that someone's negligence, recklessness, or deliberate disregard for human life shortened the days of someone deeply loved. In these deaths, grief does not arrive alone. It arrives with a companion that refuses to be quiet: *the demand for accountability.*

In the agonizing aftermath, loved ones and neighbors have found themselves holding two unbearable things at once: the private devastation of personal loss, and the searing, collective rage of a community that believes justice has been denied. This is not garden-variety grief. This is grief and anger locked in an embrace that neither can escape—and it requires its own pastoral theology.

The Legitimacy of Communal Anger

Let us be clear from the outset: communal anger in the face of injustice is not sin. It is not a failure of faith. It is not immaturity. It is the human soul's instinctive cry that something sacred has been violated—and that cry has deep biblical roots.

In Matthew 2:18, the prophet Jeremiah's ancient lament is invoked again at the slaughter of the innocents: *"A voice was heard in Ramah, weeping and great mourning, Rachel weeping for her children; and she refused to be comforted, because they are no more."* This was not a private grief. It was communal catastrophe—an entire generation of children taken by state violence. And Scripture does not rush to silence Rachel. It records her anguish and calls it by name.

In Revelation 6:9–10, the souls of those who had been slain cry out from beneath the altar: *"How long, O Lord, holy and true, until You judge and avenge our blood?"* These are not voices of rebellion. They are the voices of those unjustly killed, demanding that heaven itself answer for what earth has done. God does not rebuke them. He tells them to rest a little longer—and He promises that their cry has been heard.

Communal anger after wrongful death is, at its deepest level, a demand for the restoration of divine order. It is a community's refusal to accept that a human life had no value. That refusal is not only understandable—it is holy.

What Makes This Grief Different

When a loved one dies of illness or old age, grief arrives with the quiet understanding that loss is part of the human condition. It is devastating, but it carries no perpetrator. When a loved one is killed wrongfully—especially by those sworn to protect them—grief arrives with a companion that refuses to be quiet: the demand for accountability.

This compound grief carries unique physiological and psychological characteristics that counselors, pastors, and caregivers must understand:

The stress cascade discussed in Chapter 5 is intensified by ongoing exposure—news cycles, trials, public debates, and community confrontations keep the nervous system in a perpetual state of hypervigilance that normal bereavement does not produce.

The search for meaning that normally begins weeks after loss is often short-circuited by a clear, external cause. The "Why?" is not metaphysical—it is moral. "Why did they do this?" replaces "Why does God allow suffering?" and can redirect grief energy into fury before it has had time to become lament.

The identity earthquake described in Chapter 1 becomes communal. An entire neighborhood must renegotiate its sense of safety, its relationship to authority, and its understanding of its own worth in the eyes of those who govern them.

Moral injury—a deep wound to one's sense of what is right and good—overlays the grief. Survivors and witnesses carry not only sorrow but also a shattered assumption: that the institutions they were told to trust can be trusted.

Righteous Anger Versus Destructive Rage

The Apostle Paul drew a line in Ephesians 4:26 that is essential here: *"Be angry and do not sin; do not let the sun go down on your anger."* The verse does not forbid anger. It commands its stewardship. There is a form of anger that protests injustice without becoming injustice itself—and there is a form of anger that, left unprocessed, consumes its host and harms the innocent.

Righteous anger names what is wrong. It marches, it speaks, it demands accountability, it refuses to let a death pass unremarked. It keeps the memory of the victim alive in the public square. It has a face and a direction. History's great movements for justice were fueled, in large part, by communities who chose to transform communal grief into righteous, organized, purposeful protest.

Destructive rage, by contrast, turns inward and sideways. It destroys neighborhoods, fractures families, and ultimately dishonors the memory of the one who was lost. It harms people who had no role in the original injustice. And it gives those who wished to dismiss the grievance a convenient distraction. When anger crosses that line, it no longer serves the victim. It consumes the living.

The pastoral task is not to suppress communal anger—that would be toxic positivity of the worst kind, dishonoring both the living and the dead. The pastoral task is to help communities channel that anger toward righteousness rather than ruin. As I noted in Chapter 4, anger refined by grace becomes fuel for mercy. It can build foundations, fund scholarships, reform laws, and comfort new mourners. The history of every justice movement confirms it.

The Role of the Faith Community

In moments of communal grief and rage, the faith community faces perhaps its most demanding calling. It cannot offer easy answers. It cannot minimize the pain. It cannot retreat to sanitized theology that pretends the Cross was tidy. What it can offer—what it must offer—is what Job's friends offered before they opened their mouths: presence.

Practically, this means:

Open the doors. The church building is not merely a place of worship on Sunday mornings. In a community convulsing with grief and anger, it must become a sanctuary in the oldest sense of the word—a safe place for people to weep, to shout, to sit in silence, and to feel held.

Hold space for lament before you offer hope. Read Lamentations aloud. Pray the imprecatory Psalms together. Give the community permission to feel what it feels before asking it to move toward anything else. Hope offered too soon becomes pressure, not promise.

Name the injustice from the pulpit. Silence from spiritual leaders in the face of wrongful death is its own wound. The community needs to hear its shepherds say: "This was wrong." Not "God has a plan"—not yet. First: "This was wrong."

Accompany the grieving through every public stage—the vigil, the march, the trial, the verdict, the silence after the verdict. Do not disappear when the cameras leave. Sustained presence is the medicine, and it must outlast the news cycle.

Offer practical help that honors dignity. Meals, legal referrals, counseling, childcare, and financial assistance are all forms of bearing one another's burdens (Galatians 6:2). They say, without words, that this community will not be abandoned.

A Word to Those Who Grieve with Rage

If you are reading this in the aftermath of a violent and wrongful death—perhaps the death of someone you loved, perhaps someone in your neighborhood, perhaps a stranger whose face has become the symbol of your own fear—hear this:

Your anger is not un-Christian. Your anger is not a sign that your faith has failed. Your anger, offered honestly to God, is one of the most ancient forms of prayer in the Bible. The Psalms are full of it. God preserved every cry. He has preserved yours.

But anger, like every powerful force, must be stewarded. The same energy that can march for justice can—if unguided—destroy the very community it set out to defend. So let your anger be directed, not dissipated. Let it ask, *"What can I build from this? What can I change? What can I do that honors the one I lost?"*

And know this: grief does not require you to forgive on a schedule. Forgiveness, as I noted in Chapter 11, is the decision to release the emotional grip that keeps you tied to what hurt you. It does not mean pretending no injustice occurred. It does not mean abandoning the pursuit of accountability. It means refusing to let the perpetrator's action also claim your future. That distinction matters enormously, and only you—with God's help—can navigate when and how you arrive there.

Faith Window — Appendix

"How long, O Lord, holy and true, until You judge and avenge our blood?" Revelation 6:10

The martyrs beneath the altar did not pray polite prayers. They cried out for justice. And God's answer was not rebuke but promise: "Rest a little longer… until the number of your fellow servants… was completed." Heaven holds every cry for justice.

Not one is lost. Not one is forgotten. Not one goes unanswered
in the fullness of time.

In the meantime, the God who sees every sparrow that falls also saw the life that was taken. He saw the face of your loved one. He knows their name. He kept count of their days. And He is not indifferent to the manner of their ending.

Bring your rage to Him. He is large enough to hold it. He will not flinch. He will not correct you too quickly. And in His time—always in His time—He will turn your mourning into something neither injustice nor death could ever have predicted: *a life that still carries meaning, and a love that refuses to be extinguished.*

A Note for Pastors, Counselors, and Community Leaders:

If you are walking alongside a community in the aftermath of a wrongful death, the full resources of this book remain available to you. Chapters 4 (anger), 10 (community in recovery), 13 (presence and listening), and 14 (meaning after loss) are especially relevant. Do not be afraid to name both the grief and the injustice from the same breath. God is the God of the broken heart and the God of justice. He is not confused by the intersection of the two. Neither should we be.

And for every community waiting for justice that has not yet come: weeping may endure for the night. But joy—and justice—are coming in the morning.

My Journal

Control your grief before it controls you.

Get a Grip on Your Grief!

Journal

Control your grief before it controls you.

Support Contacts

(Please input contact details ASAP)

	NAME	TELEPHONE
Reliable friend		
Reliable friend		
Reliable friend		
Medical Doctor		
Counselor		
Clinician		
Therapist		
Pastor/Priest/Elder		
Pastor/Priest/Elder		
Imam/Qazi/Sheikh		
Pandit/ Swami/Guru		
Grief Hotline		

About the Author

Godfrey E. McAllister spent the first two decades of his life in Guyana, South America, the country of his birth. In 1972, he migrated to Jamaica to study at the Jamaica Theological Seminary. Four years later, he graduated with his Bachelor's degree, majoring in Theology and minoring in Psychology. He simultaneously acquired a Diploma in Guidance Management.

His first employment in Jamaica was as a Guidance Counselor with the Ministry of Education. Two years later, he made a career switch and entered the world of Insurance Sales with **Life of Jamaica** in October 1978.

Godfrey knew nothing about sales, and so he invented most of what he did. Apparently, his strategies, which he credits to his love for people, paid off. In his first three months at Life of Jamaica, he shattered the New Agent's record and qualified for the Million Dollar Round Table (MDRT) in 1978. He again qualified for MDRT in 1979, and in 1980, he qualified for the ultimately prestigious Top of Table section of the international Million Dollar Round Table.

After a psychologically induced reversal in fortunes, resulting in the unpardonable industry sin of zero sales production for three consecutive years, Godfrey was fired by Life of Jamaica but was immediately hired by **American Life Insurance Company**'s Jamaica operations. A breath of fresh air was all it took to revive him, and in the year he was hired, he topped the company's Jamaica production charts. He topped ALICo's Caribbean production charts in his second year and, in his third year, became ALICo's worldwide Personal Accident Insurance Sales Agent. This time, he cemented his legacy by retaining ALICo's worldwide #1 position for 7 consecutive years, breaking his own record each year.

Throughout his life, Godfrey has been involved in a wide variety of Christian Ministries at the church level and in para-church organizations such as Youth For Christ and **Child Evangelism Fellowship**. But his experiences have by no means been limited to Christian activities. Godfrey worked in numerous 'people' organizations, and among others, founded **United Consumers In Action** (UCIA), Jamaica's most aggressive

Consumer Advocacy group. Godfrey enjoys an enviable record of successfully resolving Consumers' complaints at 96%, without ever needing to go to court. He even laid the foundation for Jamaica's first Consumer Protection Law, now enshrined in his published Human Relations major Doctoral thesis, "***Winning the War? Consumer Survival in a Free Market Economy***".

Additionally, Godfrey has authored several other books including, "***You've Got All it Takes to Succeed***" — his published thesis for his Master's degree in Theocentric Counseling; "***Young Consumer Power***", "***Put Him Back America***!", and "***Think… Speak… Dominate in 15 seconds or less***."

Dr. McAllister is a Chartered Life Underwriter, a Chartered Financial Consultant, a Supreme Court Mediator, and a Journalist. He has hosted several radio programs, including "***The Children's Bible Club***", "***Friend in Need***", "***Consumer Power Hour***", and has produced and hosted the Television series, "***A God Pickney Dem – The Show that Listens to Children.***"

Godfrey is a Motivational Speaker, a Distinguished Toastmaster, and Toastmasters International's 6-time multi-District Impromptu Speaking Champion, and World Champion of Public Speaking Finalist from a field of 30,000 contestants from 140 countries.

Drawing on his vast and varied life experiences, inspired by his forays into Neuroscience, and concerned about the potential harm that uncontrolled grief can cause to millions of people of all ages, genders, ethnicities, and socio-economic status, Godfrey embarked on writing the most challenging book of his life. Three years later, he now offers to the world – "**Get a Grip on Your Grief!** *Control your grief before it controls you.*" His work merges God's wisdom enshrined in the Bible with endorsements by Scientists across many disciplines. This book is where theology, psychology, physiology, sociology, and neuroscience converge. David may not have been able to explain, but he concluded accurately in Psalm 139:14, "I will praise You, for I am fearfully *and* wonderfully made; Marvellous are Your works, and *that* my soul knows very well.

Glossary

Comprehensive Glossary of Specialist Terms

used in

Get a Grip on Your Grief!

Godfrey E. McAllister, Ph.D.

The terms defined in this glossary reflect an integrated framework that draws on neuroscience, psychology, pastoral theology, and lived human experience. Clinical terms referenced from the DSM-5-TR are included for clarity and diagnostic literacy, not to reduce grief to pathology. Theological interpretations are presented as complementary perspectives alongside established scientific descriptions. Clinical classification does not imply spiritual failure or moral deficiency.

A

Acceptance

Often described as the final stage in Kübler-Ross's model, though Kübler-Ross herself later clarified that the stages were never linear or prescriptive.
Critiqued for oversimplifying the endpoint, the book argues that grief involves integration rather than acceptance.

Acute Grief Response

The immediate physiological and psychological reaction to loss, characterized by shock, disbelief, and heightened stress response

Acute Stress Disorder (DSM-5-TR)

A trauma-related disorder involving intrusive memories, avoidance, negative mood or cognition, and heightened arousal occurring 3 days to 1 month after a traumatic event. May precede PTSD.
Describes the body's emergency state in early bereavement

Acute Stress Reaction (ASR)

Built-in emergency reflex that floods the bloodstream with adrenaline and cortisol when devastating news strikes. Common features include dissociation, hyperarousal, emotional numbing, and cognitive narrowing.
Explains why the body outruns the intellect during initial loss

Adaptive Dependency

Healthy reliance on others that protects against prolonged grief while still maintaining personal agency
Contrasted with maladaptive dependency; involves accepting help while taking small steps independently

Adrenaline

Stress hormone released during fight-or-flight response; increases heart rate, blood pressure, and energy
Part of the stress cascade is activated during acute grief and bereavement

Affect Labeling

The practice of naming emotions to reduce limbic reactivity and engage prefrontal regulation

Reduces amygdala activity when processing grief emotions

Amygdala

The brain's alarm system processes emotional responses, especially fear and threat detection
Becomes hyperactive during grief; quiets when emotions are named, or safety is established

Anger (in Grief)

Grief with teeth: a protest response when love collides with loss
Described as grief's witness to the violation of something sacred; can be sanctified rather than suppressed

Anticipatory Adaptation

The mind's ability to rehearse adversity and build emotional elasticity before impact
Biblical examples include Joseph storing grain, Noah building the ark before the flood

Anterior Cingulate Cortex

Plays a central role in processing emotional pain and distress, overlapping with, but not identical to, physical pain pathways. Usage: Activated when emotional rejection or bereavement occurs

Anxiety (Grief-Related)

A heightened state of physiological arousal where the threat-detection system remains hyperactive after loss
Body acting as if everything is a threat; the nervous system's survival response to an unsafe world

B

Bereavement

The state of having lost someone significant through death encompasses grief and mourning
Distinguished from grief (emotional response) and mourning (cultural expression)

Bereavement-Related Immune Suppression (Grief Effect)

Biological marker of bereavement showing reduced lymphocyte activity and immune suppression
Based on a 1977 British study showing that widows are more vulnerable to infections after loss

Biology of Bereavement

The measurable physiological state involving stress hormone cascades, immune suppression, and organ system disruption
Shows grief is not "just sadness" but a biological emergency

Broken Heart Syndrome (Takotsubo Cardiomyopathy)

Temporary heart failure triggered by emotional shock; the left ventricle balloons, mimicking a heart attack
Demonstrates that intense emotional pain can literally reshape the heart muscle

C

Cognitive Behavioral Therapy (CBT)

A form of psychotherapy that helps identify and modify unhelpful thought patterns. Used in grief therapy to address rumination, guilt, and maladaptive beliefs about loss

Cognitive Dissonance

Psychological discomfort arising from holding conflicting beliefs, information, or realities simultaneously
Explains the "This can't be true" response during the acute bereavement window

Cognitive Pre-Appraisal

The alignment of thought and spirit before impact through meditation and wisdom practices
Prepares the soul for crisis; what counselors call cognitive reframing in advance

Cognitive Reframing

Changing how stress is interpreted to alter emotional outcomes; "renewing the mind" in biblical terms
Shifts from "Why me?" to "What now, Lord?"; transforms mental battlefield

Complicated Grief

Grief that locks onto the nervous system and does not release; persistent, impairing yearning and functional decline
Requires professional intervention when normal grief becomes chronic and disabling

Cortisol

Primary stress hormone released by adrenal glands; suppresses inflammation in the short term but breaks down tissues with chronic exposure
Doubles or triples baseline in the recently bereaved; chronic elevation weakens immunity

Covenant Love

Deep, stubborn desire to stay with God even when you don't understand Him; survives emotional collapse
Distinguished from emotional clarity; Peter's "to whom shall we go?" (John 6:68)

Covenant Memory (Theological)

Recollection that God who raised before will raise again, stands on history, not sentiment
True Christian hope; divine certainty walking with human ache

D

Default-Mode Network

The brain network governing reflection and meaning-making shows reduced activity after acute loss
Explains blankness/numbness that many describe as "feeling nothing."

Denial

Not lying but pacing; a protective story that helps the soul face pain in increments. In clinical psychology, denial is understood as a defense mechanism that reduces immediate psychological threat.
Moderates autonomic arousal; allows grief to be absorbed gradually rather than all at once

Depression (Grief-Related)

Depletion rather than hopelessness; emotional temperature lowered to survive shock; not only sorrow but absence. Distinct from major depressive disorder unless symptoms persist, intensify, or generalize beyond the grief context
Natural neurochemical response when the brain's reward system takes a blow from relational connection loss

Disbelief

The mind's emergency brake keeps the psyche from collapsing by throttling emotional input until cortisol drops

First safety valve; not denial of reality but the brain's protective circuit

Disenfranchised Grief

Grief that is not socially acknowledged or validated, such as grief over a miscarriage, pet loss, or non-traditional relationship. Lack of social support intensifies suffering.

Disorientation

Collapse of orientation when disbelief and denial wane; vestibular system alterations under high emotional stress
Feeling of "falling into a hole"; pressure that dissipates when equalized through honest expression

Dissociation

Automatic buffering state, where the mind distances itself from reality to prevent psychological overload
Temporary suspension of normal emotional processing; peritraumatic dissociation

Dopamine

Neurotransmitter associated with reward, anticipation, and resilience; levels drop during prolonged grief
Reactivated through small, purposeful engagement; helps the brain relearn the expectation of the future

Dual Process Model

The framework showing grief involves oscillation between loss-oriented focus and restoration-oriented focus
Healthy grieving moves between processing pain and engaging daily life; not a linear progression

E

EMDR (Eye Movement Desensitization and Reprocessing)

A psychotherapy technique using bilateral stimulation (eye movements, tapping) to process traumatic memories. Used when grief is complicated by trauma.

Embodied Cognition

Physical acts of prayer (kneeling, raising hands, breathing deeply) that translate faith into physiology
Shows how body participation in spiritual practice creates measurable biological change

Embodied Hope (Theological)

Belief manifested through the physical body; grief is embodied theology
Every heartbeat slowing, sigh releasing, tear finding peace is evidence that the Shepherd tends the flock

Emotional Granularity

The ability to name and distinguish specific feelings rather than vague terms reduces amygdala activity
Saying "I feel angry" vs. "I feel bad"; activates the prefrontal cortex to calm the alarm center

Emotional Aftershocks

Irregular involuntary pulses of emotion that strike after initial impact; the nervous system recalibrates under pressure
Not regression but normal integration of trauma into conscious reality

Emotional Flattening

Temporary protective dissociation when the emotional system burns too hot for too long — Brain reducing overload; described biblically as "spirit grows faint" (Psalm 142:3)

Endogenous Opioids

The body's natural pain-relieving and soothing agents, including endorphins
Released during crying, especially when it occurs in supportive social contexts

F

Five Stages of Grief

Kübler-Ross's model (denial, anger, bargaining, depression, acceptance) was originally for terminally ill patients, not bereaved survivors
Critiqued as misapplied, oversimplified, and harmful when treated as prescriptive rather than descriptive

G

Grace (Greek: χάρις, charis)

The unmerited favor and enabling power of God are freely given to humanity. In grief, grace provides strength to endure suffering, forgiveness for guilt and regret, and the gradual restoration of hope. Not the removal of pain but the presence of God within it, sustaining the bereaved through what feels unbearable (2 Corinthians 12:9).

Grief Response Matrix

Three interconnected parts (body, mind, spirit) that form a circle where each speaks and listens to others
Guides holistic care during grief; illustrates how healing requires attending to all three domains

H

Heart Rate Variability (HRV)

Variation in time between heartbeats; higher variability indicates better autonomic regulation and resilience
Improved through prayer, gratitude, and meaning-making practices

Hematidrosis

A rare stress response where fragile capillaries rupture under extreme pressure, causing sweat to become like drops of blood
Jesus in Gethsemane (Luke 22:44); shows Christ entered same crisis state humans experience

Homeostasis

The body's ability to maintain stable internal conditions despite external changes. Grief disrupts homeostasis across multiple systems (sleep, appetite, temperature, mood).

Hope (Psychological Definition)

Cognitive-emotional skill is made of pathways (seeing routes forward) and agency (believing you can take the next step)
Can be trained through small repeated acts; physically remodels brain circuits

HPA Axis (Hypothalamic-Pituitary-Adrenal Axis)

The Major stress system that sends chemical signals from the brain's hypothalamus to the adrenal glands to release cortisol
Becomes dysregulated within days of profound grief; chronic exposure breaks down tissues

Hypervigilance

State of heightened sensory sensitivity and exaggerated alertness; scanning for threats even in safe spaces

Like a deer remaining alert hours after the predator disappears, part of anxiety's companion role in grief.

Hypothalamus

A small brain region that regulates body temperature, hunger, thirst, sleep, and the stress response. Sends signals to the pituitary gland during the stress cascade.

I

Immune Collapse

Significant, but often temporary suppression of immune markers (reduced lymphocyte activity) following bereavement.

Part of the stress cascade; bereaved spouses and parents more vulnerable to infections

Implicit Regulation

Theologically interpreted as unseen alignment of body and soul through divine empathy (Spirit interceding with groanings)

When feeling faithless, a person may be most carried; Romans 8:26

L

Lament

Grief with direction; an honest cry that begins in pain but moves toward petition and eventually praise

Faithful cry, bringing confusion to God; restructures emotion from chaos toward communion

Limbic System

The brain's seat of emotion; includes the amygdala, and works with the hypothalamus to bridge physical and spiritual

Bridge that shakes during grief; grace steadies it

Loneliness (in Grief)

Not just absence of people but absence of a particular person whose presence shaped the world; irreplaceability

Three forms: relational (missing specific person), identity (missing version of self that existed with them), social (out of sync with unchanged world)

M

Major Depressive Disorder (DSM-5-TR)

A mood disorder defined by ≥5 symptoms during the same 2-week period (including depressed mood and/or loss of interest/pleasure), causing clinically significant distress/impairment; not attributable to substances/medical conditions and not better explained by bipolar disorder.

Maladaptive Dependency

Unhealthy dependence, expecting others to carry what only God and time can heal

Linked with complicated bereavement; contrasted with adaptive dependency

Meaning-Making

Process of converting pain into narrative; narrative into testimony; finding a coherent story within loss

Psychologists call it post-traumatic growth; believers know it as sanctification through suffering

Mourning

Cultural expression and outward manifestation of grief
Distinguished from grief (internal response) and bereavement (state of loss)

N

Neuroplasticity

The brain's ability to change its own wiring through experience, new connections supporting new stability
Small repeated acts of hope physically remodel circuits regulating attention, emotion, and stress

Nocebo Effect

When negative expectations heighten pain and stress responses through neurochemical pathways

Ominous inner sentences ("I will never sleep again") function like nocebos; they can be re-trained

Norepinephrine

A stress hormone and neurotransmitter that increases alertness, arousal, and focus during threat or loss. Works alongside adrenaline in the fight-or-flight response.

Numbness (Psychic)

Neurological protection; brain mechanism that shields from experiences that would overwhelm if felt all at once
Not weakness but design; traumatic shock or dissociation

O

Oscillation (in Grief)

Healthy pattern of moving back and forth between engaging loss and turning toward restoration tasks
Not regression when emotions return; it's how the nervous system regulates between processing pain and rebuilding balance

Oxytocin

A bonding hormone that returns through contact, touch, and community after stress
Part of the renewal process; released during crying in supportive contexts

P

Parasympathetic Nervous System

Body's calming system; releases body from siege state; activates during prayer and soft worship
Triggered by slow exhale breathing, lowers heart rate and blood pressure

Peritraumatic Dissociation

Temporary suspension of normal emotional processing to prevent psychological overload
People describe "watching from outside" or "functioning automatically."

Pituitary Gland

A pea-sized gland at the base of the brain that releases hormones regulating growth, metabolism, and stress. Part of the HPA axis.

Placebo Effect

When positive expectation recruits real neurochemical pathways (endogenous opioids, dopamine) to reduce pain
Expectation changes physiology; belief can speak back to the body

Pneuma (Theological)

Spirit: seat of meaning, conscience, connection to God

In the Trinity of healing (spirit, mind, body), the pneuma gives mind meaning

Pneumopsychosomatic Model

The author's framework examines the interplay between spirit (pneuma), mind (psyche), and body (soma). This model is theological-integrative, not yet a formal medical diagnostic system. True recovery requires wholeness across all three dimensions; spirit gives mind meaning, mind gives body instruction, body gives spirit expression.

Polyvagal Theory

A theory by Stephen Porges describing how the vagus nerve regulates the body's stress response and social engagement. Explains why presence, voice, and safe connection calm the nervous system during grief.

Post-Traumatic Growth (PTG)

Positive psychological change following profound disruption appears in five areas: appreciation for life, deeper relationships, increased strength, new possibilities, and spiritual deepening
Not that trauma was good, but that capacities/insights emerge that didn't exist before

Post-Traumatic Grief Mitigation (PTGM)

The author's term for preparing the heart before it breaks; building resilience before loss
Anticipatory adaptation grounded in the theology of preparedness

Post-Traumatic Stress Disorder (DSM-5-TR)

A trauma-related disorder characterized by re-experiencing, avoidance, negative mood or cognition changes, and hyperarousal persisting beyond one month after trauma exposure.

Prefrontal Cortex

The brain's reasoning center is responsible for planning, sequencing, and emotional evaluation
Temporarily impaired during shock; regains function as stress subsides

Prolonged Grief Disorder (DSM-5-TR)

A diagnosable grief condition marked by persistent yearning, identity disruption, emotional pain, and functional impairment lasting 12 months or longer after a loss.

Protective Dissociation

Brain reducing overload by temporarily flattening emotional response
When the emotional system burns too hot, too long; allows vital functioning to continue

Psyche (Theological)

Mind: translator of experience into perception; organizes memories, constructs narrative
In the healing trinity, gives body instruction; cognitive renewal rewires loops toward hope

Psychic Numbness

Early response to significant loss; neurological protection shielding from overwhelming impact

One of the most immediate and universal reactions allows survival of the first hours/days

Psychophysiological Coherence

Harmony between body rhythms and emotional states; synergy between the nervous system and the spirit
Gratitude, singing, and worship synchronize heart rate and respiration, reducing stress hormones

Psychoneuroimmunology

The study of how psychological states (stress, grief, social connection) affect the nervous system and immune function. Explains why grief increases vulnerability to illness.

R

Resilience

Sanctified elasticity; ability to bend under pressure without breaking; the capacity to recover equilibrium after disruption
Not stoicism but rebalancing; common grace rather than rare gift

Resilience Spectrum

Continuum from emotionally immobilized to oscillators to adaptive mourners; most people move through all three zones
Removes guilt from the equation; shows grief fluctuates rather than progresses linearly

Resilience Trajectories

Bonanno's finding that recovery doesn't move in straight lines but through waves—decline, stabilization, partial recovery, renewed strength
Multiple healthy patterns exist; chronic disabling grief is a minority pattern

S

Serotonin

Neurotransmitter involved in mood regulation, affected by grief-related depression

Synthesis is disrupted when chronic cortisol affects the gut microbiome

Shattered Assumptions

When life no longer fits the old map, meaning feels unstable after loss
The gap between what you believed and what you now experience

Shock (Physiological)

State where body recognizes danger while mind struggles to interpret; split sensation of stunned awareness
Protective shutdown; God-designed mercy allowing survival of the first blow

Soma

The body houses both spirit and mind; stores emotional memory
In the pneumopsychosomatic model, gives spirit expression and mind instruction

Somatization

The process by which psychological pain manifests as physical symptoms
Body speaking for voiceless soul; chest pain, headaches, GI distress as grief's voice

Stress Cardiomyopathy

Medical term for broken-heart syndrome; the left ventricle weakens after extreme emotional shock
Recovery improves when patients engage in spiritual practices evoking peace

Stress Cascade

Driven by the sympathetic nervous system and the HPA axis; floods the bloodstream with stress hormones
Begins moment bereaved perceives loss; dysregulates over time

Survivor Guilt

Irrational sorrow for merely being alive when another is not
Distinguished from moral guilt, grievers punish themselves for circumstances they never commanded.

Sympathetic Nervous System (SNS)

Floods the bloodstream with adrenaline and norepinephrine; breathing quickens, pupils dilate, and blood diverts to muscles
Part of the stress cascade during a bereavement emergency

T

Toxic Positivity

Compulsion to silence sorrow, replace lament with slogans, hide pain behind smile; pressure to "stay positive" that suppresses negative emotion
Promotes emotional suppression and shame; worsens psychological distress; short-circuits healing

Traumatic Grief

Grief is complicated by the traumatic nature of the death (sudden, violent, unexpected, or witnessed). Often includes PTSD symptoms alongside bereavement.

Traumatic Shock

Universal reaction to significant loss; neurological protection creating unreal, detached, and insulated feeling
Same as psychic numbness or dissociation

V

Vagus Nerve

The body's main calming pathway slows the heart during prayer and soft worship, according to polyvagal theory (Porges), though aspects remain debated
Polyvagal theory; physiological route through which spiritual practices create biological change

Vestibular System

System governing balance; shows altered patterns under high emotional stress
Explains why mourners sway, stumble, feel light-headed or dizzy

W

Wolff's Law

A biological principle that bones healing after a fracture often grow stronger at the break site. Used here metaphorically to illustrate post-traumatic growth.
Metaphor for post-traumatic growth; spirit discovering resilience where pain once was.

Endorsements

Get a Grip on Your Grief! offers a compassionate guide for navigating loss through a distinctly Christian lens. McAllister invites readers to reframe their pain within God's redemptive story, helping them process sorrow without suppressing faith or emotion. The book is both pastorally sensitive and practically grounded, making it a helpful companion for those seeking meaning, hope, and spiritual anchoring in the midst of grief.

Lance Woodley, Th.M., MSW, CAGCS
Certified Advanced Grief Counseling Specialist
Chaplain | Therapist | Educator

❖

Get a Grip on Your Grief! is a thoughtful and compassionate work. I believe it offers real value for anyone seeking spiritual grounding and support during a time of grief.

Dr. Sherry Schachter,
President, National Widowers' Organization

❖

This book offers a thoughtful, compassionate, and theologically rich guide to grief, blending Christian faith with insights from psychology and neuroscience in a way that feels both gentle and practical. It honors the complexity of grief by rejecting simplistic stage models, presenting grief as recurring seasons, validating anger, numbness, doubt, and ongoing sorrow as normal, and not spiritual failure. It offers small, doable practices for those with limited energy. With a pastoral tone and clear hope that does not deny pain, the book provides a slow, realistic path for learning to carry both love and loss with greater stability and hope.

Rupert A. Bromley, M. Div, Ph.D, PsyD.
Evangelical Expansion Manager
FOOD FOR THE POOR, INC.

❖

A must-have for every home, teacher, therapist, community leader, and anyone in a position to offer counsel or leadership. Get a Grip on Your Grief! is an insightful and compassionate work that resonates deeply with readers from all walks of life. It is a true page-turner—thoughtful, relatable, and profoundly human.

Dr. McAllister addresses the subject of grief in a manner that transcends class, education, or social status, making the book accessible and meaningful to everyone.

What stands out most is the author's ability to cover the many dimensions of grief with clarity and simplicity, offering guidance and comfort in a language that speaks to the heart. This book is not only valuable for those currently experiencing loss, but also for anyone seeking to better understand the human experience and to support others through difficult times.

Silvana Trinidad, DTM
Communications Expert & Government Policy Advisor
The Kingdom of the Netherlands

❖

I found the reflections for grieving individuals to be particularly poignant: they are gentle, permissive, and deeply attuned to the complex and overwhelming nature of loss. They offer solace while validating the very real emotions that accompany profound grief. Individuals grieving any kind of loss will find hope and understanding in these pages. The book's further exploration of grief from a biblical perspective offers a thoughtful framework for those who walk alongside bereaved people seeking to lean into their faith while grieving tremendous loss.

Jennifer Stachula, B.A.
Executive Director — Share Pregnancy & Infant Loss Support

❖

Get a Grip on Your Grief! integrates faith, biblical scripture, empirically based studies, and modern-day psychology in a clear, concise, and understandable manner. It is a book for those who are looking to understand their grief and maintain their faith while navigating the grief and loss process. It is also written for those professionals looking to understand the interrelationship between faith, religion, spirituality, and grief.

Brad Lindell, Ph.D.
President — American Academy of Experts in Traumatic Stress

❖

What if, even in a limited way, we could successfully neutralize the sting of death and the victory of the grave that will otherwise plunge us all into the grief that nobody wants?

In his groundbreaking sequel, Dr. Godfrey McAllister advances a proposition as radical as it is scientifically grounded: that the human brain, already wired to grieve, can be intentionally rewired in the best interest of all, before the inevitable loss of a loved one occurs.

The benefits are not theoretical and extend beyond the grieving period. They are measurable, they begin immediately, and they may even contribute to delaying the very loss you are preparing for. Dr. McAllister removes death from the shadowed corner of human experience where most people refuse to look. He places it squarely in the light as a reality that demands thoughtful, loving preparation.

On this reframing of death, he lays a foundation that transforms everything. The quality of the years shared with loved ones, the depth of connection built before goodbye, and the nature of grief itself are all revolutionized. "Goodbye" becomes potentially less devastating, less isolating, and far more richly celebratory of a life that mattered deeply.

This is not a book about the inevitability of dying. It is a book about living so intentionally, loving so completely, and preparing so thoroughly, that when loss finally arrives — as it will — it finds you ready, not to capitulate… but celebrate. God wired your brain to grieve. He also empowered you to rewire your brain. This could be the greatest adventure of your life. August 2026 cannot come soon enough.